Captured Confederates at Gettysburg, Pennsylvania

Mississippi Memorial, Vicksburg National Military Park, Mississippi

Maj. Gen. Philip Kearny, U.S. Volunteers, Arlington National Cemetery, Virginia

Confederate Monument, Shiloh National Military Park, Tennessee

Confederate Monument, Augusta, Georgia; Maj. Gen. W.H.T. Walker of Augusta on left, Brig. Gen. T.R.R. Cobb of Athens on right

124th Pennsylvania Monument, Antietam National Battlefield, Maryland

Lee Monument, Richmond, Virginia

THE BLUE
AND
THE GRAY

By Thomas B. Allen

Photography by Sam Abell

Prepared by the Book Division
National Geographic Society, Washington, D.C.

THE BLUE
AND
THE GRAY

By Thomas B. Allen
Photography by Sam Abell
Foreword by Shelby Foote

Published by
The National Geographic Society

Gilbert M. Grosvenor
President and Chairman of the Board

Michela A. English
Senior Vice President

Prepared by
The Book Division

William R. Gray
Vice President and Director

Margery G. Dunn, Charles Kogod
Assistant Directors

Staff for this book

Leah Bendavid-Val
Project Editor and Illustrations Editor

Mary Ann Harrell
Text Editor

Marianne R. Koszorus
Art Director

Bonnie S. Lawrence
Research Editor

Carolinda E. Hill
Senior Researcher

Elizabeth W. Fisher
Kimberly A. Kostyal
Researchers

Margery G. Dunn
Elizabeth L. Newhouse
Contributing Editors

Edwin C. Bearss
Jay Luvaas
Principal Consultants

Karen Huntt Mason
Illustrations Researcher

Melanie Patt-Corner, William
T. Spicer, Anne E. Withers
Contributing Researchers

Leslie Allen, Leah Bendavid-Val,
Toni Eugene, Mary Ann Harrell,
Carolinda E. Hill, Catherine
Herbert Howell, Edward
Lanouette, Gene S. Stuart,
Jean Kaplan Teichroew,
Jennifer C. Urquhart
Picture Legend Writers

Sandra F. Lotterman
Editorial Assistant

Karen Dufort Sligh
Illustrations Assistant

Karen F. Edwards
Design Assistant

Richard S. Wain
Production Project Manager

Lewis R. Bassford, Heather
Guwang, H. Robert Morrison
Production

Elizabeth G. Jevons, Artemis S.
Lampathakis, Teresita Cóquia
Sison, Marilyn J. Williams
Staff Assistants

Susan G. Zenel, *Indexer*

*Manufacturing and
Quality Management*

George V. White, *Director*

John T. Dunn, *Associate Director*

R. Gary Colbert, *Executive Assistant*

Cartography by
R. R. Donnelley & Sons

*HARDCOVER STAMP: These flags flew over
Fort Sumter in April 1861. The U.S. flag
carried 33 stars in a popular pattern of
the time. The Stars and Bars, accepted in
March by the Confederacy's provisional
Congress, bore seven stars for the seven
states that had seceded.*

*OPPOSITE: Confederate pickets at
Fredericksburg, Virginia*

*TITLE PAGE: 128th Pennsylvania
Monument, Antietam National Battlefield,
Maryland*

Chapter Portfolios

The Instruments and
Elements of War
by Richard Deutsch

The Great Army of the Wounded
by Leah Bendavid-Val

The Nations in Alliance
by Philip Kopper

At Greatest Risk: Black Servicemen
by Mary Ann Harrell

Wartime Mapmaking: Art, Craft,
and Victory
by Jay Luvaas

The Women of a House Divided
by Leslie Allen

Biographies by
Mary Ann Harrell
Bonnie S. Lawrence
Jay Luvaas
Elizabeth L. Newhouse

Contents

Foreword

The American Civil War—April to April, Sumter to Appomattox, 1861 to 1865—pervades the national conscience and excites the interest of much of the rest of the world. This is not only because of the carnage, though of carnage there was plenty. Of the nearly three million men under arms in the course of the struggle, afloat and ashore, Union and Confederate, more than a million were casualties. About half of them died of various diseases, infections, and off-the-field mishaps. The rest were killed or wounded in some 10,000 military actions, including 76 full-scale battles, 310 engagements, 6,337 skirmishes, and a number of more casual encounters that the troops themselves called "dust-ups" or "squabbles," any one of which could kill a man as dead as Gettysburg. The effect was devastating—particularly southward, where the state of Mississippi, in the first year of peace, spent a solid fifth of its meager revenues for the purchase of artificial arms and legs for its returning veterans.

For all the steepness of the butcher's bill—one out of ten men of conscription age was a casualty in the North, as against one out of four white males in the South—the perverse attraction extends in other directions, similarly doleful. When Douglas Southall Freeman, the distinguished seven-volume biographer of R. E. Lee and his chief lieutenants, moved on (or, strictly speaking, back) to writing about George Washington and the Revolutionary era, he was surprised to find not only how different that period was from the one he had spent the past twenty-odd years examining, but also how much like our own time the late 18th century was. Religion, for example, seemed not to be a main concern of the participants in the Revolution, whereas in the later conflict, even in the midst of battle, unit commanders often called on God in their dispatches and reports. Moreover, in the Revolution the Patriots had a feeling of moving from darkness into a new dawn, while in the Civil War one side was slogging toward defeat and the Ku Klux Klan, and the other toward the assassination of its great leader and the triumph of the robber barons. It was, according to Dr. Freeman, as if the clear stream of American history had flowed into "a muddy, bloody lake" and then emerged clear again on the other side.

I too got that impression in the course of my own twenty-year exploration of the surface and depths of that bloody lake—and something else as well, which I think accounts, at least in part, for abiding interest in that cataclysmic struggle. At "four score and seven" the nation was into its adolescence, so to speak, and this terrible four-year ordeal entered the national memory, the national conscience and unconscious, much as some horrendous family tragedy—the violent loss of a brother or sister by fire or flood, the suicide or public disgrace of a parent—can enter the mind of some individual at a highly impressionable age. It lurks there, waiting to be called up. At the slightest suggestion, even a passing, seemingly unconnected remark or gesture, its scar is pricked. Wanted or unwanted, there it is, insisting on being pondered. And so it is with us as a nation, even for those whose forebears became part of the national entity after the conflict itself had ended. It was, as I have said elsewhere, "the crossroads of our being." To a considerable extent, in good ways and bad, it not only made us what we are, it also continues to play its part in shaping what we are to become.

This in itself makes that war worth all the study we can give it lest we summon back its horrors. But there are other appeals, including certain far-ranging innovations in the very tools with which the grisly thing was waged.

In a single brief March afternoon the Confederate ironclad *Virginia* (ex-*Merrimack*) demonstrated the obsolescence of wooden navies—only to be neutralized by the U.S.S. *Monitor,* which showed up next morning with the patness of a plot twist out of light fiction. Soon afterward the railway gun made its appearance, another Rebel contrivance. The telegraph gave an army commander all but instantaneous communication not only with his own dispersed elements or other armies but also with the capital to his rear. Railroads provided rapid all-weather supply lines and made possible the sudden shift of massive reinforcements even from one theater to another, hundreds of miles apart. The observation balloon; "hasty entrenchments," fieldworks thrown up during a battle; the breech-loading repeating carbine—the list of innovations is long.

But perhaps the deadliest was the simplest, the rifle bullet—the so-called minié ball, already battle-proven in Europe—which quadrupled the 50-yard effective range of the old smoothbore musket. Thus modified, the primary infantry weapon was far ahead of the tactics that

Behind Confederate defense lines at Petersburg, Virginia

employed it. Generals believed that to mass their firepower in the attack, they had to mass their men. The resultant shoulder-to-shoulder charges produced the interminable casualty lists, which in turn produced in their readers, then and now, two tandem disbeliefs: first, that so many men had fallen and, second, that anyone at all involved in all that madness had survived.

All this you will find detailed, along with much else, in the pages that lie ahead, including the illuminating maps and identifying photographs, old and new, whose excellence has long been the hallmark of the National Geographic Society. Yet of all the pleasures that lie in wait none is greater than the company you'll keep, the men you will meet or get reacquainted with during your four-year journey through that war. U.S. Grant and R.E. Lee, Tecumseh Sherman and Stonewall Jackson, George McClellan and Joe Johnston, Phil Sheridan and Jeb Stuart—listed thus, these blue- and gray-clad leaders seem to hunt in pairs in

their quest for fame, but I could find no counterpart for Bedford Forrest; militarily, for me at least, he stands alone. These are only a representative handful. The men under them, all the way down to the lowest-ranking soldier or sailor, have a fascination that deepens as it expands. I think of the Prussian "Leatherbritches" Dilger, for example, who sniped Bishop Polk off the crest of Pine Mountain with a 12-pounder during the Atlanta Campaign, or the unnamed Union private, sent wounded to the rear amid the chaos of Shiloh, who presently returned to confront his company commander. "Captain, give me a gun!" he cried, shouting to be heard above the uproar. "This durn fight ain't got any rear!"

Civilians too await your pleasure and bemusement, beginning of course with Abraham Lincoln and Jefferson Davis—great men both, though the latter was grievously overmatched by an opponent who was a genius—and working your way along, past the Cabinet members and bureaucrats and the various martyrs and patriots, scamps and scoundrels, to the factory workers and farmers on the home fronts, the women who waited—perhaps the hardest job—and the slaves north and south of the firing line, who also waited for the issue to be settled, or else took the oath of service—some 87,000 of them, all told—and joined the struggle for their own freedom. It makes a great story for winners and losers alike, in and out of uniform, and though any truly told war story, given the nature of war, must in the end be anti-war, this one at least has a satisfactory if not in fact a happy ending. It became known in time as the Great Compromise: admission on the part of the South that it was probably best for all concerned that the Union had been preserved, and admission on the part of the North that the erstwhile Rebels had fought bravely for a cause they believed was just.

It makes, as I said, a great story; I know of none since the *Iliad* that rivals it either in drama or in pathos, and I wish you hours of joy in its unfolding.

Shelby Foote

THE MYSTIC CHORDS OF MEMORY

Created equal . . . endowed with certain unalienable rights . . . Turbulence cut new channels with these words.

At Charleston, at Norfolk, at Baltimore, the refugees arrived. They had seen the unthinkable: slaves in revolt, black men armed and vengeful, killing white masters, violating their wives, brandishing machetes and marching behind a standard—the body of a white baby impaled on a pike.

The stories came from French, British, and American citizens who had sailed out of a flaming Haiti. There, between 1791 and 1804, slaves stirred by the idea of *liberté* nearly wiped out the French. One army of slaves, a young survivor wrote, "numbered about 6,000, some naked, some in tatters, and some grotesquely draped in rich apparel taken from our wardrobes. They were armed with guns, knives, sticks, and all the sharp utensils of kitchen and farm."

Saint-Domingue, or San Domingo, or Haiti—by any name the island colony meant terror. Accounts of its massacres spread rapidly throughout the South, especially in Carolina rice-growing areas where slaves outnumbered whites eighty or ninety to one. Here a code word had been passed down for years: *Remember Stono,* planters would say.

On a September Sunday in 1739, near Charleston and the Stono River, a man called Jemmy led fellow slaves on a raid for firearms. Many may have been soldiers in a West African kingdom; they marched in disciplined style, and fought stubbornly against hastily mustered militia. Some 40 slaves and 25 whites died before the rebellion was crushed. The story lived on long after America's white colonists had triumphed in a rebellion of their own.

When Haiti won independence in 1804, slaveholders saw a chilling new reality: a victorious black nation in the New World. That victory led to Napoleon's decision to sell French possessions in North America. The United States purchased the Louisiana country: reaches of the Gulf coast, the Mississippi Valley, vast unexplored plains beyond. It also acquired new problems involving slavery.

Each of the 13 rebellious colonies had slaves and free blacks, many or few, in 1776. When delegates began framing a new constitution in 1787, four New England states and Pennsylvania had abolished slavery on their own soil. Would the new Union do as much? A Pennsylvanian argued that "misery and poverty" prevailed in slave regions; but slave states to the south were wealthier than all the northern ones and exerted great strength in argument. "South Carolina and Georgia cannot do

Cradled between the Potomac and Shenandoah Rivers, Harper's Ferry recalls its past as a thriving industrial community—site of an arsenal and, in Carl Sandburg's words, "a meeting place of . . . rocks and ranges." A heavily guarded President Lincoln takes his oath of office on March 4, 1861.

PRECEDING PAGES: A forest of derricks rises near Titusville, Pennsylvania. Edwin Drake struck oil here in August 1859, and kerosene distilled from the crude petroleum soon supplanted whale oil and turpentine to light the nation's lamps; oil kept its machines running.

A factory window gives a worker's-eye view of the Boott Mills clock tower in Lowell, Massachusetts, built in 1864. New England's burgeoning textile industry took wing after the War of 1812. Much of the cloth was woven from cotton grown in the South. "Mill girls," the daughters of Yankee farmers, worked 12-hour days 6 days a week to keep the looms clacking. Before 1840, Lowell was turning out 750,000 yards of cloth a week—enough to reach from there to Washington, D.C. By the mid-1800s, shoemaking had been revamped— especially in Massachusetts, which soon dominated the industry. Heavy-duty sewing machines and other equipment made old-time cobblers and their hand tools (opposite) obsolete. From turning out six pairs of shoes a week, a worker using one of the new machines could double-peg up to 400 pairs a day— at less than a penny a pair.

Bustling and boisterous, pre-war New York City had begun to flex its muscle and its wealth—as seen by this heavy traffic on Broadway, even then one of the world's busiest streets. By 1860 this city of more than a million people had become a major gateway to the United States—either as a new home for thousands of European immigrants who stayed in the city or as a springboard to the West, a journey made less arduous by the opening of the Erie Canal in 1825.

without slaves," said a former general. In the final compromises, these states agreed that the importing of slaves could end in 1808. To determine representation in Congress, free persons counted as whole numbers and each "other" individual as three-fifths of a human being. (By this ratio, each group of 30,000 citizens in a free state had one congressman. In a slave state, 12,000 citizens who among themselves owned 30,000 slaves also had one congressman.) Slave, bondsman, chattel—the words did not appear in the finished Constitution, for many found them abhorrent.

This was the era of America's intellectual jubilee over liberty. Not a few owners freed their slaves as an act of conscience. The largest such act known came in 1791 when Robert Carter III, one of Virginia's wealthiest planters, began the gradual freeing of more than 500 slaves; he believed that owning them was "contrary to the true principles of Religion & Justice." George Washington, Thomas Jefferson, James Madison—all were champions of liberty, holders of slaves tormented by contradiction. In their time slavery seemed likely to die out.

That attitude changed when the cotton gin made cotton the new Southern cash crop. Slavery hovered like a wraith over the growing country, as states entering the Union came in free (Vermont, Ohio) or slave (Kentucky, Tennessee). This one-for-one admission scheme maintained a Senate balance between free and slave states. By 1820, with New York and New Jersey free and 9 new states added to the original 13, the Senate's balance remained unchanged. But the slave states were losing their strength in the House of Representatives and votes in the electoral college.

Now the lands of the Louisiana Purchase introduced a threat to the Senate's uneasy equipoise, for Missouri, carved from that purchase, wanted to enter as a slave state. Northerners objected. If Missouri were thwarted, a Georgia congressman shouted, "the Union will be dissolved. You have kindled a fire which all the waters of the ocean cannot put out, which seas of blood can only extinguish." A New York opponent cried "Let it come!" Southern legislators hinted at unspeakable horrors threatening their states, their homes, and their families.

Senator Henry Clay of Kentucky, born in the America of the Revolution and a hero of the frontier, saw a genuine threat to his beloved

RAILROADS | *Westward—by rail and by water—spread the course of empire, made swifter by the application of steam to transportation. Here, railroad tracks accompany a slough of the Mississippi River near Savanna, Illinois. Steam engines, in widespread use by the 1850s, made it possible for boats to buck river currents and carry goods upstream; railroads added speed. Opposite, a line of hopper cars weaves through Galena, Illinois, long a center of lead mining. By 1860, nearly a third of the nation's rail lines extended into the Great Lakes region. Illinois alone counted 2,867 miles of track, and Chicago had become the hub of 11 different railroads.*

Union. In 1820 he negotiated a compromise. Maine would come in as a free state, Missouri as a slave state—but in the rest of the Louisiana Purchase north of Missouri's southern border, slavery would be prohibited.

Tempers cooled. Citizens turned to everyday topics and possibilities: building up trade, improving the farm, moving west to develop new land. Rituals of patriotism brightened the year. On Washington's birthday, on the Glorious Fourth, militia drills and fireworks and spread-eagle speeches entertained the most fortunate people on earth. But the last veterans of the Revolutionary War were passing away, the cold realism of its statesmen was obscured, and new enthusiasms were flourishing.

Then the old terror flared again. In August 1831, in southeastern Virginia, Nat Turner, a slave preacher and man of visions, entered his master's house and murdered the family. With other slaves he recruited, he killed nearly 60 whites, many of them women and children. For weeks Virginia militiamen, aided by volunteers and Federal troops, hunted him down. They killed scores of slaves out of hand, many of them innocent. Turner and 20 others were tried and hanged.

Many Southerners blamed agitators in the North for inciting slaves to revolt. Yet it seems coincidence that William Lloyd Garrison had begun publishing his anti-slavery newspaper, *The Liberator,* eight months before Turner struck. The linking of Garrison and other abolitionists to Turner was the linking of fear and hate.

Abolitionists' words seethed with anger and scorn. Garrison despised Southerners. He saw the planter "from the cradle to the grave" living a life "of unbridled lust, of filthy amalgamation [a polite term for masters having their way with slave women], of swaggering braggadocio . . . of boundless dissipation, of matchless insolence, of infinite self-conceit, of unequalled oppression, of more than savage cruelty." His first tenet was that "every slaveholder has forfeited his right to live."

Freedom of speech and freedom of the press did not go unscathed. The postmaster of New York City refused delivery of the *Liberator* and other anti-slavery publications. The Postmaster General, Massachusetts-born, endorsed the ban. In the 1830s state legislators in Connecticut, Maine, and New Hampshire introduced bills to restrain abolitionist publications. Southerners often took more direct means. In

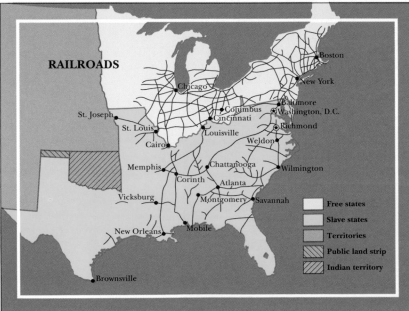

RAILROADS

Boston
New York
Chicago
Columbus
Baltimore
Cincinnati
Washington, D.C.
St. Joseph
Richmond
St. Louis
Louisville
Cairo
Weldon
Memphis
Chattanooga
Wilmington
Corinth
Atlanta
Vicksburg
Montgomery
Savannah
New Orleans
Mobile
Brownsville

☐ Free states
☐ Slave states
☐ Territories
▨ Public land strip
▨ Indian territory

The Kentucky River throws a smoking loop through Bluegrass country en route to its rendezvous with the Ohio. Rivers would become a help—or a hindrance—to moving goods and soldiers. At this palisaded gorge of the river, a ferry and road would become a strategic funnel for troop movements of both armies. Cincinnati (below), an Ohio River jumping-off point for westward-bound pioneers, became a center for trade and commerce with the introduction of steamboats. Near the mouth of the Mississippi, New Orleans (lower) by 1860 prospered as a busy shipping point for goods from the interior—and, with nearly 170,000 people, it ranked as the South's largest, most cosmopolitan city.

1835 a mob in Charleston broke into the post office, carried off mail sacks full of anti-slavery literature, and burned them.

The most famous work in the anti-slavery tradition, *Uncle Tom's Cabin,* was banned in the South in the 1850s, but it lacked the hate that tinged most abolitionist writing. Harriet Beecher Stowe lived for 18 years in Cincinnati, just across the Ohio River from slave soil, and portrayed her Southerners by observation, not contempt. Her cruel plantation owner, Simon Legree, was a Yankee. As a child in Connecticut she had been stirred by a recital of the Declaration of Independence, and she resolved "to fight for my country, or to make some declaration on my own account." She stood for the Union not as an enemy of anyone but as a citizen of a Christian nation; she wanted slavery to end because she wanted a republic of unstained integrity.

That ideal had again come under strain. The dazzling idea of manifest destiny—dominance of the continent—had swept the nation in the 1840s. President James K. Polk's administration had increased its domain by two-thirds. In the far northwest the border enclosed the Oregon country, acquired by treaty. The Mexican War, a triumph for the small professional army and eager volunteers, added California and the New Mexico region. In the midst of the war Senator Tom Corwin of Ohio had denounced it. If we conquer "a single acre of Mexican land," he said, "the North and the South are brought into collision on a point where neither will yield"—the old question of slavery in the new lands. He foresaw a "bottomless gulf of civil strife."

By 1850 that seemed entirely possible. Some of the more fiery Southerners declared that unless slave-owners could take their "peculiar institution" of bondage into the western territories, they would take their states out of the Union. South Carolina did more than talk of secession; she bought 64 cannon from the Tredegar Iron Works in Richmond, and some were installed at Charleston.

The city of Washington, and even the crimson-and-gilt Senate Chamber, witnessed wild scenes and resounded to venomous words. Henry Foote of Mississippi scuffled with a Pennsylvania senator, threatened to hang a senator from New Hampshire, and, during a speech on the floor, pulled a gun on Senator Thomas Hart Benton of Missouri. Senator Jefferson Davis of Mississippi got into a fistfight with

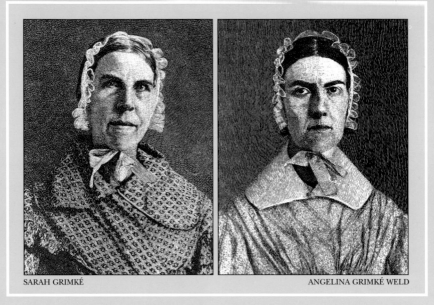

SARAH GRIMKÉ

ANGELINA GRIMKÉ WELD

THE GRIMKÉ SISTERS

As a Southerner I feel that it is my duty to stand up here tonight and bear testimony against slavery. I have seen it— I have seen it. I know it has horrors that can never be described. . . . I have *never* seen a happy slave. I have seen him dance in his chains, it is true; but he was not happy."

Outside the new lecture hall a Philadelphia mob threw stones at the windows, shouted, and banged against the locked doors. Inside, a frightened woman of 33 addressed several thousand attentive men and women. It was May 16, 1838. The hall was being dedicated as a forum for reform; the next day, rioters burned it down. The speaker was Angelina Grimké Weld. After that night, she never again lectured on abolition in public.

Sarah and Angelina Grimké were the daughters of a wealthy, aristocratic family of Charleston, South Carolina. They were brought up in luxury, in the most exclusive society. Both were uncomfortable with social gaiety, and with the formalism of the Episcopal Church. From girlhood they expressed abhorrence of slavery.

Their father's profession, the law, appealed to Sarah, but as a woman she could not enter it. When she was 27, Judge John Grimké fell ill; she went with him to Philadelphia and there nursed him until he died. Impressed by the Quakers she met, discontented at home, concerned about her spiritual welfare, she became a Quaker convert and settled in Philadelphia. Angelina, 12 years younger, became an active Presbyterian and tried to reform her family. Failing in this, she followed Sarah to Philadelphia and membership in the Society of Friends.

In 1835 Angelina wrote a letter of support to the abolitionist leader William Lloyd Garrison, who published it—including her name. The following year she wrote an anti-slavery appeal to Southern women. In Charleston the postmaster burned copies in the mail. The mayor warned her mother that if Angelina came home to visit her family, she would be arrested and imprisoned.

Abolitionists invited the sisters to address groups of women in their parlors. Then, in 1837, the Grimkés stirred New England by lecturing in more than 60 towns. This was indeed a phenomenon: ladies of quality addressing "promiscuous audiences"—audiences of both sexes as well as white and black. Once a clergyman opened the meeting with prayer, but left vowing he would "as soon rob a hen-roost" as hear a woman speak. The issue of women's rights complicated the anti-slavery cause; conservatives, especially in the South, were shocked by both.

The sisters had to assert the right of women to assume a role in public affairs and to use a public platform. In 1838 Angelina became the first woman to address members of an American legislature, that of Massachusetts. She defined her ideal in a private letter: "I recognize no rights but human rights. I know nothing of men's rights and women's rights; for in Christ Jesus there is neither male nor female."

At the height of their fame the sisters retired from the lecture circuit. Angelina had married abolitionist Theodore Weld and the couple, joined by Sarah, devoted their lives to teaching. After the war the sisters learned of Negro nephews, sons of their brother and a family slave. Freely acknowledging the relationship, they offered help with higher education: Archibald Grimké became famous as a lawyer, Francis as a clergyman. Sarah died in 1873, Angelina in 1879. They were unique: among Southern white women, the only abolitionist speakers.

Bearing their work upon their heads, field hands bring in a day's pickings near Charleston, South Carolina. The cotton gin, invented by Eli Whitney, a Yankee, quickly combed seeds from the fibers and by 1820 made cotton the king of Southern cash crops.

Foote and challenged an Illinois congressman to a duel with muskets.

Once again a compromise was cobbled up. By one provision, California became a free state; by another the Fugitive Slave Act let slave-owners call on Federal officials to capture runaways. A "filthy" law, said Ralph Waldo Emerson; "I will not obey it, by God!"

Again, a lull. A briefer one, this time.

In some respects the nation had changed dramatically. By 1850 the population of the free states was 13.5 million, growing as European immigrants arrived. New industries and inventions were boosting the economy. Political power was growing accordingly.

The South had 6 million whites and 3.2 million slaves. Only 384,884 whites appeared in the 1850 census as slave-owners, and many were yeomen farmers with a house servant and a few field hands. Just 46,274 ranked as planters, with 20 slaves or more; great planters with 100 slaves or more made up a tiny, proud elite. A white's dignity might be skin deep, but undeniable; the free person of color had a precarious status, which new laws were eroding. And in four of the free states—Illinois, Indiana, Iowa, and Oregon—white voters wanted to see free blacks excluded from their soil by explicit law.

One point made for stability. The old Missouri Compromise had come to seem part of the order of things. Then, in 1854, Congress repealed its limits on slavery. The Kansas-Nebraska Act let settlers in an organized territory vote on whether their new state would be slave or free. When the Kansas Territory opened up on July 1, 1854, pro-slavers led the wave of settlers. The free-soil partisans included a man who believed he was Heaven-sent to rid America of the scourge of slavery. His name was John Brown.

His eyes were hard, unblinking. His brow at 55 was creased by what seemed to be eternal anger. For much of his life he had wandered, a failure at many trades. In two marriages he fathered 20 children and buried 9 of them in infancy or early childhood. Five of his sons went into Kansas. Warned that abolitionists faced death there, John Brown said, "We are prepared not to die alone."

President Franklin Pierce recognized a pro-slavery legislature in Kansas and placed U.S. Army units under the control of the governor. Abolitionists shipped in boxes of Sharps rifles—"Beecher's Bibles." The

nickname honored Henry Ward Beecher, Mrs. Stowe's brother, a clergyman who had said that on the Kansas plains a rifle might be a more powerful moral agent than a Bible.

In May 1856 pro-slavery bands sacked Lawrence, a free-soil town. In swift retaliation John Brown and seven men, including four of his sons and a son-in-law, dragged a pro-slaver and two sons from their home, shooting the old man and hacking the sons to death. That night his party found two more pro-slavers and killed them too. Such incidents were far from rare.

"Bleeding Kansas" now dominated American politics. In the 1858 senatorial campaign in Illinois, Republican Abraham Lincoln, a fairly successful lawyer, was challenging the Democratic incumbent, Stephen A. Douglas. They agreed to make seven joint appearances and debate the issues. Douglas argued for "popular sovereignty": Voters in any state or territory should choose between free soil and slavery. He accused Lincoln of wanting "negro equality." Lincoln denied this. He believed that the white race was superior to the black and that the "physical difference" between the races would "probably forever forbid their living together upon the footing of perfect equality." He would free all slaves if he could, and send them to Liberia, settled in 1822 as an African nation for freed American slaves. Yet he had "no purpose directly or indirectly" to interfere with slavery where the Constitution protected it; he was no abolitionist. Nevertheless, he insisted, blacks were "entitled to all the natural rights enumerated in the Declaration of Independence, the right to life, liberty and the pursuit of happiness."

Douglas won the election, but Lincoln's eloquence was attracting nationwide attention. Some Republicans were thinking of him as a presidential candidate whose views would appeal to mainstream voters.

Many voters would certainly prefer moderate men and means; but the two sections defined "moderate" differently, and saw each other in disparaging terms. Southerners looked northward and saw meddling Puritans, strong-minded females, money-grubbing men. An algebra book for the Southern market set problems about cheating Yankee merchants and cowardly Indiana volunteers in Mexico. Proud "Southrons" sneered at greasy-handed "mechanics" slaving in factories, the poor "mudsills" of society. If war came, said the governor of Georgia, the white laborers of the North would rise up against their bosses.

Northerners looked southward and saw a region of romance, a land of languor and jasmine, a perennial nuisance of complaints about its rights and bragging about its valor. Frederick Law Olmsted, the designer of the U.S. Capitol grounds, traveled through the South and wrote candidly of what he saw: the great plantations with their mansions and work gangs; slovenly taverns and bad transportation; raw little farms where Southern hospitality had its price—"Dollar, I reckon"— for a night with fresh cornbread and stale bedding. He admired the authentic gentleman but not the numerous would-bes: "constantly drinking, smoking and chewing; card-playing and betting; and unable to converse upon anything that is not either grossly sensual or exciting, such as . . . projects of disunion or war."

Men of the latter sort had made a hero of Congressman Preston Brooks of South Carolina when the war on the Kansas plains spread to the Senate floor. In May 1856 Charles Sumner of Massachusetts, denouncing the "crime against Kansas," grossly insulted his fellow Senator Andrew P. Butler, calling him a man besotted with "the harlot, Slavery." Butler and Brooks were kin. Brooks caught Sumner at his Senate desk. Before he broke a cane on Sumner's head he had landed "about 30 first class stripes," he said. Moderates were appalled, partisans angrier than ever. Each section felt increasing contempt for the other.

In July 1859, John Brown rented a vacant farmhouse in Maryland, across the river from Harper's Ferry, Virginia, site of a rifle factory and a Federal arsenal. For weeks men and arms arrived at the farm by night. In August he met secretly with Frederick Douglass, an escaped slave who had become a great orator of abolition. "Come with me, Douglass," pleaded Brown. "When I strike, the bees will begin to swarm, and I shall want you to help hive them." Douglass refused.

On Sunday, October 16, Brown rose earlier than usual and called his men to a Bible reading. He also explained the plan shimmering like a fever vision in his mind. They would seize weapons from the arsenal, rally supporters, establish bases in the southern Appalachians. From these outposts they would storm down upon plantations, free the slaves, and arm them with pikes. Their forces would overwhelm the South and exterminate human bondage forever.

DRAYTON HALL | *In a reflective mood, Drayton Hall admires its stately image near Charleston, South Carolina. Completed in 1742, the house has survived the years virtually unchanged— including the Great Hall (opposite) with its carved mantel and cypress paneling. It would be the only Ashley River plantation to survive the war intact. While Union troops torched neighboring estates, legend has it, a family member posted smallpox warnings—a successful ruse. At the outbreak of the war, 14-year-old Charles Drayton would run away to join the Confederate forces. Two of his Drayton cousins would fight at Hilton Head—brothers on opposing sides.*

About eight o'clock, Brown led 13 whites and 5 blacks into a cold, rainy night. At a covered bridge over the Potomac, they cut telegraph wires and overpowered a watchman. Brown and one party entered Harper's Ferry, successfully taking over the armory and other sites.

Another band broke into the nearby home of Col. Lewis Washington, great-grandnephew of George Washington. Brown had planned to make the colonel a hostage. The colonel owned a pair of pistols that Lafayette had presented to the great hero and a sword said to have been given to him by Frederick the Great. To symbolize a transfer of authority and a moment of liberation, the raiders forced him to place these heirlooms in the hands of a free black, Osborn Anderson. At the armory, the first victim had been slain—a free black who was shot when he refused a raider's order to halt. When militiamen closed in, Brown, two sons, and others with him retreated to the fire-engine house.

On Monday night, 90 Marines arrived, sent by President James Buchanan. Lt. Col. Robert E. Lee, U.S.A., took command of all forces, including militia. Next morning Lee sent his aide, 1st Lt. J.E.B. Stuart,

On Monday evening, August 16, 1841, a young mulatto rose to his feet in a shingled building on the island of Nantucket, Massachusetts. He was embarrassed; never before had he spoken in front of such an audience. "The truth was, I felt myself a slave," Frederick Douglass later wrote, "and the idea of speaking to white people weighed me down. I spoke but a few moments, when I felt a degree of freedom, and said what I desired with considerable ease."

What he desired to say electrified the crowd. It was the story of his life in captivity and of his recent escape. Others had told similar stories, but no one with such passion and persuasion. It was a moment of triumph for the young fugitive—and the start of a career that would bring him world renown.

Frederick Douglass had traveled far that Nantucket evening, though perhaps not as far as he would have had his audience believe. Yes, he'd been born a slave on Maryland's Eastern Shore in 1818. But from childhood his looks and intelligence had marked him as exceptional, and he'd been very lucky.

At age eight Frederick was sent to Baltimore to live with relatives of his master's son-in-law. Of "Miss Sophia" Auld he would write: "No mother's hand could have been more tender than hers." He stayed in Baltimore for most of the next dozen years, and taught himself to read and write. In the 1830s, the city boomed in commerce and shipbuilding. Always more than a slave town, it held about one-fourth of Maryland's 60,000 free blacks. Frederick mixed with free people on the Fells Point docks and gradually began to think of his own liberty.

His luck held out in September 1838, when, dressed as a sailor, he boarded a train headed north. Soon he found himself in New Bedford, Massachusetts, whose abolitionist population made it a safe haven. In the spring he heard William Lloyd Garrison speak and discovered what he himself would become: an orator.

FREDERICK DOUGLASS

After his success in Nantucket, Douglass signed on as an agent for the Massachusetts Anti-Slavery Society and before long was speaking a hundred times a year. Eloquent, impassioned, hyperbolic, he held himself up as a tortured victim and the Aulds as symbols of despicable slave-owners. In the propaganda war against slavery, Douglass's speeches and his best-selling 1845 autobiography, *Narrative of the Life of Frederick Douglass*, were powerful and effective tools. Though his two later autobiographies tried to correct the record, it was the horror of the first account the world remembered.

In the British Isles, Douglass was a celebrity. On his return he moved to Rochester, New York, and started a newspaper, the *North Star*. When the war began, he urged the enrollment of black soldiers, writing sarcastically in 1862: "Colored men were good enough to fight under Washington. They are not good enough to fight under McClellan. . . . They were good enough to help win American independence, but they are not good enough to help preserve that independence against treason and rebellion." And with other abolitionists he ceaselessly pressed Lincoln to make emancipation a war aim. When the Emancipation Proclamation was finally issued, Douglass turned it into a call for equality. After the heady early post-war days, he saw his dreams dashed by Black Codes, Jim Crow, and lynch mobs.

A more personal hurt dogged him to his death in 1895. A loyal Republican, who worked tirelessly in presidential campaigns and naively refused to acknowledge the party's surrender to white supremacists, he was never awarded high office. Again and again he thought it would come his way, but beyond a few minor posts—secretary of the Santo Domingo Commission, marshal for the District of Columbia, minister to Haiti—the most honored black of his time never received the recognition he deeply craved.

A street of shattered hopes in Atlanta heard the steady beat of the auction hammer that often broke up slave families, scattering their members to toil on plantations of the Deep South. By 1860, with some four million slaves in the South, a prime field hand sold for $1,800; a blacksmith for $2,500.

Kansas becomes "Bleeding Kansas" as Free Staters (manning the artillery piece, opposite) vie with pro-slavery forces for territorial control. Opened to settlement in 1854, the territory grew with river traffic (below). Settlers were to vote for statehood with or without slavery, but bitter feelings soon led to warfare—and the loss of some 200 lives. Free-soilers set up a capital in Topeka (lower). In the nation's capital, Preston Brooks caned Charles Sumner in the Senate Chamber.

to the engine house with a flag of truce and a call for surrender. Brown, with one son dead and another dying, refused to yield. Marines battered down the door and captured him, freeing Colonel Washington and other hostages.

Convicted of murder, criminal conspiracy, and treason against the Commonwealth of Virginia, John Brown was hanged at Charles Town on December 2, 1859. Among the 1,500 militiamen on guard to fight off abolitionists was a young actor named John Wilkes Booth.

Relayed by telegraph, news of the raid had spread through the South—faster than the old stories from Haiti but to similar effect. Examples of Brown's pikes were distributed in Southern cities. Memories of Nat Turner heightened new fears. The governor of South Carolina warned of "secret emissaries inciting our slaves to insubordination and insurrection." The legislature enacted laws to control such potential agents of abolition as traveling salesmen and touring circuses.

In April 1860 the Democrats assembled in Charleston to nominate a presidential candidate. After years of conciliation, free-state delegates balked at adopting a pro-slavery platform. Southern delegates stalked out. The Democratic Party split in two. A new party sprang up, the Constitutional Union Party, made up of aging moderates.

The beneficiary of this was the six-year-old Republican Party. It convened in Chicago and, on the third ballot, chose Abraham Lincoln to run for President. He accepted a platform that called for barring slavery from the territories but left it unchanged in Southern states.

After a campaign remarkable for its intensity and confusion, 1,866,452 citizens voted for Lincoln. He received 39 percent of the popular vote but won 180 electoral votes—all from free states—to his three opponents' combined total of 123.

Prudence would dictate, said the Declaration of 1776, that long-established governments not be changed for transient causes. But all Americans agreed that the governed may withdraw from a government that threatens their rights. South Carolina had warned that Lincoln's election would mean the breakup of the Union. On December 20 a special convention unanimously proclaimed secession. The next day Charleston newspapers began reporting events in Northern states as "foreign news." (Continued on page 46)

NEW SALEM | *A frontier settlement when Abraham Lincoln moved here as a young adult in 1831, this community on the Sangamon River in Illinois prospered awhile, then faded away. Settlers pushed west in Conestoga wagons like the one in this re-created village. Young Abe, into whose hands an ax was put at age eight, spent part of his life hewing wood and splitting rails— work that would steel his frame for life. In later years, he would awe companions by holding an ax at arm's length—head out. In New Salem, Lincoln engaged in a variety of businesses and odd jobs. Here, too, his life would find direction in studies of the law—and his first venture into politics as an elected legislator.*

GALENA | *Boomtown of the frontier West, Galena grew rich on lead in the 1830s and '40s. Even though played-out mines could not meet Civil War contracts, the Illinois town claimed nine generals—including Ulysses S. Grant,* *whose red-brick house grateful citizens bestowed on him after the war. Despite declining lead production, Galena remained a thriving market town, its wharves busy with river traffic. Mansions lined the nearby hills.* *But the river silted up; railroads bypassed the town, siphoning trade to Chicago. After the war, General Grant settled in Washington. Modest homes trimmed with mill-work "gingerbread" took their place near the red-brick mansions.*

As a sovereign realm, South Carolina demanded possession of all Federal real estate within her borders, particularly three forts in Charleston harbor: Pinckney, a minor one; Moultrie, whose guns aimed toward the sea; and Sumter, a formidable threat to the city as well as to shipping. A stronghold on an artificial island, it commanded the harbor. It was unfinished, after 30 years' work; some of its 78 guns had yet to be mounted.

President James Buchanan was fretting over the issue of secession; the Secretary of War had singled out 55-year-old Maj. Robert Anderson to command U.S. forces at Charleston. A Southerner and former slaveholder, he had been wounded in the Mexican War. He had mustered young Abraham Lincoln into service, and out of it, in an

Bonfires blaze, rockets resound, and a flag of the first Revolution flies at a secessionist rally in Johnson Square on the night of November 8, 1860, when news of Lincoln's election two days earlier reached Savannah, Georgia.

The band strikes up the French anthem of revolution, "La Marseillaise." In little more than a month—on December 20—South Carolina delegates meeting in Charleston would vote for secession, dissolving their bond to the union of

states, as proclaimed within minutes by newspaper headlines. A few weeks later, six other states of the Deep South would follow South Carolina's lead—an act lampooned by Northern cartoonists.

THE U.S.
BEFORE SECESSION
1860

Free states
Slave states
Territories
Public land strip
(Status undefined until 1890)
Indian territory
(Land restricted to Indian ownership and use)

1832 Indian conflict, and served with Jefferson Davis, an old friend from West Point days. Davis had called him a "true soldier and man of the finest sense of honor."

When the crisis began, Anderson, based at Moultrie, commanded 7 officers, 75 men (including 8 musicians), and a slow-moving construction crew. As unofficial envoy and sharp-eyed soldier, he visited friends in town to take the pulse of the community. He watched volunteers streaming into Charleston and realized he might have to fight. Moultrie, he knew, could not be defended. He spiked its guns on the night after Christmas and secretly moved his stores and men, in rowboats and barges, to Sumter. There, the next day, he held a solemn ceremony. He knelt at the flagstaff while the chaplain prayed for a reunited country. Then he rose, and raised a flag whose stars numbered 33 states. His move had stunned Charleston and angered his friends there.

South Carolina militia promptly seized the other two forts, the customs house, and the U.S. arsenal. This improved their supply of weapons, and sharpened the defiance of the new republic.

Buchanan sent an unarmed merchantman, *Star of the West,* with troops and food for Sumter. She was driven away by cannon fire.

By February 4, the states of the Cotton Kingdom—Alabama, Florida, Mississippi, Georgia, Texas, and Louisiana—had also seceded. They had taken over post offices, customs houses, arsenals, and coastal forts. Delegates gathered in Montgomery, Alabama, to create a provisional government for the Confederate States of America and to write an interim constitution. Jefferson Davis, who had resigned from the Senate in January, became provisional president.

Slaves at Charleston worked night and day to build gun emplacements that would bring Sumter into range. On January 6, Anderson reported to Washington: "We are now, or soon will be, cut off from all communications. . . ." The question of relieving him remained unanswered—by the outgoing administration and the prospective one.

Late in February, Lincoln reluctantly obeyed advisers worried by rumors of assassination—he slipped into Washington for his Inauguration. Southern legislators had made flowery farewells to their former colleagues and returned to their new country. Southern officers were resigning to serve their states.

Loyal Army officers lined the streets of Washington with troops. Sharpshooters stood poised on roofs. To keep some enemy from planting a bomb, soldiers huddled under the platform where Lincoln took the oath of office and gave his address. The Union, he said, "is unbroken; and, to the extent of my ability, I shall take care . . . that the laws of the Union be faithfully executed in all the States. . . .

"We are not enemies, but friends. We must not be enemies. . . . The mystic chords of memory, stretching from every battle-field and patriot grave, to every living heart and hearthstone, all over this broad land, will yet swell the chorus of the Union, when again touched, as surely they will be, by the better angels of our nature."

During the celebration a report came in from Anderson. He had enough bread for only 28 days. Lincoln temporized; his Cabinet was split on whether to evacuate Sumter or reinforce it. Confederate emissaries in Washington huddled informally with his aides, trying to negotiate an agreement on independence and the peaceful transfer of U.S. property. Anderson, baffled by the indecision in Washington, sent increasingly desperate dispatches. Finally, Lincoln acted. On April 8 a courier from Washington read his message aloud to the governor of South Carolina: "an attempt will be made to supply Fort Sumter with provisions only. . . ." If the effort met no resistance, no reinforcements or weapons would be sent.

At Sumter, the bread was gone. The defenders were down to salt pork, crackers, and some moldy rice. On April 11 a small boat, bearing uniformed men under a flag of truce, approached the fort. The men, Confederate officers, brought a message from one of Anderson's former artillery pupils at West Point—Brig. Gen. Pierre Gustave Toutant Beauregard. He demanded evacuation of the fort but added, "The flag which you have upheld so long and with so much fortitude, under the most trying circumstances, may be saluted by you on taking it down."

Anderson assembled his officers and asked their response. All agreed there could be only one answer. Anderson wrote it: Evacuation "is a demand with which I regret that my sense of honor, and of my obligations to my Government, prevent my compliance."

As the Confederates were about to row away, taking the formal reply, Anderson said, "I shall await the first shot. . . ."

The Instruments and Elements of War

War is progressive," said U.S. Grant, "because all the instruments and elements of war are progressive." As he saw it, the components of victory included all new technology—a novel, and characteristically Northern, insight.

By 1861, Americans were using steam and electricity to tame the distances of the continent. They were dispatching steam locomotives along new-laid rails. Steam-driven paddle wheelers thrashed along the rivers; steam challenged sail on the high seas; immigrants could find work in factories ringing with the noise of steam-powered machines.

Men were stringing telegraph wires from horizon to horizon. Telegrams carried news of secession and Sumter and Lincoln's call for volunteers, and "the cars" (rail carriages) took men into service. (During the war, "train" usually referred to the horse- or mule-drawn wagons that carried supplies on the march, but the modern meaning often appears in veterans' memoirs.)

Both rails and wires proved their value in the first major battle: at Bull Run, in July 1861. P.G.T. Beauregard deployed his Confederates north and east of Manassas Junction: "We had a railroad approach in

our rear for the accumulation of reinforcements, while another (the Manassas Gap) railway gave rapid communications with the fertile valley of the Shenandoah." From Winchester, in the lower valley, Gen. Joseph E. Johnston brought 8,340 men and 20 cannon. They marched all night to the rail stop where Beauregard had sent "all possible railway transport." Two of the engineers, a Marylander recalled, were Yankees who "treacherously concocted a plan

to collide their trains." Few were hurt, and two-thirds of Johnston's troops arrived in time for the fight.

During the battle, Brig. Gen. Irvin McDowell, U.S.A., kept mounted couriers galloping to Fairfax Court House, where a telegrapher relayed messages to Washington. In the telegraph office at the War Department on Pennsylvania Avenue, senior officials gathered, the President among them. Lincoln "waited with deep anxiety for each succeeding dis-

patch," noted office manager David Homer Bates.

Until early afternoon McDowell's messages were encouraging. Then they stopped. At first this suggested an advance, but "as the silence became prolonged, a strange fear seized upon the assembled watchers.... Suddenly, the telegraph instrument became alive again" and clicked out a sentence in Morse code: "Our army is retreating."

At the telegraph key in Springfield, a boy of 16 saw the flight and informed Bates's office that he would join it. He got this reply: "If you keep your office open until you have permission to close it, you will be rewarded. If you close it without such permission, you will be shot." He remained.

Both civilian and uniformed specialists had their place in the Union war effort. Soon after Bull Run the government seized all telegraph systems near the capital, and Congress later authorized the takeover of all lines needed by the new Military Telegraph Service. This had a thousand civilian members by 1864. The uniformed signal force was one man, Maj. A.J. Myer, at Bull Run; his improvised branch became the U.S. Signal Corps in March 1863.

Pontoon survey raft floats its inventor, Brig. Gen. Herman Haupt, field chief of Union railroads. Superiority in rail transport aided Northern victory. The locomotive "Firefly" tests frame trestles near Union Mills, Virginia, under the supervision of Haupt's foreman, E.C. Smeed.

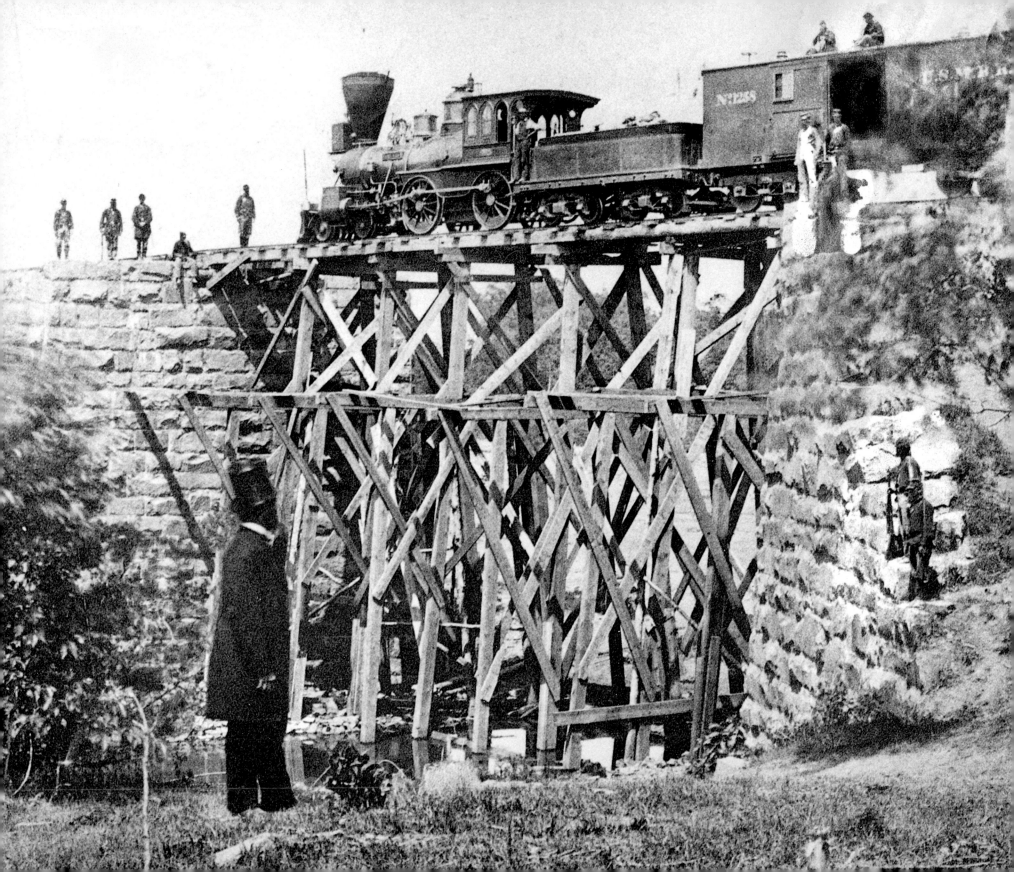

In 1862 Myer's men tested a field telegraph powered by George W. Beardslee's newly invented magneto. Small and light enough to be taken onto the battlefield, this expensive new device proved temperamental in practice and went out of use. Its insulated wire, however, became standard issue.

Wire was spooled off reels lashed onto the backs of mules or carried by men. Then it was draped over trees and bushes or just laid on the ground—where curious soldiers might snip out a sample. They got a shock if the wire was connected to the covered "battery wagon" that supplied electricity. Underwater lines came into use in 1862, and remote-control detonators for mines became possible.

The Confederacy also relied on telegraphy, but had less wire, only one wire factory, and fewer trained men. In 1863 a Texas private saw a clicking instrument for the first time, assumed it was some infernal Yankee device, and trampled it. "Boys!" he cried, "they is trying to blow us up. I seen the triggers a-working, but I busted 'em."

Among the pioneers of electronic warfare was a more sophisticated Rebel, George "Lightning" Ellsworth. When John Hunt Morgan raided Union-held Kentucky, Ellsworth kept the Federals confused by tapping their lines and impersonating their operators. Once he listened in for an hour or two before identifying himself as a "Federal operator" dodging Morgan's men. He claimed to be hiding in a darkened office, "reading by sound of my magnet," and tapped out disinformation for another couple of hours.

Both sides took to sending important dispatches in code, known as cipher. The Rebels never cracked the best Union system, but were first in the field with visual signals.

A. J. Myer had developed a wigwag system of signal flags for use against the Plains Indians. His associate E. P. Alexander took it into Confederate service and employed it to great advantage at Bull Run; he spotted a Union advance and gave the warning: "Look out for your left. You are flanked."

Both sides spelled out letters by holding the flag upright, then waving it to the side or dipping it to the front. At night, a torch doused in turpentine traced the same patterns.

Visual systems demanded elevations: hilltops, treetops, towers. In the siege of Port Hudson, eight of ten stations were in tall trees or on the masts of David Farragut's ships in the Mississippi. Operators relayed messages between the admiral and Maj. Gen. N. P. Banks, commanding ashore, and even directed artillery fire: "The rebels from opposite me are firing." "Are they together?" "No; one is 600 yards, the next 1,000 yards, and the next 1,200 yards

from your battery. . . . Your last shot was very good; a little to the right."

High in a balloon, an aeronautical telegrapher helped Federal gunboats concentrate their fire in a successful attack on Island No. 10; but balloons never found a place in the military practice of the 1860s. Signal towers, even on mountaintops, didn't offer such fat targets.

In the Antietam Campaign, a correspondent for a Richmond newspaper reported that Federal signal stations kept the Southern columns in view and "no doubt enabled the enemy to concentrate his force against our weakest points."

Eyewitness accounts from the front were common; more than 125 journalists covered the Union forces

Though Southerners were first to use signalmen—at Bull Run in 1861—Union forces established the Signal Corps. Below, a Signal Corps officer and his men stand ready with torch-capped staffs to wigwag nighttime signals from Army Headquarters in Washington, D.C., to forces across the Potomac River. Near Fredericksburg, Virginia, in 1863, corpsmen eye Confederate movements through telescope and binoculars.

alone. Steam-powered presses had reduced printing costs, and by 1860 the nation had 3,725 newspapers—387 of them dailies.

For anxious families everywhere, the telegraph and the newspaper brought the conflict home. But for the embattled governments, the railroad was supremely important. This was the first major war in which railroads gave long-distance logistical support from start to finish; and with less than a third of pre-war trackage, the South was limping from the beginning.

Both regions suffered from lack of common gauge—no fewer than 11 were in use—but Northern lines could cope more easily, laying new track or altering axles or diverting shipments to alternate routes. The Union had three major trunk lines between the West with its raw materials—grain, meat, ore—and the Eastern industrial centers.

Most Southern railroads were built for the short haul, conveying crops to rivers or seaports. The companies had relied on Northern factories for rails, spikes, and rolling stock. No new engines were constructed during the war, while a Northern line could easily triple its supply. To open a new line or repair an old one, Dixie's crews had to rob old track. Thus a crucial 48-mile link between Danville and Greensborough was constructed: two years in the making and then plagued by

breakdowns and wrecks. Moreover, many of the skilled employees of the 1850s were Yankees, and most of them went north in 1861.

Perhaps the most skilled of all was Herman Haupt, who ran the Union's military railroads from April 1862 until September 1863. A West Pointer, he had won fame as a civilian construction engineer. His first war assignment was to repair the line between Aquia Creek Station and Fredericksburg, which the Rebels had wrecked. He had its longest bridge ready in just nine days.

Its spindly trestles made a great impression on President Lincoln when he saw the new span; he called it "the most remarkable structure that human eyes ever rested upon. That man Haupt has built a bridge across Potomac Creek, about 400 feet long and nearly 100 high, over which loaded trains are running every hour, and . . . there is nothing in it but beanpoles and cornstalks."

Late in 1862, Haupt warned of "tough times" ahead, worse than the problems of supplying McDowell. "That was in June when grass could be obtained; now 60,000 animals must be fed exclusively by rail. . . ." Other requirements were now four to five times greater. "Expect plenty of grumbling, but I shall go ahead."

Generals grumbled, bureaucrats fretted, and privates did their bit by taking baths: "Soldiers would . . . wash clothes and persons with

soap in the springs and streams which supplied the water stations, and many engines were stopped on the road by foaming boilers caused by soapy water." Despite such hazards—not to mention enemy action—Haupt's system performed such feats as moving 1,500 tons of supplies a day to Gettysburg.

When Jefferson Davis left his plantation to take office in Montgomery, about 200 miles away, he had to travel nearly 700 miles by rail. He never gave anyone a role like Haupt's, and inept private management bedeviled a feeble system. Wheezing engines wobbled cautiously along flimsy rails as tons of supplies piled up behind the front.

Armor plates for the hull of the *Merrimack*, being rebuilt at Norfolk as an ironclad, lay around in Richmond for four weeks in 1861 because of a shortage of flatcars.

Moving troops by rail was a struggle in itself. When a corps was sent from Virginia to reinforce the Army of Tennessee in 1863, E. P. Alexander noted that the artillery traveled some 852 miles in 182 hours and missed the victory at Chickamauga.

Man for man, the Rebel soldier would have driven out every invader, a veteran insisted later, but he had to fight resources "afforded by the network of railways in the country north of him" and supplies from around the world. In the end, new instruments and elements prevailed.

1861

TOO POWERFUL TO BE SUPPRESSED

At 4:30 a.m. on Friday, April 12, a Confederate mortar a few miles south of Charleston fired a single shell. Its sputtering fuse traced a high arc across the starry sky. Then, in a cascade of red and white light, the shell exploded directly over Fort Sumter. Responding to the signal, a crescent of heavy guns roared and a torrent of shells fell upon Sumter.

The cannon fire awoke Mary Boykin Chesnut, the wife of former Senator James Chesnut. She "sprang out of bed. And on my knees—prostrate—I prayed as I never prayed before." Later, she and hundreds of others climbed to rooftops to watch the bombardment.

About 7 a.m., Major Anderson's garrison, undermanned and outgunned, feebly but gallantly returned fire. Soldiers crawled around, handkerchiefs to their faces, gasping in the smoke engulfing the fort. They improvised powder bags from their own clothing, risked death to haul powder from magazines. The Confederate gunners, who included one of Anderson's brothers-in-law, fired more than 3,000 rounds of shot and shell, smashing the masonry walls.

After 34 hours, his barracks ablaze and his ammunition nearly spent, Anderson surrendered. General Beauregard had given his old West Point instructor the privilege of firing a 100-gun salute to Sumter's tattered flag. After about 50 guns, a cartridge ignited in a hot barrel, touching off explosions that killed one Federal soldier and wounded five others, one mortally. These were the first casualties of the Civil War.

To the tune of "Yankee Doodle," Anderson marched his men out of the rubble of the fort and through a shattered gate to a wharf. There they boarded a steamer that would take them to the relief fleet, which had helplessly stood off the Charleston bar during the bombardment. From the deck of the ship the grimy defenders of Sumter watched the wild celebration ashore and the raising of the Stars and Bars over the fort. When the steamer finally headed out of the harbor, Confederate gunners lined the beach and silently doffed their caps.

Word of the surrender of Fort Sumter spread through North and South by telegraph, still a wonder of the age. Beyond the last telegraph pole, the Pony Express carried the news westward. At Camp Floyd in the Utah Territory, the rider from Fort Kearney handed an officer a dispatch. "There were the silent anxious faces" as he read it aloud. "All were quiet, serious and thoughtful, as we (Continued on page 66)

Lightning echoes the fiery conflict of the war's first major land battle at Manassas in July 1861, in view of a monument to Stonewall Jackson.
Defense units at Washington, D.C., only 30 miles away, include militia (above) and the 1st Connecticut Heavy Artillery (following pages).

"Sphinx of the Confederacy," an Alabamian called Jefferson Davis; "a strangely muffled man," concluded a modern biographer. Davis's life held drama enough for a long summer novel, but he is remembered mainly as an overmatched counterpart of Abraham Lincoln. If Davis had led the Union and Lincoln the South, one noted scholar has said, the Confederate States might well have won their independence.

Born like Lincoln in Kentucky, in 1808, youngest of ten, he grew up on a Mississippi farm. He spent two happy years as the only Protestant in a Catholic boarding school, four fractious years at West Point. In 1828 he graduated 23rd in a class of 32, with 327 demerits on his record. From plebe year to deathbed he was restive under discipline, touchy, quite humorless, quick to assert dignity and to take offense.

In 1835 he resigned from the army to marry Col. Zachary Taylor's daughter Sarah Knox. They were wed in June; malaria struck both and killed her in September. For ten years Davis lived alone with a few slaves on a Mississippi plantation called Brierfield. Then he married Varina Howell, 18 years younger than he; in 1845 his neighbors sent him to Congress.

Davis rushed off to the Mexican War the following June as elected colonel of the 1st Mississippi Rifles, a volunteer unit of the rich and highborn, and came home a hero. President Franklin Pierce made him Secretary of War. His army grew from 10,745 to 15,752, and his reputation grew as well. Davis became a senator again in 1857, and served as chairman of the military affairs committee. Nothing suggests that he gave much thought to the industrial basis of war. A moderate as Southern politicians went, he championed slavery and states' rights.

With dismay Davis learned in February 1861 that he had been elected provisional President of the Confederate States of America. "I thought myself better adapted to command in the field," he confessed.

JEFFERSON DAVIS

Probably, say specialists, the South could not have chosen better. Admirers called Davis "honest, pure, patriotic." He appointed some able men—including the first American Jew to hold Cabinet office, Judah P. Benjamin. He could take decisive action. In private he charmed strangers with his insight, candor, and courtesy. Brig. Gen. Arthur Middleton Manigault of South Carolina said such occasions showed Davis "to greatest advantage." The President often exerted this power "when in a good humor, and with persons that have never offended him."

Good humor faltered with poor health. Digestive ills, eyestrain, headaches, and facial neuralgia laid him low. Under stress he took offense quicker than ever. Strain mounted as the government grew—70,000 civilian employees, about 4,000 men in the Navy, and more than 300,000 in the Army—and its domain shrank. Davis never spared himself, but mired himself in detail. In 1863 the head of the Bureau of War called him "no administrator—the worst judge of men in the world." As Commander in Chief he clung stubbornly to such miscast friends as the calamitous general Braxton Bragg. In both military and civilian affairs he scorned the arts of conciliation, like a mechanic disdainful of grease. He did little to sustain public morale.

In desperation, Davis tried to gain recognition from France and Britain by offering to emancipate the slaves. He called on Congress to use slaves for military service. These measures came too late. On April 4, 1865, he proclaimed "a new phase" of the struggle: guerrilla warfare. R. E. Lee and U.S. Grant, and other commanders, prevented that.

Captured, held in solitary confinement at Fort Monroe, for a time chained like a felon, Davis became a martyr of the Lost Cause. Freed in 1867, he dictated his apologia, *The Rise and Fall of the Confederate Government*. He died in 1889. It may be said of him, as Lincoln said of John Brown, "It could avail him nothing that he might think himself right."

Barely visible at the doorway of the State House in Montgomery, Alabama, Jefferson Davis takes the oath of office as provisional President of the Confederate States of America on February 18, 1861. Despite the buoyant hopes of onlookers, Davis foresaw "trouble and thorns innumerable."

wended our way back to our quarters to tell our wives and children that all our hopes of peace were blasted. . . ."

At Floyd and at Army posts elsewhere, Southern officers quietly resigned: 197 of the 1,100 officers leading the 16,300-man U.S. Army. With 99 from the retired list, they gave the Confederate Army an elite. Of those who resigned it was simply said, "He went with his state."

The garrison at Floyd began getting ready for what would be a two-month march eastward to war. Among them was Capt. John Gibbon of North Carolina, who remained loyal to the Union. His three brothers joined the Confederates.

Another Pony Express dispatch went to Lt. Edward Porter Alexander, U.S.A., in San Francisco. He was ordered to report to Lt. James B. McPherson for work on fortifications on Alcatraz Island. McPherson, an Ohioan and a friend, tried to talk Alexander, a Georgian, into staying in California on coast defense duty, eloquently arguing that his cause could not possibly succeed. But Alexander resigned his commission and sailed to New York City.

As his train rattled across New York, Pennsylvania, and Ohio, "everywhere there were camps & soldiers in regiments & brigades. And they were all fine healthy looking men, with flesh on their bones & color in their cheeks, thoroughly well uniformed, equipped & armed." In Tennessee and north Georgia, "the villages were few & small, & the troops I saw nowhere more than one or two companies together. These were generally poorly & promiscuously uniformed & equipped & they were even still more poorly armed. . . . Our men were less healthy looking, they were sallower in complection & longer & lankier in build, & there seemed too to be less discipline & drill among them. . . . But I lived to see that our men had a spirit which more than made up for all their deficiencies. . . ."

McPherson had argued that in population and economic power the agricultural South could not match the industrial North. Alexander's faith was that of a Southerner: *Spirit* would prevail over scarcity. The regional differences were not that simple.

According to the 1860 census, Northern factories turned out 30 times as many pairs of shoes and boots as the South, and 32 times as many guns. In the North, about 1.3 million worked in factories, in contrast to the South's 110,000. Workers in the 23 states that stayed in the Union produced some 90 percent of industrial goods.

King Cotton ruled the farm fields of the Deep South, and planters were slow to turn to the food and fodder crops needed for war. Southern farmers grew enough peas, beans, rice, corn, and sweet potatoes to feed armies. But the South lacked the factories to can food or a system of distribution. Only about 9,000 miles of the nation's 31,000 miles of railroad served the Confederacy.

In February 1861, three days after he was sworn in as provisional President, Jefferson Davis had sent Confederate purchasing agents north to buy ammunition, artillery, and machinery for making munitions and rifles. Arms merchants accepted their orders—and not just in Virginia. The seven seceding states had also armed themselves from seized Federal arsenals, which yielded about 159,000 guns (some

of them flintlocks), about 400 cannon, nearly 500,000 pounds of gunpowder, and millions of cartridges. If the Yankees prolonged a struggle, the Confederacy would need her own source of munitions and matériel. "A misplaced but generous confidence" in the North, said Davis lamely, had kept the South from preparing for war.

The Confederate government expanded the Augusta Powder Works in Georgia and began to set up shipyards. Ironworks increased production. Agents scoured the countryside for caves containing deposits of nitrate, essential for gunpowder.

Southerners welcomed "the Second War of Independence"—a deliverance from the economic tyranny of the North—while some lamented the end of the American dream. "The United States! the star country! . . . her glory has departed!" wrote a Tennessee woman to her sister soon after Sumter. A Georgian said, "Is it not strange that we should fire cannons, illumine cities, raise bonfires, and make noisy the still hours of the night with shouts over the destruction of a government infinitely greater than Rome ever was!"

Many slaveholding Indians renounced the Union. In the Indian Territory between Arkansas and Texas, the Chickasaw legislature declared its alliance with the Confederacy, saying that "as a Southern people we consider their cause our own."

For Northerners, Sumter's fall was the first act in a drama that mystically combined Union and Justice. Frederick Douglass, disheartened by the apparent failure of the anti-slavery crusade, had been thinking of moving to Haiti when he heard about Sumter. "God be praised!" he exclaimed, and decided to stay. Other abolitionists took up the cry, "Crush the Slavocracy!" They were still a minority; the majority were determined to avenge the insult to "the old flag."

Ted Upson and his father were working an Indiana cornfield when a neighbor brought the news. "We did not finish the corn," Ted wrote in his diary; "Father looked ten years older." When Ted tried to enlist, his father withheld permission. "I was so mad I bawled," Ted wrote. In 1862 his father would relent, and Ted would go off to war.

Southerners and Northerners were ready to die for their faith. A Cincinnati lawyer, Rutherford B. Hayes, explained why he volunteered: "I would prefer to go into it if I knew I was to die, or be killed in the course of it, than to live through and after it without taking any part in it." Hayes's regiment, the 23rd Ohio, typified the Northern citizen army, in which men from many occupations pooled their talents to fight. Lincoln later remarked that "a president, a cabinet, a congress, and perhaps a court" could be plucked from many a Northern regiment. He was prophetic about the 23rd, whose men included two future Presidents—Hayes and William McKinley.

When Sumter fell, Lincoln asked the state militias for 75,000 men. They would serve, he proclaimed, for 90 days. They would probably be used mainly to "repossess" the forts and other Federal properties seized by the seceded states, "combinations too powerful to be suppressed by the ordinary course of judicial proceedings." Each of the states still in the Union was asked for a quota of 780-man regiments.

The governor of Virginia refused to send troops because, he said, Lincoln had "chosen to inaugurate civil war." Arkansas refused, as did North Carolina. Tennessee said it would not send any men to Lincoln but would send "50,000, if necessary, for the defense of our rights and those of our Southern brethren." Unionists in these states fell silent. "All of a sudden," said one, "I felt very southern."

All four of these states quickly seceded. Virginia's troops went into action, capturing the Norfolk Navy Yard and the arsenal and armory at Harper's Ferry but losing Alexandria and Arlington Heights.

Kentucky's governor refused to aid "the wicked purpose of subduing her sister Southern States." Missouri's labeled Lincoln's actions "illegal, unconstitutional, and revolutionary . . . inhuman and diabolical." Delaware's governor replied that his state had no militia—her volunteers would offer themselves. Maryland reflected the divided sympathies of the border states. Baltimoreans isolated Washington by cutting telegraph lines, ripping up railroad tracks, destroying bridges.

Lincoln had Maryland's secessionist lawmakers arrested, and the state remained in the Union. The Confederate Congress would admit Missouri and Kentucky, significant sources of troops and invaluable suppliers of mules and horses, but the role of these states would be determined by force. Federal control of the border states would threaten the upper South's industrial and grain belt. Within 150 miles of the northern border of Tennessee and Virginia were almost all of the

FOURTH REGIMENT
NEW HAMPSHIRE

DOWN
WITH THE REBELLION.

VOLUNTEERS.
ABLE BODIED MEN WANTED
FOR THE FOURTH REGIMENT.

The subscribers having been appointed Recruiting
Officers, will open a Recruiting Office at

On both sides, volunteers of all kinds and conditions rushed to their colors in '61, answering broadside appeals for "able bodied men" (right). The well-known Sussex Light Dragoons (below, lower) formed in January, nearly four months

before Virginia's secession. Nameless Rebels, possibly in Louisiana, relax in their "den" (below, upper). Soldiers of a New York Zouave regiment (opposite) sport stylish uniforms inspired by those of French infantry in North Africa.

FOLLOWING PAGES: A journalist found these 9th Mississippi infantrymen fixing supper—"uniformless in all save brightly burnished arms and resolute purpose."

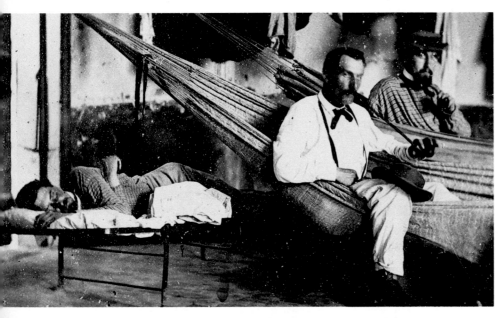

South's grain crops, flour mills, hogs and cattle for market, and key sources of salt for curing meat. This region also held coal, ironworks, lead mines, and the Confederacy's main source of copper—essential for percussion caps—at Ducktown, Tennessee.

Few in the North or South went to war worrying about logistics. The war began in a whirl of tailors sewing gaudy uniforms, of ladies stitching silk flags, of veterans of the Regular Army trying to make soldiers out of what an exasperated drill instructor from Europe called "one dam herd of goose." Seeking battle and glory, the recruits got sore feet and diarrhea. Going to war meant learning to drill and wearing little military caps that let your ears get sunburned.

Soldiers were expected to march 5 miles in 60 minutes at double-quick time. They were not to fire until "they distinctly perceive the objects at which they aim, and are sure that those objects are within proper range." They had to learn more than 40 bugle calls, which rang out for such orders as "Fix Bayonet" and "Retreat."

The North's first volunteer regiments entrained to Washington, camping in and around the Capitol, roasting meat in marble-manteled Senate fireplaces, sleeping in the Rotunda. The new Confederate capital of Richmond also drew protective garrisons. But thousands of Confederate troops headed for the little Virginia town of Manassas, a railroad junction about 30 miles southwest of Washington. Many did not have uniforms or army boots. Supplies of ammunition were limited to about 50 to 70 rounds per soldier, although regulations called for 200 rounds. Inefficient quartermasters and a rickety railroad system slowed down the delivery of tents, blankets, and food.

In June, two small encounters cast long shadows. In western Virginia, 2,000 Federals under Maj. Gen. George B. McClellan routed 1,500 Confederates at Philippi. The victory gave instant fame to the 34-year-old McClellan, dubbed the "Young Napoleon" by the Northern press. And the military rout led to a political one; Philippi and Virginia west of the Alleghenies would be lost to the South with the creation of West Virginia in 1863. And near Boonville, Missouri, a Union force of 1,700 routed secessionist militia. "We were both missionaries and musketeers," a Union soldier wrote, sensing the significance of the encounter: It kept Missouri in the Union and secured the Missouri River.

Streams and fords near Manassas, Virginia, figured in major actions in 1861 and '62. On July 18, 1861, Rebels kept Federals from crossing Bull Run at Blackburn's Ford. Three days later, Union columns forded the stream farther to the north, crossed Catharpin Run at Sudley Springs Ford, and attacked the Confederates' left flank. Here, Union cavalrymen revisit the ford the following March as children watch and play.

Another minor affair, hailed as a major triumph, heartened the South. In Virginia, Confederates at Big Bethel Church repulsed a Union sortie from Fort Monroe, the Federal stronghold overlooking Hampton Roads. By now considerable forces were deployed in Virginia. For the Union, Brig. Gen. Irvin McDowell had about 37,000 men at Arlington, across the Potomac from Washington. Another 18,000, under Maj. Gen. Robert Patterson, occupied the lower Shenandoah Valley. At Fort Monroe were 15,000 men under Benjamin F. Butler, a Massachusetts lawyer with a major general's commission. For the Confederacy, Beauregard had assembled about 22,000 men at Manassas, a well-chosen spot. Here a railroad from the south met a line from the Shenandoah, where Gen. Joseph E. Johnston with 12,000 was keeping an eye on Harper's Ferry.

Congress and newspaper strategists prodded Lincoln to end the war quickly by a march on Richmond, just a hundred miles south of Washington. But Lincoln's chief military advisor, Lt. Gen. Winfield Scott, had conceived a strategy based on a naval blockade that critics called the "Anaconda Plan," after the snake that slowly crushes its prey. The South at first saw one aspect of the blockade as a boon: inadvertent enforcement of the cotton embargo. The South had cut off cotton from export to idle the textile mills of Britain and France, hoping these nations would decide to aid the Confederacy.

Scott's plan to patrol some 4,000 miles of coastline had gotten off to a bad start. Only 3 of 42 warships were at hand in home waters. Federal forces had to evacuate the Norfolk Navy Yard, scuttling the out-of-commission *Merrimack*. And the commandant of the Washington Navy Yard joined the Confederate Navy. But that service got no Federal warships. When a Southern officer in command of a U.S. Navy ship returned, he took his ship to a Union harbor—and then resigned. In April 1861 the Confederate Navy consisted of 2 small steamships, 4 captured Federal revenue cutters, and 3 commandeered slave ships.

Pressure on Lincoln to launch an offensive grew as July neared, for then the 90-day enlistments of many Union volunteers would expire. The men were ill-organized, not yet fully equipped. But the calendar could not be denied. On July 16, McDowell sent some 35,000 troops toward Manassas on what was billed as a campaign to take Richmond.

Field maneuvers had no place in American doctrine. An army would learn the skills of campaigning by trial and error if it learned at all. In straggly columns the Union troops jammed dusty country roads. Strolling soldiers, many of them teenagers, wandered off the road to pick blackberries. The "trains"—subsistence and ordnance wagons—lumbered along behind the divisions. It took the army two and a half days to cover the 20 miles to the hamlet of Centreville, about 3 miles east of a meandering creek called Bull Run.

From here, for two days, McDowell sent out reconnaissance units. He planned feints at Confederates arrayed near a stone bridge over Bull Run while his main force swooped down on the Rebels' left flank.

At 2 a.m. on Sunday, July 21, McDowell launched the complex attack, sending two diversionary thrusts toward the Confederate line while his main force of about 13,000 men headed to a ford at Sudley Springs, north of the stone bridge. Thus began the battle that the South would call Manassas and the North, Bull Run. The Rebels saw through McDowell's plan and, from signal stations on hilltops, passed a warning by "wigwag," the semaphore-flag communications system.

Confederate defenders at the stone bridge across Bull Run wheeled and headed for high ground that would face the Federal main body, which had crossed the ford and entered a thick woods. When they emerged, the Confederates raked the ranks with withering fire—and stopped them. Union reinforcements, led by Col. William Tecumseh Sherman, arrived late in the morning. Outnumbered and outgunned, the Rebels fell back to a bare hill topped by a house owned by Mrs. Judith Henry. The 85-year-old widow insisted on staying there; she was mortally wounded when a shell hit the house.

As the Confederates scrambled up the hill, Brig. Gen. Thomas J. Jackson, a former professor at the Virginia Military Institute, was already there, calmly organizing his brigade along a swale that gave them cover against Union artillery. Seeing the panic swirling around him, Jackson suggested to Brig. Gen. Barnard Bee that his men form around Jackson's brigade. Bee—who would die that day—rode into the retreating swarm and, legend says, shouted, "There stands Jackson like a stone wall! Rally behind the Virginians!" From that moment on, the professor was Stonewall Jackson.

Among the troops in Jackson's brigade were Virginia Military Institute cadets in dress uniforms. Someone yelled, "Come on, boys! We can whip them!" And the boys rose from wrinkles of the land to attack the enemy. Bullets or canister felled many. After the battle, Joseph Norris of the Loudoun Artillery found his dead brother, Cadet Charles R. Norris, who was serving as captain of Company B, 27th Virginia Infantry, and bore the body home to Leesburg.

Beauregard rode among his men on the hill, rallying them and directing fresh troops—among them the last of the men arriving from the Shenandoah, via the Manassas Gap Railroad. (Patterson had done nothing to stop them.) About 4 p.m., the reinforced Confederates launched a flank attack and drove the enemy back down the hill.

Confederate artillery fired into the retreating ranks. At this point the Regulars proved their worth. Four companies of U.S. Cavalry had fought steadily, as had nine batteries of U.S. Artillery; now eight companies of the U.S. Infantry formed a fighting rear guard. Under Maj. George Sykes, they withdrew in good order under heavy fire—meeting the cruelest test of discipline. By now the volunteers were a fleeing horde. A shell smashed a wagon blocking the Cub Run bridge near Centreville; Federals leaped into the creek or scattered into woods, hoping to make their way back to Washington.

Lincoln feared that the Confederates would attack the capital. But their pursuit ended in darkness and rain. "The want of food and transportation," Beauregard complained, "had made us lose all the fruits of our victory."

Porter Alexander, the former Union officer who had made his way home to Georgia from San Francisco, was now a captain of engineers on Beauregard's staff. Like many West Point officers, he saw war as chess. He said he observed few skillful moves this day, and concluded, "Neither of us played the game as well as it might have been done."

On the fields lay the bodies of 387 Confederates and 481 Federals. About 1,500 Southerners and 1,100 Northerners were wounded, and many of them would die. The glory of battle had summoned men to Bull Run, and glory still would summon them. Now, shadowing the glory, was the reality of the battlefield—torn limbs, dying screams, cowardice, the living picking the pockets of the dead.

MANASSAS | *Chinn Ridge (below, foreground) saw action in both the battles here. In '61, the troops of Col. O.O. Howard, just off a long march and outflanked by firing Rebels, broke ranks and ran, launching a chaotic retreat across tree-lined Bull Run (opposite page). Wounded soldiers at a Federal field hospital in the stone house (below, center) were captured.*

At the war's onset, both sides lacked two important elements: accurate maps and trained troops. More than five months after its 1861 defeat at Bull Run, the Union published the first comprehensive survey of northern Virginia. This map of the battlefield at Bull Run (below), compiled from maps prepared under Generals Beauregard and McDowell, appeared after the war. It shows Federal positions in blue, Rebel ones in red. During the battle on July 21, many raw recruits fled at first fire. The monument to the 14th Brooklyn (opposite) honors New York infantry who served gallantly in First and Second Manassas.

Capt. John Gibbon, still marching eastward through the Utah Territory, got the news of Bull Run from a Pony Express rider. The column halted while an officer began reading aloud to a group of eager listeners. The report described "how our troops had forced the rebels back from position after position driving everything before them in the most gallant style." The reader paused and one of his listeners muttered, "Great God, the thing will be over before we get there." The reader went on to announce "an unaccountable stampede" and a Federal retreat "in great confusion." He stopped, stunned, and the same voice spoke up: "Good God, there will be no Government when we get there." They resumed marching.

Lincoln reacted to the Bull Run debacle by reaching for a victorious general—he summoned McClellan and ordered him to expand and reorganize the army. In November, McClellan would replace the ailing, 75-year-old Scott. With the Young Napoleon in Washington, Lincoln looked at his political problems. They included keeping Kentucky in the Union, keeping Maryland and Missouri out of the Confederacy, and keeping Britain and France out of the war.

Lincoln the Commander in Chief worked smoothly with Lincoln the politician. He cracked down on Maryland. Anyone deemed an "adherent of the rebel Government" was taken off to a military prison. If a lawyer applied for release of a political prisoner, Federal officials regarded this "as additional reasons for declining to release."

Kentucky, Lincoln's birthplace, got gentler treatment. According to one story, the President answered an assurance of divine blessing by saying he could do without it "but I *must* have Kentucky." Kentucky in the Confederacy would make the Ohio River a national boundary. Kentucky in the Union offered the Tennessee and the Cumberland, waterways running deep into the South. Lincoln tacitly accepted Kentucky's profession of neutrality but covertly slipped arms to the Home Guard, a pro-Union militia.

In the summer of 1861, Maj. Gen. Leonidas Polk, a West Point graduate and former Episcopal bishop of Louisiana, took over temporary command of the Confederacy's heartland—Tennessee, north-central Alabama, northern Georgia, and northeastern Mississippi. With luck, it might include Kentucky. *(Continued on page 86)*

Oh, what a battle must have been raging in Heaven, when the Archangel of the Lord needed the services of Stonewall Jackson!" So one mourner took the news that the great Rebel general had died on May 10, 1863—shot mistakenly by his own men in the dark at the hour of victory. His flanking marches, staunch defense, and bold attacks had become as famous as his unfaltering Christian faith.

Thomas Jonathan Jackson had won his longest, slowest campaign in his youth. Born in Virginia's backcountry hills in 1824, an orphan at age seven, he was raised by his kin. He entered West Point in 1842: an awkward, big-footed yokel in homespun, with all his goods in his saddlebags and the scantiest of schooling. Despite desperate study, he almost flunked in his first lonely year; he finished 17th of 59. Given another year, said classmates, he would have been first. Adult traits were already clear: rigid obedience to duty; scrupulous honesty; doggedness; oddities of posture and diet to relieve his obscure ailments; generous kindness.

With the field artillery in Mexico, he won glory and promotion. He learned to dance and speak Spanish with young ladies, and learned something of the Catholic faith. Later, on a tour of Europe, he admired fine art between visits to battlefields. His experience was wider than might appear from his austere life as a professed Presbyterian after November 1851. In that year Jackson left the army to teach at the Virginia Military Institute in Lexington. He married Elinor Junkin in 1853, but soon lost her to death. In 1857 he married Mary Anna Morrison, whose memoir tells of his happy, playful, tender ways at home.

In 1855, Jackson started a Sabbath school for Lexington slaves, recruiting ladies and gentlemen to help him teach. Among his pupils were the parents of Dr. Lylburn Liggins Downing, who as pastor of a Roanoke church commissioned a stained-glass window in Jackson's

THOMAS JONATHAN JACKSON

memory—a scene of mountains, and a river, and a tranquil soldiers' camp.

The general dazzled his people—and the enemy—with his little Army of the Valley. Often he showed brilliance as a corps commander. "Such an executive officer the sun never shone on," said Robert E. Lee. Could he have filled Lee's role? Probably not, say military analysts. Jackson handicapped subordinates by keeping them ignorant of his plans, and he had a way of quarreling with his best second in command—notably the hard-fighting A. P. Hill. Just once, in the Seven Days, he faltered badly, perhaps because of sleep deprivation. That one time, said a younger artillerist, cost the South her best chance to win a conclusive battle, and the war, and independence. Jackson never discussed it. In setbacks he saw God's providence; in victories, God's blessing. He made his plans with prayer; he got up several times to pray on a night before battle. Considering his career, mused an official in Richmond, "it might be fair to suppose him equal to any untried test."

In combat Jackson applied the unflinching logic of Calvinism. Once he rebuked a junior for ordering his men not to fire at an easy target, a Federal officer of heartbreaking gallantry. The general was adamant: "Shoot them all. I do not wish them to be brave."

His own death brought tributes from many quarters. Lee praised his daring, his skill, his energy. Old acquaintances in Union service spoke freely of their personal regret, calling him one of the purest, most honorable, most conscientious men who ever lived. A Southern civilian called his "a character of antique beauty, simple and severe." Perhaps the most Jacksonian of honors came from a Federal private. There was something so daring and noble in Jackson's way of fighting, wrote the youth, that it made his enemies love him, but they would not hesitate for a moment to send a bullet through his heart.

Yankee prisoners from First Manassas relax under casual guard of Charleston cadets at Castle Pinckney (opposite). They bunked cozily in the fort's casemates and shared the cadets' provender, royal treatment compared to later conditions in the squalid open stockade at Andersonville, Georgia.

In May 1861, Maj. Gen. Benjamin Butler, U.S.V., commander of Fort Monroe, Virginia, refused to hand over three escaped slaves, declaring them "contraband of war" (below). This doctrine, accepted by Lincoln, spurred thousands of slaves to flee toward Union lines. Before Second Manassas in 1862, slaves evading Jackson's advancing troops ford the Rappahannock (right) to reach a Union camp.

Meanwhile, the Confederates would not yield Missouri without a fight. In August an 11,000-man Rebel force marched on Springfield. About 5,400 Union troops intercepted the invaders at Wilson's Creek, ten miles southwest of the town. In five hours of fighting, each side suffered more than 1,200 casualties. The Federals pulled back, leaving the Confederates a large chunk of southwestern Missouri.

Union forces in the West were under the command of Maj. Gen. John C. Frémont, the flamboyant "Pathfinder." He had run for President in 1856, the first Republican nominee, and saw himself as the ruler of his military domain. While Confederate recruiting agents went about Missouri, Frémont threatened to execute any Rebel bearing arms. He issued a proclamation confiscating the property of pro-Confederate Missourians and emancipating their slaves. Lincoln annulled this edict and relieved Frémont of command in November.

Guerrilla fighting tormented Missouri, but the state remained in the Union. So did Kentucky, thanks considerably to the blundering of Leonidas Polk. In September, Polk put his vast and vital region at risk by impulsively sending troops into Kentucky and seizing Columbus. Brig. Gen. Ulysses S. Grant, newly in command of Federal forces in

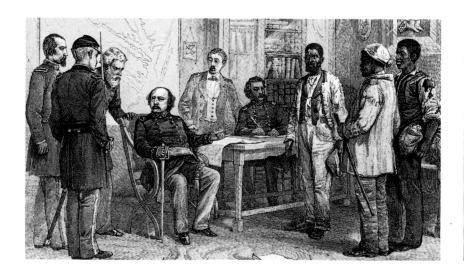

southeastern Missouri, swiftly countered this move. He landed troops from gunboats and transports and took the Kentucky river city of Paducah without a fight. Kentucky's governor ended his state's neutrality and ordered the Confederates off its soil.

As a prelude to a drive on Columbus, Grant on November 6 loaded about 3,000 men aboard transports and, with an escort of two gunboats, sailed down the Mississippi from Cairo, Illinois, toward Belmont, Missouri, the steamboat landing opposite Columbus. The next day Grant captured Belmont, and Polk responded by sending about 5,000 men across the river and overwhelming the Federals.

Under protective fire from the gunboats, Grant's troops scrambled back aboard ship. The raid accomplished little, but it foreshadowed the traits of Grant on larger battlefields: a quick eye, a decisive mind, and an unflinching acceptance of casualties as the price of action.

On the same day that Grant arrived at Belmont, Flag Officer Samuel F. du Pont, U.S.N., sailed into Port Royal Sound, South Carolina, with 77 vessels—the largest fleet an American had ever led. His gunners poured devastating fire into two Confederate forts. Percival Drayton commanded one of the warships; his brother Thomas commanded one of the forts. Du Pont landed marines and sailors to hold the forts until army troops could be landed from transports. Later, du Pont captured Beaufort, South Carolina, cutting off seagoing communication between Charleston and Savannah.

This success gave the U.S. Navy a southern base for the Atlantic blockade. The Confederates were buying swift blockade-runners in Europe and trying to build ironclad ships for coastal defense. Jefferson Davis hoped that Britain and France would put diplomatic pressure on Lincoln to end the blockade.

The Confederate Department of State named two former U.S. Senators, James M. Mason of Virginia (author of the 1850 Fugitive Slave Act) and John Slidell of Louisiana, as Special Commissioners to Britain and France respectively. They slipped through the blockade and sailed to Havana, where they boarded the British mail steamer *Trent*. On November 8, off Nassau, Capt. Charles Wilkes, commanding officer of the U.S.S. *San Jacinto*, stopped the *Trent* with a shot across her bow, then sent a boat to pick up the envoys. After a two-hour standoff,

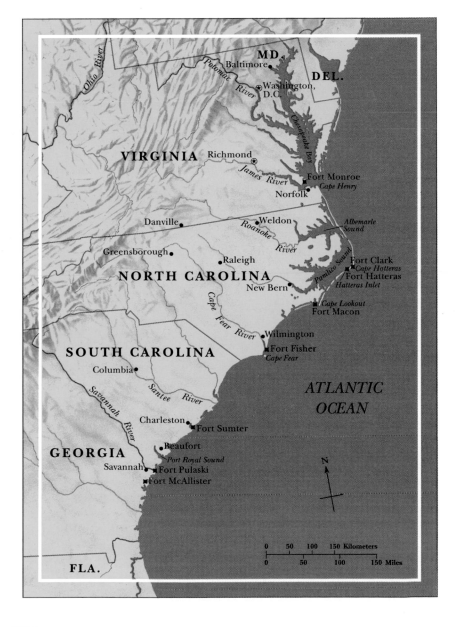

War in the West began in Missouri, a border state that Lincoln was determined to keep in the Union, despite its slave-owning and secessionist tendencies. At Wilson's Creek in August 1861 (right), a surprise Union attack on larger Rebel forces resulted in a Federal defeat. Yet the Union kept formal control, even in the face of incessant, bloody border raids by guerrillas on both sides.

the boarding party took Mason and Slidell and their secretaries to the *San Jacinto*—a breach of international law and an insult to Britain.

When Wilkes deposited Mason and Slidell at Fort Warren in Boston Harbor, the North hailed him as a hero and the U.S. House of Representatives voted him a gold medal. Britain's infuriated prime minister ordered 8,000 troops to Canada, strengthened naval forces in the West Indies, and rattled the sabers of diplomacy. Washington assured London that Wilkes had acted on his own. The "*Trent* affair" quietly ended when the prisoners were sent off aboard a British steamer.

Lincoln's first war year had begun with him riding in an open coach from Willard's Hotel to the Capitol for his Inauguration. Seated with him was Senator Edward Dickinson Baker of Oregon, a longtime friend and the namesake of Lincoln's second son. Just after sunset on October 21, Lincoln stumbled out of a military communications office, tears streaming down his cheeks. The telegraph had just brought the news that Baker, simultaneously a senator and a colonel, had been killed that day in battle. Lincoln's year ended with the U.S. Senate, outraged at Baker's death in the botched battle, setting up a Joint Committee on the Conduct of the War.

The mismanaged struggle that brought the war to the Senate had been fought on Ball's Bluff, high ground on the Virginia shore of the Potomac. Federal troops, probing Rebel deployment around Leesburg, had been mauled. They reeled back to the bluff. A Confederate soldier watched as the Federal soldiers "rolled, leaped, tumbled over the precipice" until "the side of the bluff was worn smooth by the number sliding down." Small boats carrying the wounded were swamped as the fugitives tried to board. Scores drowned. Of the 1,800 Federal troops who fought at Ball's Bluff, 921 were killed, wounded, captured, or lost in the bloody river waters.

Bull Run . . . Belmont . . . Ball's Bluff. The Senate wondered why so many Federal volunteers, sent off wreathed in hometown glory, had died in shameful defeats on Southern soil. After the battle of Belmont, an editorial writer had printed a question over the casualty lists: "They have fallen, and to what end?" Both sides could give ideological answers to the question. But in that first year of war, there was, for the Union Army, no military answer.

Hoping to avoid the fate of Sumter, several Illinois volunteer regiments fortified the town of Cairo, at the confluence of the Mississippi and Ohio Rivers (below). They worked feverishly, building barracks, earthworks, and batteries. Coast-defense guns stood at the ready for a Confederate attack from downriver that never came. Instead, the soldiers kept busy thwarting river-borne cotton smugglers.

FOLLOWING PAGES: The 2nd Maine parades on Christmas Day 1861. Of McClellan's attempts to season his recruits, one wrote, "The drowsy lion must have time to collect itself."

The Great Army of
the Wounded

In a letter to his cousin Phebe dated November 23, 1862, Massachusetts volunteer Samuel Nichols wrote from Virginia, "Everything here concerning sickness and its management seems so repulsive that the thought of being sick or having one of your friends in the Hospital, is filled with gloom."

Throughout the war, on both sides, private letters and newspaper accounts told of filthy hospitals, drunken doctors, callous attendants, patients uncared for or dying untended in unnecessary pain. Soldiers often hid minor wounds rather than resort to their doctors.

But most medical men did what they could within the limits of the age. "Germ theory" lay in the future; no one understood the role of microorganisms in spreading disease and infection, or the connection between sterile conditions and healing.

Recruits from rural backgrounds usually had no immunity against infectious diseases such as measles and chicken pox, which spread rapidly in crowded camps. Dysentery and typhoid fever spread as well, a direct result of unsanitary conditions. Many volunteers did not understand the importance of washing themselves and their clothes and bedding,

or placing garbage pits and latrines away from their water supply. Regular Army units in the North, with time-tested rules and strict discipline, had a better health record.

Doctors treated malaria and vaguely diagnosed fevers with quinine. They gave opium mixtures for diarrhea and rhubarb or jalap or calomel as cathartics. In massive doses, however, calomel caused permanent harm from mercury poisoning. Laudanum and morphine worked as painkillers, but their sustained use led to addiction.

By the end of the war, disease had killed two Confederate or Union soldiers for every one who was killed or mortally wounded in combat. This was an improvement over previous wars. Still, the sick overwhelmed Civil War medical services even before the first wounded were carried off the battlefield.

A few months before Samuel Nichols wrote his letter, a reporter for the *New York Herald* filed his story on the wounded of the Peninsula Campaign: "All the cow-houses, wagon-sheds, hay-barracks, hen-

coops, Negro cabins, and barns were turned into hospitals," and the patients lay on corn shucks and fodder. At one of the largest hospitals, "an amputation was being performed, and at the door lay a little heap of human fingers, feet, legs, and arms. I shall not soon forget the bare-armed surgeons, with bloody instruments, that leaned over the rigid and insensible figure, while the comrades of the subject looked horrifiedly at the scene."

But surgeons had little choice. Often amputation was the best they could do for a limb wrecked by a "minny ball," the notorious bullet named for Capitaine C.E. Minié of France. A heavy, slow, .58-caliber slug of lead, it crushed soft tissue and splintered bone.

The Confederacy, accustomed to relying on Northern manufactures, suffered from medical shortages of every kind. Patriots tried to help. Blockade-runners imported European supplies; travelers smuggled drugs through the lines. Native remedies, produced in newly founded pharmaceutical laboratories, were tried in desperation.

Almost from the start, hospitals ran short of soap. One in a variety of substitutes was a mix of boiled meat

A Union soldier kneels to offer water to a wounded Zouave comrade (above). Flags and garlands could not alleviate the suffering of soldiers in Washington's crowded Carver Hospital, but these men stood a better chance of recovery than those treated in makeshift field hospitals.

scraps, bones, skins, and lye held together with ashes. It worked, but attracted flies in warm weather.

Hospital space, too, was in short supply. After the first battle at Manassas, South Carolinian Samuel P. Moore, 26-year veteran of the U.S. Army, took charge of the medical effort of the Confederate States Army. He called for several large general hospitals (so labeled because they admitted men from any regiment). In 1861, on the eastern side of Richmond, slaves built Chimborazo, the most famous and, for a time, the largest hospital in the South. Its 250 pavilions (plank shanties, conceded a surgeon) could house 40 to 60 patients each, and tents sheltered a thousand convalescents.

Only months after completion, Chimborazo overflowed with casualties from the Peninsula Campaign. In September 1862, responding to the appalling conditions there and at other hospitals, the Confederate Congress passed legislation providing for paid "matrons" to perform a wide variety of services, from supervising laundry to cooking meals and administering medicines.

Inspired by Florence Nightingale's work for the British in the Crimean War, both Northern and Southern women defied convention to volunteer for service in military hospitals. Some gave up after a few days, but many swallowed their initial shock—"all horrors, to be taken in at a glance," said one lady—and went to work.

Southern projects remained local in character, as did some Union ones. Working independently, the Illinois widow Mary Ann Bickerdyke organized hospitals and food transport along the Mississippi; admired by Grant and Sherman, she appeared at battlefields from Fort Donelson to Atlanta. Dorothea Dix, famous as a reformer of insane asylums, became the Union's superintendent of female nurses and recruited thousands, insisting on mature years and homely faces. And the legendary Clara Barton joined the war effort in 1862 with the purpose of "stanching blood and feeding fainting men." The success of such pioneers shook deeply held views about women's capabilities.

At the Cooper Institute in New York City, 3,000 women met on April 29, 1861, and established the Women's Central Association of Relief, to coordinate the work of local groups and create a program for training nurses. Out of the W.C.A.R. grew the powerful United States Sanitary Commission, modeled after a British organization in the Crimean War. At first, Federal officials thought the commission superfluous and would not support it, but Lincoln gave it official status in June. As one of its founders noted, "It is out of the question for Government to do all that is to be done immediately

after severe fighting.... Hence the absolute necessity of volunteers during active operations."

When the Civil War broke out, 115 surgeons worked for the Army Medical Department; 24 of them left to establish the Confederacy's Medical Service. Each side had a Surgeon General; each set up field and general hospitals; each had arrangements for battle. When fighting occurred, noncombat soldiers such as bandsmen carried the wounded to ambulances driven by civilians. The standard vehicles were two-wheeled carts. Later, steadier four-wheeled wagons came into use, but even these gave a rough ride on bad roads. Men deposited in railroad cars sometimes remained stranded in them for days.

In 1862 boats were used to evacuate casualties from Shiloh and the Peninsula Campaign. *Red Rover,* a U.S. Navy hospital ship, served with distinction on the Mississippi during the Vicksburg Campaign. And Dr. Elisha Harris, one of the U.S. Sanitary Commission's founders, designed a hospital-style passenger car for railroad use; it had stretchers suspended on rubber cords for relative comfort, and it carried an operating table for emergencies.

In 1864 the Union gave official standing to the ambulance corps developed in 1862 by an Army surgeon, Maj. Jonathan Letterman. The system of uniformed, trained specialists became a model for European

A Federal surgeon, uniformed in hat and sword, stages a leg amputation in an open tent at Fort Monroe, Virginia (below). A lieutenant applies a tourniquet above the knee while another assistant, in Zouave uniform, grips the patient's lower leg. The assistant surgeon, also wearing a Zouave hat, administers ether or, more likely, chloroform. A catch basin rests beneath the leg. Actual amputations, like other actions, could not be captured by the photographic process of the time. At a Union forward collecting point near Fredericksburg (left), wounded soldiers, some amputees, await evacuation.

armies—and part of the war's legacy to modern medicine.

The Civil War involved an unprecedented mobilization of men and resources, and the Union's outdated, haphazardly run little Army Medical Department could not keep up as the war expanded and casualties mounted. It had to change. As a result, the department was transformed into an impressive organization that controlled the largest hospital system yet developed. Improvements were made in surgical care and evacuation procedures, in preventive medicine and record-keeping systems.

Doctors gained valuable experience and practical knowledge that ranged from splinting fractures to treating emotional trauma. Neurologist S. Weir Mitchell began the study of "phantom limb," the perception of a missing arm or leg as present and painful. He also recognized that many so-called malingerers or cowards were actually ill. He described cases of "acute exhaustion" when soldiers "gave out suddenly . . . and remained for weeks, perhaps months in a pitiable state." He prescribed "complete rest and plentiful diet," and saw that many of these men recovered to return to the front line. The symptoms he observed would be called shell shock or combat fatigue in later wars.

In its own way, the Civil War fostered the work of mercy.

1862

THENCEFORWARD, AND FOREVER FREE

Before daylight faded on September 14, Pvt. David L. Thompson of Co. G, 9th New York Infantry, walked over the churned ground at South Mountain in Maryland. "All around lay the Confederate dead. . . . As I looked down on the poor, pinched faces . . . all enmity died out. There was no 'secession' in those rigid forms nor in those fixed eyes staring blankly at the sky. Clearly it was not 'their war.' "

A few days later, on the nearby battlefield of Antietam, scene of the bloodiest one-day fight of the war, Thompson and men like him looked down and tried to fathom the carnage of 1862— the Bloody Lane, the Bloody Pond far to the west at Shiloh, and the nameless places where men by the thousand rushed at death or cowered before it.

Even on days without battles, men wondered about the meaning of the war. James A. Garfield, an officer of the Army of the Ohio, noticed "a growing hatred of slavery among the rank and file of the army." The soldiers, he wrote, were "linking slavery and the rebellion together in an indissoluble bond." Garfield, more politician than soldier, saw a cunning move for Jefferson Davis: Declare emancipation and then seek diplomatic recognition in Europe. "If he does this," Garfield wrote a friend, "the day is lost to us forever."

President Davis was not about to free the slaves of his embattled states. And, as 1862 began, neither was President Lincoln. His mind had turned from short-term crises to a longer, clouded prospect. Leaders, North and South, might have shared the reality that Bartlett Yancey Malone of Co. H, 6th North Carolina, waiting in camp day after day, set down in his diary: "we had orders to pack our knapsacks and to be ready to march at a moments warning but whar we was to go too we did not no."

No one knew. Strategies were evolving, as was the waging of war itself. New weapons, new ideas would arrive on land and sea in 1862. In the West, men would fight on swollen rivers and in narrow canyons. In the East, they would range across fertile lands, ducking behind stone walls and rail fences from Maryland to South Carolina. Survivors, like Thompson and Malone and hundreds of thousands of others, would charge forward or stumble back, then march on and fight again.

Often the land itself would determine where armies would fight or wouldn't. Richmond, for example, lay behind formidable natural defenses. But the great rivers of the West—the Mississippi, the Tennessee, the Cumberland—were potential channels of invasion.

The Mississippi got the most attention from Union strategists.

Shiloh in April in the West (opposite), Antietam five months later in the East (above): These two battles would claim 7,500 lives—and leave both sides reeling at the unutterable cost of war. At Cumberland Landing not far from Richmond, Union forces marshal their might (following pages).

"The people of the Northwest," said the governor of Indiana, "can never consent to be separated politically from the people who control the mouth of that river." Conquest of that river, said William T. Sherman, was "far more important than the conquest of Virginia."

General-in-Chief George B. McClellan, however, favored war in the East. He proposed "crushing the rebellion in one campaign" by taking Richmond, Charleston, and other cities. Prancing about the capital on a bay charger and polishing the Army of the Potomac, he sounded ready to go. But deep into January he gave no sign of taking his 100,000-man army anywhere. Winter made overland campaigns a poor bet.

On January 27, Lincoln issued his General War Order Number 1. All forces of the Union were to move against the Rebels on February 22. This would honor Washington's birthday and spoil Jefferson Davis's Inauguration Day. A few days later he issued a special order requiring McClellan to seize the railroad southwest of Manassas Junction. The junction was occupied, but the general-in-chief objected to the plans of his Commander in Chief. For some time McClellan had maintained that action in Kentucky should precede a drive to take Richmond.

In the West, strategists were planning to attack the Confederacy's "Long Kentucky Line." This ran from Columbus, Kentucky, on the Mississippi to the Cumberland Gap in northeastern Tennessee. Brig. Gen. George H. Thomas, a Virginian who chose to side with the Union, struck first. After a mud-wrestling march—40 miles in eight days—he drubbed a Rebel force at Logan's Cross Roads on January 19. This opened a path into east Tennessee, a region of cut-up terrain, small farms, few slaves, and Union loyalty, typical of the Southern highlands. But nothing much larger than a guerrilla band could operate effectively in its more mountainous areas.

Brig. Gen. U.S. Grant had easier going and specific targets. He moved against the center of the Southern cordon to take two river bastions: Fort Henry, on the east bank of the Tennessee River, and Fort Donelson, on the west bank of the Cumberland—12 miles apart by land. While winter ravaged the roads, it brought the rivers high.

In a joint army-navy operation, Grant's 17,000 men assembled at Paducah and set off aboard 13 transports escorted by Flag Officer Andrew H. Foote's 7 gunboats. The troops (Continued on page 111)

NEW ORLEANS | *Time vanquishes what Northern guns could not: Forts Jackson (below) and St. Philip (opposite), now shrouded in vines and weeds, stood as bastions of the lower Mississippi River 75 miles south of New Orleans.*

Their massive walls and heavy guns— combined with a floating chain of hulks and logs stretched across the river between them—made these defenses a formidable barrier to the city. But 13 of a Union fleet of 17 wooden warships

draped in chains, and commanded by Flag Officer David G. Farragut, ran a gap in the chain on April 24 and steamed past the forts—only lightly damaged despite mortar bombardment. New Orleans surrendered five days later.

In the early morning of April 24, 1862, two red beams flashed from the mizzen of the flagship *Hartford*. To the 17 warships assembled silently in column the signal was clear: The assault on the forts guarding the South's largest city was to begin. It was one of the Union's mightiest armadas, and its commander, Flag Officer David G. Farragut, had spent weeks preparing it for action.

"If successful . . . the rebellion will be riven in the center, and the flag . . . will recover its supremacy in every state," Secretary of the Navy Gideon Welles had written Farragut about the battle for New Orleans, hardly easing the officer's anxiety. On opposite banks of the Mississippi, Forts Jackson and St. Philip were deemed impassable by the South. Now as the Union fleet pressed forward, an alarm sounded, and soon, a reporter penned, "The river and its banks were one sheet of flame, and the messengers of death were moving . . . in all directions." "It was a time of terror," scribed another. But by dawn Farragut had cleared the barriers with only one ship lost. Even Maj. Gen. Ben Butler, not given to praising the Navy, was awed: "A more gallant exploit it has never fallen to the lot of man to witness."

Meticulous planning and a mastery of strategy, combined with boldness and supreme bravery, brought Farragut to victory; those qualities, plus tactical ingenuity, would secure his place as the nation's first admiral. Opportunity and recognition, however, had been long in coming: Farragut was 60 years old in 1862, and his naval career had already spanned 50 years. Born in Tennessee, the orphaned son of a Spaniard, he had fought in both the War of 1812 and the Mexican War; his reputation was for diligence, not leadership.

The day after Virginia announced her secession, Farragut moved his family from there to New York. He impressed his Navy superiors with a Southerner's allegiance to the Union cause. An assault on New

DAVID GLASGOW
FARRAGUT

Orleans was on their minds, and they needed an officer to lead it. Commander David Dixon Porter, whose father had reared Farragut, endorsed him for the job. "I am to have a flag in the Gulf, and the rest depends upon myself," Farragut wrote his wife.

He disappointed no one. "Not rash, but a go-ahead man," observed a newsman. "Our men will fight to the death for him." After New Orleans, Farragut hoped to move against Mobile Bay, a Gulf port much used by blockade-runners. Instead he was sent upriver to Vicksburg; at Port Hudson he proved the value of his famous principle, "The best protection against the enemy's fire is a well-directed fire from our own guns." By the end of 1862, Farragut, now a rear admiral, commanded the entire Gulf coast except Mobile Bay. Frustrated, he had to wait until 1864 for orders to capture it.

A narrow channel flanked to the west by sunken pilings, mined with explosives (or "torpedoes"), and defended by forts, the bay's entrance presented a formidable challenge. The first of Farragut's 18 ships hit a mine and sank, stalling the second; Confederate guns blazed. Aboard the *Hartford*, a report noted, "Shot after shot came through the side . . . deluging the decks with blood." Go on! signaled Farragut. Legend adds drama: "Torpedoes ahead, sir!" "Damn the torpedoes! Full speed ahead!" Boldly the flagship struck out and, with Farragut secured to the rigging, led the fleet through the passage. In three hours, Union forces held the bay, closing the entire coast to enemy ships. It was a crowning but costly victory. Battle-worn, Farragut wrote: "This is the last of my work, and I expect a little respite."

It was time to bask in honor, including the rank of admiral specially voted by Congress and a celebratory European tour. In 1870, two years after returning, the man Gideon Welles saw as possessing "the unassuming gentleness of a true hero" died peacefully at age 69.

Aboard the 24-gun Hartford, *David Farragut savors victory at Mobile Bay in August 1864. This photograph shows the great naval hero at the pinnacle of his fame, an officer willing to take "great risks to obtain great results," as Secretary of the Navy Gideon Welles put it.*

*Indians called the valley Shenandoah—
"daughter of the stars." But to most
Virginians it was simply the Valley—just
as the tongue of land between the York
and James Rivers was the Peninsula.
In both places, geography was key to
military operations. The broad, fertile
Valley in season supplied abundant
provender for foraging troops. On either
side, wooded hills, gaps, spurs, and knobs
made an ideal maze for Southern troops
familiar with the terrain. The tidal
rivers of Virginia, on the other hand,
provided ready access to the interior for
amphibious invaders. And the dense
lowland forests could conceal an entire
army poised for attack.*

went ashore about three miles below Fort Henry, and the gunboats chugged on to challenge it. Floodwater had already invaded the poorly sited earthworks, and nearly 2,500 Rebels had withdrawn to Fort Donelson. A heavy artillery company held off the ironclads for more than an hour, but the fort surrendered to the Navy before Grant's mud-stained men arrived. Three wooden gunboats went on upriver to snip off a Southern supply route by disabling a bridge on the Memphis, Clarksville & Louisville Railroad.

In one day Grant marched about 15,000 men, many of them new recruits, across the 12 miles to Fort Donelson. The weather being unseasonably warm, men discarded overcoats, blankets, and tents on the way. The Federals moved up to the Rebels' outer defense line. This was an abatis—felled trees with tangled and sharpened branches facing the enemy—with a cleared zone behind it for easy shooting. The fort itself was an enclosed earthwork, guarded on land by a 2.5-mile semicircle of rifle pits and a network of parapets and trenches. On the high bluff by the river, a dozen heavy guns poked from U-shaped embrasures.

The transports and escorts took more than two days to arrive from Cairo, Illinois, with six regiments. On February 14, Foote's gunboats moved upriver, four ironclads abreast, followed by two oak-sheathed "timberclads." (To damage an ironclad, enemy gunners had to hit the pilothouse, gunports, or hull below the armor.) The Southern gunners, though hastily trained, did well. They forced the vessels to withdraw after about 90 minutes: two ironclads out of control, two leaking badly; 11 dead, 41 wounded. Rebel casualties: 0. Long after dark the Confederates were still celebrating.

That night, winds howled under a burden of sleet and snow. Federal orders prohibited campfires. Men who had no coats or blankets froze to death. Meanwhile the Confederate commanders held a council of war. These were John B. Floyd, who had been Secretary of War under Buchanan; Gideon J. Pillow, who had been a general of volunteers in Mexico; and Simon Bolivar Buckner, a professional under amateurs. They decided to try for a breakout and a 75-mile dash to Nashville.

At dawn on the 15th, the Rebels attacked; by midday they had an escape route. Then the generals fell into a wrangle and pulled the men back to their lines. Grant, who had gone downstream to confer with

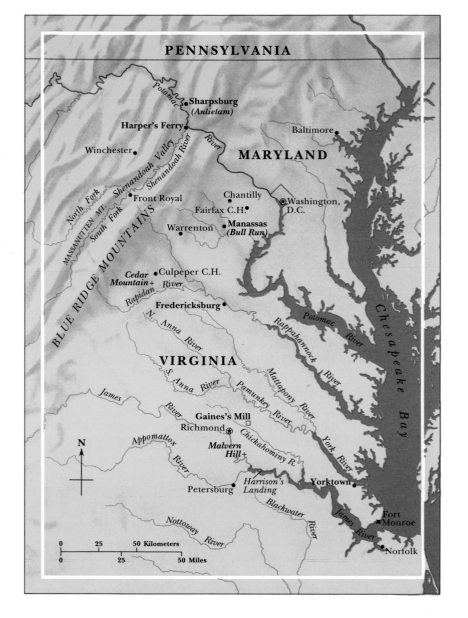

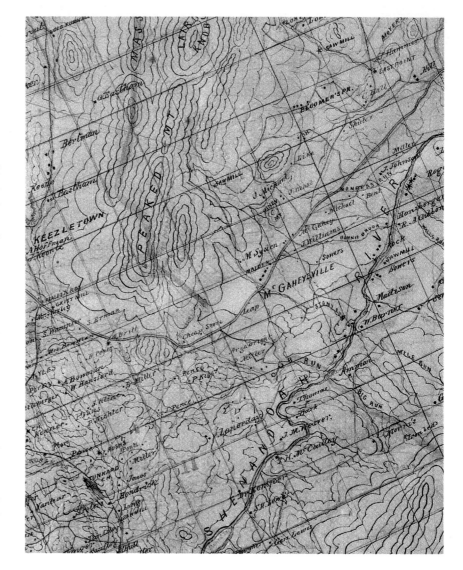

Foote, was told of the trouble by a staff officer "white with fear." Hurrying back over roads rutted with frozen mud, Grant found men milling about and out of ammunition. "Fill your cartridge boxes, quick, and get into line," he ordered. "The enemy is trying to escape and he must not be permitted to do so."

Brig. Gen. Charles F. Smith, who had been commandant of cadets when Grant was at West Point, raised his hat on the tip of his sword and led a bayonet charge that pierced the defense line. "I was nearly scared to death," one of his volunteers recalled, "but I saw the old man's white mustache over his shoulder, and went on."

By evening the Confederate generals were planning a surrender. Col. Nathan Bedford Forrest reported an escape route for his cavalry across an icy creek. Medical officers warned that the exposure would kill his troopers. Floyd, afraid of charges of treason if captured, yielded command to Pillow, who said, "I pass it." "I assume it," said Buckner. "Give me pen, ink and paper, and send for a bugler." Floyd and Pillow escaped separately, while Forrest, disgusted but not past profanity, led his men and several hundred more across the creek and away. Meanwhile Buckner wrote his request for terms; the bugle sounded a call for parley; and a truce party found Grant in his farmhouse headquarters.

Grant scanned the letter and wrote a reply: "No terms except unconditional and immediate surrender can be accepted. I propose to move immediately upon your works." Buckner surrendered. As the story spread, the North had a new hero, the South new troubles.

In Europe, Richmond's envoys reported a cooling of British and French attitudes. The Confederate Congress offered incentives to any man who signed up for three years or the duration of the war. In the West, the Confederates evacuated Bowling Green and Columbus. They had lost the keys to a region they desperately needed: middle Tennessee, with its abundant grain crops, fine bluegrass pasture and livestock, and a zone of iron ore and ironworks. Nashville—site of an arsenal, huge supply depots, and many factories—was a great loss, even though Forrest saved some machinery and supplies.

President Davis could offer nothing but moral encouragement to a proposal for conquests far to the west. This came from a former Regular who had served there, Henry Hopkins Sibley. By February, Sibley and some 2,500 Texans were fighting—and winning—engagements in the U.S. Territory of New Mexico. Then, lured into an ambush at Apache Canyon, he was battered by a sharpshooting force that included the 1st Colorado Volunteers. Many of them miners and all of them rough, they had made one of the war's epic marches: more than 400 miles through gale-swept badlands in 13 days. While fighting at Glorieta Pass, amid "huge bowlders and clumps of stunted cedars," Sibley lost his wagon train, and his men went straggling back to San Antonio. U.S. forces in the region went back to fighting Indians.

Stonewall Jackson broods over the Valley as if planning his most famous campaign. Between May 8 and June 9, he utilized ridges and gaps and roads to baffle Federal forces and to stall their advance on Richmond. With about 18,500 men, he defeated units of three Union armies (more than twice his strength, if combined) in five battles. His men earned their name "foot cavalry," marching about 350 miles. They caught N. P. Banks's 8,000 and routed them at Winchester, but were too tired to run them down. All told, Jackson inflicted almost twice as many casualties as he suffered (about 2,000), captured rich matériel, and immobilized some 50,000 Union troops. Tacticians still study his campaign. Painting in 1910, N. C. Wyeth gave him a hero's look. In fact, his field uniform was usually dingy; a brigadier described his old forage cap as "mangy." Jackson had deeper concerns: "Bear in mind in dressing, to be clothed in righteousness as with a garment."

As Southern dreams ended in New Mexico, the Union marked another victory in the Trans-Mississippi sector. At Pea Ridge in northwestern Arkansas, Federals outmaneuvered and routed Rebel troops and their allies in war paint, most of them Cherokees. Over the din of war whoops and Rebel yells, Confederates heard commands in German, proof that thousands of Yankees were not American-born.

The Southern armies contained relatively few ethnic regiments. Cajuns from Louisiana and some Irish units were conspicuous exceptions. In telling contrast, such regiments were scattered throughout the Union armies. Ohio recruited so many German regiments that the adjutant general published his 1862 report in both English and German editions. The motto on the 9th Ohio's regimental flag—"Fight Bravely for Freedom and Justice"—was in German. Other regiments mustered Irish, Swiss, Norwegians, Swedes, and Danes. The Garibaldi Guards, led by a Hungarian described as a onetime circus rider, had Spaniards, French, and Germans as well as Italians. Often such men had painful memories of poverty, oppression, and divided homelands in Europe; they were determined to defend their new country, which had offered them something better, and thereby gain acceptance.

The North's new hero, "Unconditional Surrender" Grant, was now a major general, eager to exploit his victory. Control of the Tennessee River gave him a water route south to Mississippi and Alabama. His superior, Maj. Gen. Henry W. Halleck, was bringing up troops to counter any Confederate drive.

Kentucky-born Albert Sidney Johnston, C.S.A., a full general and departmental commander in the West, bore the stigma of defeat for Donelson. Southerners were looking for a savior—and Gen. P.G.T. Beauregard was willing to oblige. He called for men, and got them. He acted as though he, not Johnston, were head of the army assembling in March at Corinth, Mississippi, yet another of the places the South desperately needed to hold. Here the Mobile & Ohio Railroad intersected the Memphis & Charleston, a crucial link in the transportation net.

Southern officers, like Northern ones, were still trying to build effective armies from batches of raw recruits and a museum collection of weapons. At Fort Henry, the 10th Tennessee carried flintlock muskets, smoothbore muzzle-loaders with an effective range of only 70 yards.

Eyes in the sky, Thaddeus S.C. Lowe is carried aloft June 1 in his hydrogen-filled balloon Intrepid *to serve as a Union observer during the battle of Fair Oaks, near Richmond. Here, crews man the tethering lines that will hold the balloon in position some 300 feet above the ground, giving the aeronaut a 15-mile range of vision. Lowe's timely warnings at Fair Oaks, and at Gaines's Mill three weeks later, helped Union troops avert disaster. Professor Lowe's innovations included developing a mobile hydrogen generator—an unwieldy but effective horse-drawn contrivance that could inflate a balloon in under three hours—and the use of airborne telegraphy to provide instant communication. A seven-balloon squadron, stitched together by 50 Washington seamstresses, grew from a demonstration a year earlier when Lowe had directed artillery fire at a Confederate position near Falls Church, Virginia—becoming the first airborne spotter in military history.*

The South had three balloons: a hot-air one that crash-landed near Yorktown and two filled with gas—the "silk dress" balloons supposedly sewn from gowns donated by Southern belles. None saw effective service.

Johnston's men had some of these, along with shotguns. They also had pre-war .58-caliber Springfield rifle-muskets, effective at 400 yards, and fine Enfield rifle-muskets imported from Britain. Percussion caps let infantrymen fire more rapidly, and in wet weather; accuracy at longer ranges expanded the killing zone. By April, Grant's forces had a fair quantity of good small arms—but Sherman's division alone required six kinds of ammunition: a quartermaster's nightmare.

Artillery improvements included long-range rifled cannon, but these had a limited role. The war was American, on rugged American land, and often in woodland, where a gunner's range was limited. The 12-pounder smoothbore Napoleon, seldom used beyond 1,000 yards, was the favorite fieldpiece; firing canister, it could disrupt or check the finest infantry at 300 yards. Moving even the smallest guns could become an ordeal on bad roads, and the roads out of Corinth were soggy when Johnston marched north to meet Grant.

Dozens of ships had brought Grant south on the Tennessee River. By April he had 35,000 men at a lonesome place called Pittsburg Landing, a position flanked by rambling creeks and deep woods, with 7,500 more at a landing about four miles downstream. He was expecting Maj. Gen. Don Carlos Buell to join him with 20,000 men.

When Johnston learned that Buell's army was nearing Pittsburg Landing, he knew he had to fight Grant immediately. He set his Rebels moving along the muddy roads, where 20-odd miles cost them three days. On the night of April 5 the Confederates bivouacked within two miles of the Union position, a scattering of encampments near a log meetinghouse called Shiloh Church.

Before daybreak the next morning, a few minutes before five, a Union patrol stumbled onto some Rebel pickets. These few men fought for about an hour before the alarm reached the main body. The Federals were tending to Sunday chores when their drummers beat the long roll, the call to battle. They scrambled into formation as the woods erupted in a firefight. Rebels swept into the thicket and met a frantic resistance. Men settled into a muddled, stubborn, day-long fight.

Some of the Southerners stopped in the camp areas to snatch up uneaten breakfasts or loot abandoned tents. Their officers tried, with varying success, to restore formations. Under orders or on their own,

Anvil chorus at Hampton Roads: The Union "cheesebox on a raft," Monitor, and the Confederate ironclad, Virginia (ex-Merrimack), hammer away in a furious four-hour battle on March 9 that ended in a draw. The Monitor had arrived at the mouth of Chesapeake Bay just in time to save a beleaguered wooden warship, U.S.S. Minnesota, from destruction. The clash of ironclads, the first ever, marked a permanent change in the course of naval warfare.

Federals fought as best they could, but entire regiments broke and ran. The Yankees fell back to a shallow wagon trace, where Brig. Gen. Benjamin Prentiss's division stopped the Confederates. Firing from behind oak trees in dense underbrush, the Federals filled the air with bullets. "It's a hornets' nest in there!" a Rebel shouted.

The sound of the guns had summoned Grant from downstream, and he had galloped into the maelstrom. He ordered Prentiss to maintain his position "at all hazards." Riding into a clearing, Grant became a likely target himself. "Go tell the old man to leave here for God's sake," one staff officer said to another. "Tell him yourself," was the reply. A third had enough courage to make the suggestion, and Grant rode off.

Johnston, dropping larger responsibilities, directed a bayonet charge in a peach orchard east of the Hornets' Nest. "Everywhere around us the storm began to rage: shot, shell . . . canister came howling and whistling through our lines," one man recalled. A minié ball struck Johnston in the right leg—apparently a minor wound, but nicking an artery. He had sent his surgeon off to care for Union wounded. Before the surgeon returned, Johnston had bled to death.

Flank attacks, or one assault in force, might have taken the Hornets' Nest. Instead, Confederate units attacked it head on, again and again. They rounded up more and more artillery until 62 cannon were bombarding the position at ranges as close as 300 yards.

With ammunition running out, the Federals tried to retreat but found themselves cut off. Men from two Rebel divisions poured into the Hornets' Nest. Prentiss had maintained the position for seven hours. More than half of the men who fought like hornets were dead or wounded. White flags were raised, and 2,200 survivors surrendered.

They and their fallen comrades had given Grant time to form new lines near the landing. Belated reinforcements came from Lew Wallace's men downriver and from Buell's army. Cold rain came on with nightfall, and the gunboats lobbed shells at the Rebels all night. Sherman found his general under a tree, and said, "We've had the devil's own day, haven't we." "Yes," said Grant, "lick 'em tomorrow, though."

Grant's and Buell's morning assault forced the Confederates back, but they resisted stoutly enough to muddle the Union advance. The two armies, Lew Wallace wrote, "degenerated into mere fighting

Fort Pulaski's battered ramparts attest to the power of a new weapon—the rifled cannon. The fort, named after the Polish hero of the Revolutionary War, stood at the mouth of the Savannah River in Georgia. It had taken 18 years,

25 million bricks, and a million dollars to build. Cannonballs fired from a smoothbore gun, then the standard heavy weapon, would bounce harmlessly off its walls. One of its engineers was a recent West Point graduate, Robert E. Lee.

At the war's outset Lee had declared the fort impregnable. But he had not reckoned with rifling—and the unprecedented range and power of the conical projectiles spun out by these spiral grooves inside a cannon barrel.

swarms." About 2:30 p.m. a staff officer approached Beauregard, now commanding in fact and form. "General," he said, "do you not think our troops are very much in the condition of a lump of sugar, thoroughly soaked with water, but yet preserving its original shape, though ready to dissolve? Would it not be judicious to get away with what we have?" Beauregard agreed, and the retreat to Corinth began.

During the battle, the wounded and the dying of both armies dragged themselves to a pond for water. By the end of the first day its red-streaked waters christened it Bloody Pond. Ambrose Bierce, not quite 20 years old when he fought at Shiloh, wrote of what he saw at Bloody Pond: "Knapsacks, canteens, haversacks distended with soaken and swollen biscuits, gaping to disgorge, blankets beaten into the soil by the rain, rifles with bent barrels or splintered stocks . . . and the omnipresent sardine-box—all the wretched debris of the battle still littered the spongy earth as far as one could see, in every direction. Dead horses were everywhere; a few disabled caissons, or limbers. . . . ammunition wagons standing disconsolate behind four or six sprawling mules. Men? There were men enough; all dead. . . ."

Grant ordered an immediate burial of the dead. In one long trench near the headquarters of Maj. Gen. John A. McClernand, some 570 Confederates still rest, buried in layers seven deep. The Union reported 1,754 men killed; 8,408 wounded; 2,885 missing. The Confederate toll, officially: 1,723 killed; 8,012 wounded; 959 captured or missing. Grant transformed the statistics into a haunting image: "I saw an open field, in our possession on the second day, over which the Confederates had made repeated charges the day before, so covered with dead that it would have been possible to walk across the clearing, in any direction, stepping on dead bodies, without a foot touching the ground."

On the day that Beauregard's men began staggering back to Corinth through rain and axle-deep mud, Brig. Gen. John Pope captured Island No. 10 on the Mississippi River. It bristled with guns—28, counting a floating battery—but Pope took it and some 7,000 prisoners in another of the land-water operations the Rebels could not match. A Southern engineer had called this "one of the finest strategic positions for the defense of the Mississippi Valley." Its loss opened the river for the Union as far as Fort Pillow, more than halfway to Memphis.

"You might as well bombard the Rocky Mountains," scoffed the chief engineer of the U.S. Army, Joseph Totten, when told of the brash plan to take Fort Pulaski. The moated fort had seven-and-a-half-foot-thick walls aimed, arrowlike, toward any seaborne invader. But in less than two days—and after 5,275 slamming shells and mortar rounds—ten of the newfangled guns with rifled barrels had breached the southeastern wall, exposing a powder magazine to catastrophe. On April 11 the commander capitulated. The quick collapse of one of the world's great forts surprised nearly everyone. As one Union officer put it, the rifled gun "must cause . . . a change in the construction of fortifications as radical as that foreshadowed in naval architecture by the conflict between the Monitor and Merrimac."

FOLLOWING PAGES: Men of the 7th Illinois Infantry proudly display their colors—and an expensive new weapon, the Henry repeating rifle. The lever-action, rapid-fire carbine carried 15 rounds and was far deadlier than the cumbersome, single-shot musket then in widespread use. Rebels came to fear the repeater as "that damn Yankee rifle they load on Sunday and shoot all week."

Shiloh: The name haunts history like morning mist drifting over Pittsburg Landing on the Tennessee River. Near here, General Grant, fresh from Fort Donelson, marshaled some 35,000 troops for a push toward the strategic railway town of Corinth, Mississippi. Confederate forces, about 40,000 strong, moved north to attack Grant's army before it could be reinforced. At dawn on Sunday, April 6, the foes collided near Shiloh Church a few miles from the river, in a hail of flying metal that raged for two days. When echoes of the last shot faded away, almost 20,000 men had bloodied the ground at Shiloh.

At the mouth of the river, Flag Officer David G. Farragut, U.S.N., was directing another complex operation against New Orleans, the South's largest and wealthiest city. Union mortar boats lobbed thousands of 13-inch shells at Forts Jackson and St. Philip, which guarded the water approach to New Orleans, 75 miles away. Union gunboat crews had cut a log-hulk-chain barrier strung across the river, and Farragut's flotilla steamed through the opening under heavy fire from the forts. Destroying several Rebel ships on the way, he secured a landing place for units of Maj. Gen. Benjamin F. Butler's army above Fort St. Philip and steamed on to New Orleans. Only one company of Confederate troops was at hand; the rest had joined the army that fought at Shiloh. Militia with "indifferent shot-guns" faced ships with a hundred naval guns, which Farragut could aim over the levee. He sent an officer ashore to accept the surrender of the city, and cruised on upriver to overawe Baton Rouge and Natchez.

The only good news for the Confederate Navy that spring was the one-day triumph of a revolutionary new ship, the former steam frigate *Merrimack*. Scuttled when the Union evacuated Norfolk, she was raised and reworked. Her hull, cut down to the waterline, carried a new superstructure. At a price of 7½ cents per pound, the Tredegar Iron Works processed more than 700 tons of iron (including B & O rails captured by Stonewall Jackson) into two-inch plates, doubled to give her sides four inches of armor. Fitted with a four-foot iron ram and renamed the *Virginia*, and compared by her surgeon to a terrapin with a chimney on its back, she went into action untested with an untrained crew.

On March 8, at Hampton Roads, Virginia, she attacked the wooden ships of the blockade fleet. Ignoring their fire and Union shore batteries, she rammed the *Cumberland*, ripping open her starboard side; crippled the *Congress*, then set her ablaze with red-hot shot; and terrified Washington officialdom. Secretary of the Navy Gideon Welles noted in his diary, with obvious delight, that Secretary of War Edwin M. Stanton interrupted a Cabinet meeting to look out a window toward the Potomac and say: "Not unlikely, we shall have a shell or cannon-ball from one of her guns in the White House before we leave this room." Welles knew that the Union's own new armored ship, the *Monitor*, was already near Hampton Roads. *(Continued on page 132)*

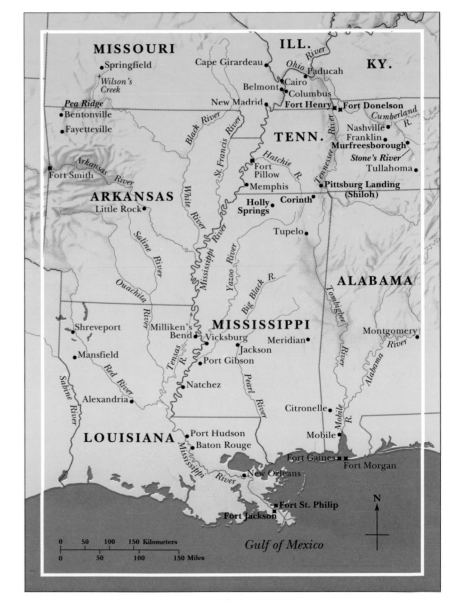

SHILOH | *Peach trees bloomed in the orchard beyond a log cabin on the afternoon of April 6, when Confederate Gen. Albert Sidney Johnston galloped up to reconnoiter a nearby Union position. Johnston directed a charge near the orchard and was struck in the leg by a minié ball—a minor wound, it seemed. But the ball had nicked an artery, and soon Johnston was dead. "The west perished with Albert Sidney Johnston," grieved a brother officer, "and the Southern country followed." Others, too, suffered the bitter sting of war that day. A spreading oak and a brace of cannon stand near the site of a Union field hospital (opposite).*

128

Lee once hinted that the Confederacy had made a great mistake—putting her worst generals in the army while her best were editing newspapers. Those experts didn't think much of him in June 1862, when he took command of the force he named the Army of Northern Virginia.

With commissioned politicians under him and William S. Rosecrans against him, he had failed in western Virginia. Then he had been sent to organize the defense of the southeastern coast. There he developed his insight in the "operational art," the art of moving troops to best advantage within a given theater. His skill in this sets him among the greatest commanders.

Although his first battle plans demanded too much of a green army and inadequate staff, he forced McClellan away from the outskirts of Richmond in just seven days of steady hard fighting.

"Lee is audacity personified," said one of his juniors. Only his shrewd understanding of his opponents accounts for some of the risks he ran; he knew the odds against him. "If you go to ciphering," he warned an officer, "we are whipped beforehand." He assessed his subordinates equally well. He boldly divided his outnumbered army when he could call on Stonewall Jackson; Jackson was "his thunderbolt," it was said, and Lee "the Jove of the war."

His past—and his family's—made Lee a perfect hero in a war for Southern independence. He came of distinguished lineage, though his father, a hero of the Revolution, had died in ruinous debt. He married Mary Custis, daughter and heiress of George Washington's adopted son. Lee had a brilliant record of his own. He stood second in the West Point class of 1829, with no demerits; won honors for gallantry in Mexico; served as superintendent of the Military Academy, and on the Texas frontier. Fun-loving and sociable in peace, he never lost the easy dignity of that Southern ideal, the high-toned gentleman. His tact

ROBERT E. LEE

covered a mountain Rebel begging a chaw of tobacco, his prickly Commander in Chief, Jefferson Davis, and anyone between—including "those people," the enemy.

One of his veterans recalled the war years: "when he loved us like a father and led us like a king, when we trusted him like a providence and obeyed him like a god. . . ." A Federal officer defined his own general's trouble as "Lee on the brain." Grant said that his juniors in Virginia seemed to expect Lee to turn a double somersault in the air and land on both Federal flanks at once. Some of Lee's feats were almost that improbable.

According to his able subordinate E. P. Alexander and competent critics since, Lee's military faults came from audacity overdone. Ordering assaults at Malvern Hill, offering battle on the Antietam, taking "the bloodiest road" without necessity on the third day at Gettysburg—these and less famous examples mark his eagerness to "strike a blow." Lee took failure upon himself: "It's all my fault. I thought my men were invincible," he said after Gettysburg, conceding that he might have asked too much of his army's prowess and valor.

After Appomattox, Lee showed his countrymen how to suffer defeat and work for the future. "The great mistake of my life," he said, "was taking a military education." He accepted the presidency of little Washington College and built up the school until heart disease claimed him in 1870. Admirers at home and abroad mourned him as a great soldier, a noble leader, a humble Christian, a moral victor. In time he was hailed as a man all Americans could be proud of.

His virtues—like Washington's—suited the image of an antique paragon, a man of marble. Nothing could be further from the truth of Lee in combat. He was the fighter whose troops forced him to the rear at the Bloody Angle, the man who could look at the victims of Fredericksburg and speak of fondness for war.

White Oak Swamp and similar terrain along the Chickahominy River complicated the fighting near Richmond. Rains could flood the low ground, close the fords, turn the roads to mud, and stop the armies.

When the *Virginia* returned to battle on March 9, she headed for the helpless *Minnesota,* which had run aground the day before. But before she could strike, the *Monitor* appeared. This strange-looking "pigmy," as a Rebel officer called her, placed herself between the *Virginia* and her prey, swung her turret toward the foe, and fired.

Gunners aboard the *Virginia* fired back as the range closed. The ships fought as close as ten yards apart, shot glancing off each clanging iron side. When some of the *Virginia*'s guns stopped firing, her captain asked why. "Our powder is precious," said the gunnery officer, "and after two hours' incessant firing I find I can do her about as much damage by snapping my thumb at her every two minutes and a half."

About 2 p.m., before the tide fell, both withdrew. "Now comes the reign of iron," said a U.S. Navy officer. In London, the *Times* declared that of 149 British warships, just 2 were now first class—both armored, and the only vessels able to engage "that little *Monitor.*"

In New Orleans, General Butler, a scowling, squint-eyed man

Daring and flamboyant, James Ewell Brown (Jeb) Stuart was a Virginia-born West Pointer who had seen action in Kansas, Harper's Ferry, and Manassas. On June 12, Lee dispatched him on a reconnaissance mission that became a bold, three-day ride around the Union army. Two weeks later, Jeb Stuart assumed command of the Army of Northern Virginia's cavalry.

FOLLOWING PAGES: Union troops reinforce one of a dozen bridges hurriedly built across the Chickahominy River. Called the Grape Vine Bridge because of its tortuous route through a swamp, it was soon washed away by floodwaters.

with a face that was a cartoonist's dream, created a sensation of his own. He had fumed over the way citizens showed their contempt for his men. Ladies made a point of gathering their skirts as if a Yankee were mud to be avoided; simpler women dumped garbage from second-story windows when Yankees went by. Butler issued a proclamation: "Any Female" who insulted a Union soldier would be "treated as a woman of the town plying her avocation." Even Yankees were shocked.

In April the Confederate Congress passed the first conscription

act in American history, calling up for three years men between the ages of 18 and 35 (eventually extended to 17 and 50). The law, like one the Union would enact a year later, allowed men of means to hire substitutes. It also exempted workers in some industries and, later, owners or overseers of 20 slaves—a clause loathed by poorer whites.

The conscription law upset advocates of states' rights. But the war itself had challenged that dogma, imposing a centralized industrial economy. The Confederate government dictated war production—and profits—in states fighting for their sovereignty. Col. Josiah Gorgas, Chief of Ordnance, controlled the manufacture and procurement of gunpowder, ammunition, and weapons. The Confederacy began to build more than 50 ironclads and dozens of other warships. The government levied taxes on land and liquor; it took over ironworks and built the Augusta Powder Works in Georgia, then the world's largest nationally owned factory. Confederate officials, regularly denounced as tyrants, bought farmers' crops at fixed low prices. The Congress, however, never imposed strict controls on railroads. The rail companies sometimes refused to cooperate with frantic army supply officers; they generally refused to carry fodder or other bulky materials.

Loss of trade with the North cut off foodstuffs as well as factory goods. Meat prices climbed. The blockade made tea and coffee scarce. Salt—the only preservative for meats—created an authentic crisis. Southerners used some 50 pounds of salt per person per year, and most of that had been imported. Coastal residents tried to get salt from seawater, only to see Union naval forces raid the works. Farmers tried to cure beef with saltpeter and bacon with wood ashes. Congress added salt makers to the list of men exempt from the draft.

Fine horses and horsemanship were idolized in the South, but much of the army stock had come from Missouri, Kentucky, and Tennessee—areas under Northern occupation. A Confederate officer or cavalryman rode his own horse with his own saddle, and received 40 cents a day in compensation. If he had a horse shot out from under him, he got money to buy another. But that payment often was not enough, especially as horses became scarce.

"The most dashing trooper," a cavalry officer wrote, "was the one whose horse was the most apt to get shot, and when this man was unable to remount himself he had to go to the infantry service and was lost to the cavalry. Such a penalty for gallantry was terribly demoralizing." As the war went on, one Rebel cavalryman in four came to lack a horse.

Amplifying a proverb, Ben Franklin traced the loss of a kingdom to the loss of a battle for want of a horseshoe nail. The South did not lack riders or, as Shiloh proved, men who could fight. But it was short of horses and almost destitute of nails. The North was beginning to suffer from want of a rider to lead the troops. On March 11, Lincoln relieved McClellan as general-in-chief but retained him as commander of the Army of the Potomac, with a single mission: march on Richmond.

McClellan planned to move by sea and land, ferrying men to Fort Monroe and then thrusting overland up the tongue of land called the Peninsula, between the York and James Rivers. He obtained transport ships without difficulty, but his slow advance through the spring mud called for a prodigious supply train—about 45 wagons per 1,000 men (compared with Napoleon's standard of 12). Some 25,000 horses and mules hauled the supplies of the army. Each four-horse team was expected to pull 2,800 pounds on a good road, as little as 1,800 on a rough one. The animals hauled roughly half the fodder they needed; foraging was supposed to provide the rest, but grass would not be adequate until May. Quartermasters struggled to cut down the number of wagons. By the fall, officers were forbidden to load trunks or boxes of personal items; enlisted men had to carry their own blankets and tentage.

The army knew little about the swampy land ahead. The maps were as bad as the roads. Defenders barricaded roads with felled trees—a primitive device, but effective against lumbering wagon trains.

McClellan met his first resistance at Yorktown, where the Confederates had superimposed new earthworks on those thrown up during the Revolution. About 15,000 Rebels manned the defenses. With about 100,000 men, the Young Napoleon chose to besiege rather than attack. Nearly a month later, the Confederates slipped away.

At Williamsburg, on May 5, the armies finally fought. A Union soldier described the action: "They immediately opened fire upon us . . . from their rifle-pits came a hum of bullets and crackle of musketry. Their heavy shot came crashing among the tangled abatis of fallen timber, and plowed up the dirt in our front, (Continued on page 144)

SEVEN DAYS | *Malvern Hill (below), an open, mile-wide plateau surrounded by swamps and creeks, provided an almost ideal redoubt for Federal fieldpieces during McClellan's retreat from the Chickahominy. On the* *crest of the hill, Fitz John Porter's Fifth Corps on July 1 opened a devastating fire against wave after wave of attacking Rebels. The fight at Gaines's Mill (opposite) on June 27 was the largest and costliest engagement in a week of* *bloody duels—seven days that would see some 37,000 men killed, wounded, or missing. Here, soldiers in Yankee regiments came to realize the value of protective breastworks erected during the heat of battle.*

CEDAR MOUNTAIN | *Little more than a wooded knob jutting above sprawling wheat fields, Cedar Mountain (below and opposite) near Culpeper, Virginia, bore witness to a clash that foreshadowed bigger, bloodier battles to come. After the Peninsula Campaign, Lee feared that McClellan's men would be redeployed to buttress John Pope's new army, so he dispatched Stonewall Jackson on a preemptive strike. On August 9, in blistering heat, Jackson's hard-marching "foot cavalry" met the enemy—and would have been driven from the field had not Jackson rallied his troops and had not A.P. Hill arrived with reinforcements just in time to turn the tide of battle in favor of the Confederates.*

FOLLOWING PAGES: *Union troops of Irvin McDowell's corps enjoy a respite from sultry summer heat in a grassy field near Blackburn's Ford on Bull Run. McDowell's men would soon return here—in circumstances far less pleasant.*

rebounding and tearing through the branches of the woods in our rear. The constant hissing of the bullets, with their sharp *ping* or *bizz* whispering around and sometimes into us, gave me a sickening feeling . . . and a sort of faintness. . . . The little rifle-pits in our front fairly blazed with musketry, and the continuous *snap, snap, crack, crack* was murderous."

Fighting desperately, the Confederates retreated, buying time for the ultimate defense: Richmond. To protect the capital, Gen. Joseph E. Johnston called in troops from Norfolk. They burned the navy yard and scuttled the *Virginia*—she was unfit for the open sea, and her draft of more than 20 feet kept her from going up the James. The Confederate capital seemed doomed, and Johnston knew it.

Two events changed the odds. Johnston was wounded in a battle at a railroad station called Fair Oaks, near Seven Pines; Robert E. Lee became commander. And Stonewall Jackson was on the march in the Shenandoah Valley. This created much alarm in Washington, and troops McClellan wanted with him were held back for its protection.

Between March 23 and June 9, outnumbered three to one in the region, Jackson marched 676 miles, eluding or defeating forces sent to trap him. His swiftly marching "foot cavalry" fought skirmishes almost

Pressing his advantage after Second Manassas, Robert E. Lee divided his forces and carried the war into Yankee territory. On September 15, Stonewall Jackson swept into Harper's Ferry and blew up the B & O bridge across the Potomac. (The span would have to be rebuilt nine times during the war.) Below, Union supply wagons cross Middle Bridge over Antietam Creek. The stream would give the Union its name for the bloodiest one-day battle of the war.

FOLLOWING PAGES: Confederate dead lie near the Dunker Church at Antietam. War's grisly reality, captured by photographer Alexander Gardner, shocked a public accustomed to artists' romanticized portrayals.

every day, won five of six battles, and tied up some 50,000 men who otherwise would have been helping McClellan. "All Old Jackson gave us," one of his men said, "was a musket, a hundred rounds, and a gum blanket, and he druv us like hell."

On June 23, with Union troops only a few miles from Richmond, Jackson arrived in secret to confer with Lee, who laid out his plan. It would trigger a series of battles that would become famous as the Seven Days. Its first weapons were picks and shovels. Grumbling soldiers called Lee "King of Spades" as they dug miles of trenches.

Brig. Gen. James Ewell Brown (Jeb) Stuart did his part with dashing horsemanship. Ordered to reconnoiter McClellan's right flank, Stuart and his 1,200 troopers headed almost due north, wheeled east, then completed a three-day ride around the Union army. Among his hard-riding but frustrated pursuers was his father-in-law, Brig. Gen. Philip St. George Cooke. Stuart's exploit heartened Richmond, tormented McClellan—and gave Lee valuable information: The Federal position was split by the Chickahominy River, and the right flank was "in the air," unprotected.

Lee called in Jackson's veterans, and the Seven Days began. Oak Grove, June 25: The Federals score a minor success. Mechanicsville: In the swamps of the Chickahominy, Lee fails to wipe out an isolated Union force; but McClellan, certain that he faces overwhelming numbers, falls back. (Lee has roughly 90,000 men, McClellan about 100,000.) Gaines's Mill: Disjointed attacks by 56,000 Rebels flail at 35,000 Federals on high ground near another of the Peninsula's hellish swamps; 8,800 Confederates and 6,800 Federals become casualties. Savage's Station: Belated Confederate attacks fail to crush the Yankees' rear guard. Glendale: The creeks in White Oak Swamp bedevil Rebel efforts to overwhelm scattered Federal forces, and McClellan withdraws to high ground near the James. Malvern Hill: Federal cannon overwhelm Rebel artillery and repel Southern infantry. "It was not war—it was murder," a Confederate general says afterward. The Federals withdraw downriver to a new base at Harrison's Landing.

"My men have proved themselves the equals of any troops in the world, but they are worn-out," McClellan telegraphed Lincoln. He had "failed to win," he said, because he had been "overpowered by superior

numbers." He also sent the President a long letter of advice. The war should be conducted by the ideals of "Christian Civilization," and "forcible abolition of slavery" should not even be thought of. He did concede that "contraband" slaves might have military protection.

That useful formula came from Ben Butler. Commanding at Fort Monroe in 1861, he had refused to return three fugitive slaves to a Virginia owner who demanded them back, invoking the Fugitive Slave Act of 1850. A lawyer in civil life, Butler parried this easily: "I replied that the fugitive slave act did not affect a foreign country, which Virginia claimed to be, and that she must reckon it one of the infelicities of her position that . . . she was taken at her word. . . ." Any enemy property of military consequence might be taken as contraband of war.

Federal units had no common practice about blacks. Some protected any fugitive who turned up. Some followed to the letter rules about respecting civilian property. Once, in Alabama, a Union brigade was marching by a field where some *(Continued on page 153)*

ANTIETAM | *Tranquillity surrounds the Dunker Church, wrecked by a storm in 1921 and carefully reconstructed 40 years later. Opposite, first light flares from a star on a monument to the 128th Pennsylvania; barely five weeks old, this unit stood up well to confusion and to enemy fire. The 137th Pennsylvania, honored by the statue beyond, saw less action and suffered fewer casualties.*

Bloody place on the bloodiest day, the sunken road (in the background) doglegs past a zigzag fence and a clump of trees at Antietam. Today, monuments to those who fought dot the battlefield, and cannon stand on stony outcrops rising from a furrowed field on the Piper farm. The road, a farm lane leading to a nearby gristmill, had been rutted into a trench by decades of heavy wagons rumbling along. On September 17 the road would earn its battle sobriquet— Bloody Lane. On this day, near the little town of Sharpsburg, Maryland, nearly 23,000 men fell. In one howling storm of lead and thunder near the Dunker Church, the Union lost 2,300 men in 20 minutes. "Try to imagine us laying there, the balls going whiz, whiz, whiz . . . over our heads. . . ," recalled a survivor. When the smoke and dust of battle cleared, neither side could find solace worthy of the carnage. Yankees outnumbered Rebels almost two to one, but had been too uncoordinated and too slow to wrest a decisive victory. And Lee's planned raid into Union territory had been halted in its tracks.

40 slaves were toiling. The slaves saw the blue uniforms and rushed to the road, throwing their hats in the air and cheering. One shouted, "Now we are free." He offered to join the brigade and fight. A colonel rode up, drew his pistol, aimed it at the would-be volunteer, and said, "Go back to your work or I will put a bullet through your blue heart."

Lincoln was pondering new perspectives on the issue of slavery. In March he suggested to Congress that the Federal government should help any state "which may adopt gradual abolishment of slavery"; the state would get Federal money to use at its discretion. A joint resolution came of this. In July he invited senators and congressmen from the slaveholding border states to the White House. The value of slave property was disappearing, he said, from "the mere incidents of the war." The border states should decide "at once to emancipate *gradually*," accept Federal compensation, and dishearten the states in rebellion. That came to nothing.

Gideon Welles noted in his diary a private discussion with the President: Lincoln "had about come to the conclusion that it was a military necessity absolutely essential for the salvation of the Union that we must free the slaves. . . ."

Lincoln finally decided, in those dismal summer days, that a proclamation to this effect should not sound like "our last *shriek*, on the retreat." He would announce it after a military victory. A battle came in August, but it was not a victory for the Union.

When the Peninsula Campaign faltered, Lincoln had called Henry Halleck in from the West to be general-in-chief. "Unconditional Surrender" Grant took charge of the Army of the Tennessee in the West. Lincoln also summoned John Pope, the conqueror of Island No. 10, and gave him command of a new army in Virginia.

Pope—a "bag of wind," brother officers called him—promptly made a vainglorious speech that compared the timid soldiers of the East with the stand-and-fight soldiers of the West. "I come to you from the West," he said, "where we have always seen the backs of our enemies." The easterners were not amused. He issued new orders about treatment of Southern civilians, who might be forced to pledge allegiance or lose their homes, and could be executed without trial for aiding the enemy. McClellan was shocked; Lee said Pope "ought to be suppressed."

In July Pope moved his improvised army south. Stonewall Jackson struck part of it on August 9 at Cedar Mountain. Lee decided to deal with all of it before McClellan's army returned north by water from Harrison's Landing. He divided his own force to do so.

Jackson's lean and weary men seized a mammoth Federal supply depot at Manassas Junction on the morning of August 27. "When we had appropriated all we could carry," wrote a soldier, "we found a barrel of whiskey, which we soon tapped; but as we had our canteens full of molasses, and our tin cups full of sugar, we had nothing to drink out of. We soon found an old funnel, however, and while one would hold his hand over the bottom of it another would draw it full." They also captured ammunition, tents, clothing, medical supplies—and coffins for Union officers to be shipped home in. These they passed up.

The next day Jackson picked a fight with a Federal column west of Bull Run. These men in black hats turned out to be John Gibbon's command, whose first battle proved them worthy of the name "Iron Brigade," which McClellan would soon bestow on them.

Pope misread both terrain and Confederate tactics in the two-day battle that followed. After suffering heavy casualties, he withdrew, his beaten troops slogging in the rain. (Philip Kearny, one of his best fighting generals, was killed in the rainy dark at Chantilly.) By the second battle at Bull Run, however, the men were mastering their new trade; some units broke, but this army retreated in fair order.

Fear swept Washington nonetheless. "I do not regard Washington as safe against the rebels," McClellan wrote his wife after the battle. "If I can quietly slip over there I will send your silver off." The government ordered arms and money to be shipped to New York, and a gunboat stood by to evacuate the President.

Amid the cries of alarm came whispers of treason. McClellan was back at the capital. What was he up to? Why wasn't he rushing to Pope's aid? Once again he seemed to be stalling; and many Republicans distrusted him anyway as a conservative Democrat. Stanton ordered an inquiry and lobbied for his removal. Halleck declared that McClellan had not obeyed orders "with the promptness I expected and the national safety, in my opinion, required." Washington buzzed with rumors about a coup d'état by officers of the Army of the Potomac, which idolized McClellan. The President concluded that only McClellan could rally the disheartened troops; he sent Pope out West to fight the Sioux and added Pope's men to McClellan's army. Soldiers cheered at the news: "Little Mac is back! Little Mac is back!"

On the deserted Manassas battlefield, Confederates had scavenged for food and shoes. "The night after the battle we drank a gallon of real coffee per man," a Virginia private wrote, "and filled up on salt pork, boiled beef and canned vegetables. . . ." The feasting did not last long. Lee's troops—and horses—could not sustain themselves in ravaged northern Virginia. They had to march somewhere.

Early in September, Lee crossed the Potomac at White's Ford, northwest of Washington. When the vanguard reached the northern bank, a band struck up "My Maryland." The song's opening line—"The despot's heel is on thy shore"—conveyed Southern faith that the state, given a chance, would spurn "the northern scum." About the same time, and under the same impression, Rebels in the West were invading Kentucky. The Confederacy's counteroffensives were under way.

Lee planned a thrust into Maryland, not an occupation. He knew his army could not live off the land indefinitely. Lacking railroad lines of supply, he planned his strategy to solve logistical problems. His army, he reported, was "not properly equipped for an invasion of an enemy's territory. It lacks much of the material of war, is feeble in transportation, the animals being much reduced, and the men are poorly provided with clothes, and in thousands of instances are destitute of shoes."

If some had thrown their shoes away as an excuse for straggling, others tried in vain to keep pace on blisters. But hundreds of men vanished and went home, never to return. "Our ranks are much diminished—I fear from a third to one-half of the original number," Lee wrote President Davis, appealing for stricter laws against desertion and the death penalty for straggling. Some of Lee's men, eager to defend their own nation, had conscientious scruples about aggressive war; as one Virginian noted in his diary, "I dont like to invade anybodys Country." By mid-September some regiments had only 80 or 45 or 34 men instead of the ideal 1,000. Estimates of Lee's strength in Maryland range from 55,000 to 35,000.

Nevertheless, Lee split up his army. Three columns converged on

Harper's Ferry to take the heights around the town and bombard it into surrender. He was counting on a slow reaction from McClellan.

Then, on September 13, a Union soldier picked up three cigars wrapped in paper. He unrolled the paper—and found himself reading a lost copy of Lee's orders. "I have all the plans of the rebels," McClellan telegraphed Lincoln, "and will catch them in their own trap." Slowly, he revised his own plan. It was, a Confederate said later, as if a lion decided to make "exceedingly careful preparations to spring on a plucky little mouse." Meanwhile, on September 15, the garrison at Harper's Ferry surrendered; the Confederates bagged 12,500 men, 13,000 small arms, 200 wagons, 73 pieces of artillery, and shoes and clothing.

Lee drew up his battle line at Sharpsburg. The Potomac would make retreat under fire almost impossible, but its bends would protect his flanks and Antietam Creek was a natural barrier to his front. His 40,000 men—"none but heroes are left," said an officer—hugged the

rumpled terrain. McClellan, fussing to position 75,000 men, wasted a day and revealed a plan to begin his attack against the Rebel left.

Through the dawn mists on September 17, Union infantry smashed into a cornfield defended by Confederates. "Again and again," a soldier wrote, "the field was lost and recovered, until the green corn that grew upon it looked as if it had been struck by a storm of bloody hail." Going into battle, Thomas Galwey, of the 8th Ohio Infantry, noticed that almost every blade was moving. He commented to a soldier that the ground was full of crickets. The soldier laughed. Then Galwey saw that the blades were moving because so many spent bullets were dropping among them. In four hours, artillery and musketry leveled the cornfield and sowed the land with dead, wounded, and dying. One company went into action with 32 men; 28 were wounded or killed. Of 280 men of the 6th Wisconsin who entered the cornfield, 150 were killed or wounded. Capt. Werner Von Bachelle, commanding officer

Long line of blue, this company of the 139th Pennsylvania saw scarcely any action during the December 13 battle at Fredericksburg. Burnside's ill-conceived tactic of storming the heavily defended heights, along with ambiguously worded orders and piecemeal commitment of troops, helped to bring about one of the war's great military debacles. Two nights later, under cover of a storm, Union forces melted back across the river, and Burnside himself was soon transferred.

of Co. F, was among them. His Newfoundland dog, trained to salute with its paw, also died on the battlefield and was buried with him.

Some Union troops drove toward the whitewashed Dunker Church; others fell before Confederates sheltered by a sunken road. But Federal units continued to attack the Bloody Lane, and swarmed in after men from New York had outflanked the Southern defenders. A Union soldier recorded the scene: "there lay so many dead rebels that they formed a line which one might have walked upon as far as I could see. They lay there just as they had been killed apparently, amid the blood which was soaking the earth."

On the left side of the Union line, a few hundred Rebels on high ground stopped Maj. Gen. Ambrose Burnside's four divisions at a graceful, three-arched stone span over the shallow Antietam.

"No tongue can tell, no mind conceive, no pen portray the horrible sights I witnessed this morning," wrote a Pennsylvania soldier. What he saw was the war's bloodiest day: more than 12,000 Federal casualties, nearly 11,000 Confederate. Of the 23,000, nearly 5,000 were dead.

The day ended with Lee's forces still holding, their backs to the river, waiting for the attack McClellan would launch the next day—he had more than 20,000 men in reserve. Surely his forces would surge forward, demolish Lee's army, and drive its remnants into the Potomac.

McClellan did not move. He was heavily reinforced on September 19, but the night before, Lee had slipped across the Potomac to safety.

Lincoln prodded McClellan to pursue and destroy Lee's army. Little Mac explained that for logistical reasons his army could not advance more than 25 miles from a railway or a canal. "I can't get a shoe for a man or beast," he complained in a letter to his wife.

However bloody and imperfect, Antietam gave Lincoln the victory he needed. On September 22 he declared that as of January 1, 1863, slaves in all states still in rebellion would be "thenceforward, and forever free." He also said that the Federal forces would not "repress" the slaves "in any efforts they may make for their actual freedom." Southerners denounced the proclamation as an invitation to rape and insurrection—the horror so long expected.

The off-year election continued the Republicans' control of Congress, and Lincoln relieved McClellan. Many of his men, the general claimed later, wanted to march on Washington and overthrow the government. But he stepped down, replaced by Burnside.

In the West, Rebels, subsisting on little more than green corn, were driving toward the rich larder of Kentucky. The state's Unionist legislature fled from Frankfort, which the Confederates occupied. Then Union forces defeated the invaders at Perryville. Buell failed to follow the retreating Rebels and was replaced—by Maj. Gen. William S. Rosecrans. In a year's-end battle at Stone's River, Tennessee, Rosecrans also failed to pursue. As winter closed down the war in the West, Grant's first offensive against Vicksburg was failing.

In the East, General Burnside decided that winter should see his army in Fredericksburg, a key city on the shortest land route from Washington to Richmond. Only about 500 Confederates defended the town when he started his campaign in mid-November. But while Burnside waited for pontoons to bridge the Rappahannock River, Lee established a strong defense line on hills above the town. At Marye's Heights, infantry had an ideal position behind a stone wall; artillerists had sited their guns and studied the ground.

On December 11, Union troops finally began filing across the pontoon bridges, and on the 13th they attacked, moving into the killing zone. Muskets blazed from Marye's Heights. The Confederates watched the blue ranks come up in parade-ground order, again and again, only to crumble; nearly 8,000 Union soldiers fell here. Another 4,500 Federals under Maj. Gen. William H. Franklin were cut down in an attack on Lee's right, held by Stonewall Jackson. The blood of the wounded froze, binding them to the ground. Through the night, freezing Rebels crept down to strip the bodies for the only warm clothes available. On the night of the 15th, Burnside withdrew his survivors.

Bartlett Malone of the 6th North Carolina recorded his Christmas: "a pritty day but I dident have nothing to drink nor no young ladies to talk too so I seen but little fun." During the holidays he wanted to talk with the Yankees across the river, but his officers forbade it.

In a Union camp, Maj. Rufus Dawes of the 6th Wisconsin opened canned peaches for a Christmas treat. "The army seems to be overburdened with second rate men. . . ," he wrote in a letter home. "This winter is, indeed, the Valley Forge of the war."

FREDERICKSBURG | *"Oh, those men! Oh, those men!" grieved General Burnside, "I am thinking of them all the time." Today their deaths cast a muted reverie upon the land of the national cemetery on Marye's Heights.*

On December 13 some 27,000 Union infantrymen hurled themselves in waves against 6,000 Confederates defending the heights. The onslaught proved suicidal: 8,000 Yankees fell in the assaults across open ground. Remarked

one Rebel: "A chicken could not live on that field when we open on it." From a nearby hill, Lee had watched a grand deployment of Federal troops earlier in the day and said, "It is well that war is so terrible—we should grow too fond of it."

FOLLOWING PAGES: *Riflemen guard a detachment of the 1st Michigan Engineers and Mechanics as they repair a railroad bridge across the Elk River in southern Tennessee. The bridge had been burned by retreating Confederates to slow the Union thrust into east Tennessee after the battle at Shiloh. Federal troops under Maj. Gen. Don Carlos Buell hoped to seize Chattanooga, a railway junction that linked Atlanta with supply areas to the north and west.*

The Nations in Alliance

Acomplete Civil War tapestry must include a shadow figure: the Native American. The conflict touched dwellings as varied as the bark longhouses of the Mohawk Valley, the buffalo-hide tepees of the Plains, the adobe pueblos of the far Southwest. On many fields their warriors fought valiantly for a chosen cause—and in some cases for their own nations as well.

They took part in famous and pivotal actions. For example, they fought on both sides in the confusion at Pea Ridge in 1862. Indians in gray glimpsed the forts of Washington through their gunsights when Jubal Early nearly breached the capital's defenses in 1864. A few Indians in blue fought as snipers during Virginia campaigns under Burnside and Meade.

A soldier of fortune might earn a place in the story of his outfit, as did the Mohawk sachem who joined the Confederate Kentuckians known as the Orphan Brigade. They called him Cloud, short for Flying Cloud, short for Konshattountzchette. He was a handsome man, before a bullet smashed his jaw at Chickamauga; after that the officers decided he shouldn't be set to guard captured Yankees—certainly not alone.

Many other warriors took part in hundreds of skirmishes that were barely remembered except by the survivors or the bereaved. And in the end, even in these, the winners were losers, almost to an Indian.

When the guns of Fort Sumter echoed across the land, Union officials took the loyalty of Indians for granted—or overlooked them entirely in the excitement of the hour.

The Confederacy, on the other hand, promptly sought alliances with Indians, especially the Five Civilized Tribes: Cherokee, Choctaw, Chickasaw, Creek, and Seminole. Natives of the Southeast, these nations had taken to many ways of the whites—including slaveholding—before the 1830s. Then the Federal authorities had forced them west to the Indian Territory (present-day Oklahoma). If the Union controlled this region, Dixie strategists realized, their western flank would be sorely exposed and Texas might well go its independent way.

An able envoy for the Confederacy, Albert Pike was a New Englander by birth but a leading citizen of Arkansas. In the summer of 1861 he negotiated treaties of alliance with the Five Civilized Tribes. The new Southern republic promised to assume all debts that the Federal government owed to the Indians, to honor Indian control of their own lands, to end fraud and corruption in trade, to maintain other rights for the tribes, and to accept their delegates as voting members of the Confederate Congress.

At first the principal chief of the western Cherokees, John Ross, favored neutrality, but by August he had given in to pro-Southern men.

One of those who forced his hand was an old adversary in tribal politics, Stand Watie—whose formal name, Degadoga, implied strength of character. Watie raised a company, then a regiment, of mounted riflemen; as colonel he achieved a rare excellence of discipline.

Silencing the weapons of war with words of peace, Lt. Col. Ely S. Parker (above), a Seneca, inscribed the articles of surrender at Appomattox.
Early in the war, Wisconsin Indians hope to replace rags with uniforms as a Union recruiting officer reads the oath of enlistment.

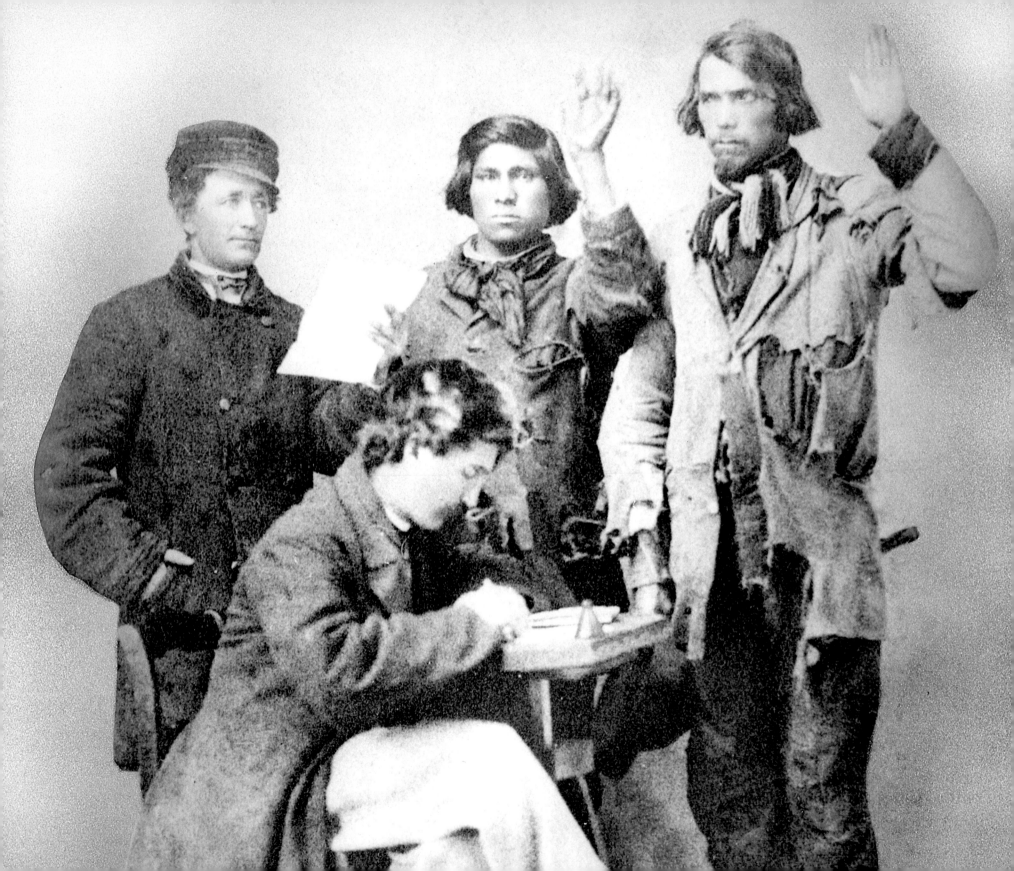

Stars within stars on the battle flag of the 1st Cherokee Rifles represent the Five Civilized Tribes and the eleven Confederate states. Not all Cherokees supported the Southern cause, but many did, including Stand Watie, who reached general's rank by war's end. In March 1862, three Indian regiments fought beside Rebel troops at Pea Ridge, in Arkansas. Though they lost the battle, they made a bold charge (left) and captured a Union battery.

At Pea Ridge, Watie's troops distinguished themselves twice in two days. On the first they charged with the 9th Texas Cavalry, brandishing guns and tomahawks, bows and arrows. Union gunners panicked and fled. The next day, when the Confederates in their turn were routed, Watie's men held their position under heavy shelling and were among the last to withdraw.

Retreating to fight another day, Watie and his men engaged in lightning raids throughout the war. In May 1864 he gained the rank of brigadier—the only Indian general on either side. By then, however, his own nation had divided; and many had renounced the Confederacy.

Nowhere was the term "war of brothers" more valid than in the Indian Territory. Old vendettas and new wrongs embittered the struggle. Some settlements sent all their able men to fight, leaving bands of women, old men, and children prey to fear and destitution at home or to misery as refugees.

Through it all, Stand Watie was undaunted. On June 23, 1865, on the soil of the Choctaw Nation, he signed a capitulation—the last surrender of a fighting force by a general of the Confederate armies.

Noteworthy Indian troops in the eastern theater were led by William H. Thomas, a man of two cultures. Born in 1805 in the North Carolina mountains, he was reared by his widowed mother and the local Cherokees, whose chief, Yonaguska, gave him a place in the tribe. He became a shopkeeper and frontier lawyer whose primary clients were Indians, individually and collectively.

When he volunteered to lead a wartime force, it naturally included his relatives by adoption, the Cherokees, who supplied two companies. By late 1862, Colonel Thomas's Legion of Indians and Highlanders numbered 2,000 men. The Cherokees had shown their mettle at a place called Baptist Gap, after being ambushed by an Indiana regiment. Second Lt. Astoogatogeh, a popular man, was killed; his avengers counterattacked—war whoops replacing the Rebel yell—and drove off the horrified Yankees, scalping several of the fallen. An exceptional incident, this spread the fame of "Little Will's force" through the mountains. His infantry and artillery joined Jubal Early without him—he was facing a court-martial for irregular dealings with deserters—but he was still in the field with 300 Cherokees when Lee surrendered.

That event brought fame to Lt. Col. Ely Parker, an adjutant on Grant's staff, who waged a minor campaign just to get into uniform. Born in 1828 on the Tonawanda Reservation in upstate New York, one of barely 2,200 Senecas, young Ely (pronounced "Eelee") took his English first name from a missionary teacher. He grew up well schooled in two traditions—at 23 he was a grand sachem of the Six Nations of the Iroquois, with the name Do-ne-ho-gawa, Open Door (in effect, chief diplomat). He studied law, but couldn't be admitted to the state bar because Indians were not considered citizens. As a civil engineer in government service, he met Grant at Galena, Illinois—and once, he said, rescued his new friend Grant from a barroom brawl.

After some wire-pulling, Parker got a commission, joined Grant at Vicksburg, and served on his staff thereafter. He could deal with engineering matters, wrote a fine clear script, and seemed unflappable.

At Appomattox, another aide began to copy Grant's terms for Lee's surrender, but found his hand too shaky; Parker wrote the official copies. His dark complexion obviously startled Lee when introductions were made; but the Seneca diplomat told of a graceful exchange: Lee saying, "I am glad to see one real American," and Parker replying, "We are all Americans."

Colonel Thomas demanded—and got—the same terms as Lee when he surrendered at Waynesville on May 9. He appeared for the peace talks dressed like his bodyguards: "stripped to the waist, painted and feathered in the style of a warrior." He tried to help his people in postwar years, but suffered repeated

Soldiers of the "Great Father at Washington. . . . are as swift as the antelope and brave as the mountain bear. . . . They will give you powder and lead. They will fight by your sides," wrote a U.S. commissioner to a Wichita chief in September 1861. Both North and South recruited Indians, promising food, clothing, arms, and money. More than 3,000 Native Americans, including the one below, took up arms for the Union. They would share little of the glory but much of the pain. After a major eastern battle, American Indians (opposite) lie beside other wounded U.S. troops on the grounds of the Marye mansion at Fredericksburg, Virginia.

breakdowns and died in a state asylum in 1893.

Stand Watie outlived a warrior son and died alone in 1871 near his old battleground at Honey Spring.

Parker, who shared the celebrity of the victors, had brighter prospects. He won the brevet (honorary) rank of brigadier. In 1869, President Grant appointed him Commissioner of Indian Affairs—the first "real American" to serve, and now arguably a citizen under the Civil Rights Act of 1866. Hounded out of office in a complicated wrangle, he turned to business, made and lost money in investments, and died a clerk for the New York City police in 1895. Union veterans raised money for his widow, left with a pension of $8 a month.

For other veterans and survivors, the post-war years were bleak indeed. Tribes whose warriors fought for the Rebels had to make their separate peace with the United States. The western Cherokee population of 21,000 had fallen below 13,000 by 1867; one study indicated that in the Union faction, one-third of the women were widows and one-fourth of the children were orphans.

Of the 3,530 men from all Indian nations known to have served in the Union army, 1,018 died in uniform. That fatality rate, 29 percent, was unmatched by the deaths recorded for soldiers of any single state.

During the war, Indians in the West had taken advantage of the conflict for ends of their own. They pinned down several regiments of Union cavalry. An uprising by the Sioux in Minnesota ignited passions among the Plains tribes. Late in 1864 a Colorado cavalry unit hit a peaceful village on Sand Creek, killing women and children; the facts appalled war-hardened Unionists in the East. Special problems among the Navajos and the Apaches remained unresolved.

Stillness had hardly fallen at Appomattox before wagon trains were creaking across the plains from horizon to horizon. Capt. Eugene F. Ware of the 7th Iowa Cavalry recalled that 36 Union regiments were ordered into his area, while veterans from North and South came "thirsting for land, gold and adventure. The Indian had to get out of the way. The lines of travel were soon garrisoned and guarded. . . . and the Indian problem was solved." Ware's outfit remained in service, but never lost another man.

President Grant had a plan for peace in the West. The Indians were to be settled on reservations, safe from whites and from each other; there they would achieve—in Ely Parker's words—"humanization, civilization, and Christianization."

In the end, the war affected the Indians more than they affected the war—but perhaps they above all others challenge its very concepts of victory and defeat.

1863

EARTHQUAKE IN THE SOUTH

The despair of Valley Forge seemed a strange image for a Federal officer to evoke. On New Year's Day the Union had 918,121 well-equipped and well-trained soldiers. Their foe, plagued by desertions, had a third as many present for duty. Lincoln's Emancipation Proclamation became effective on January 1. The freeing of slaves gave the Union a new moral purpose and foreign powers a challenge: How could nations that long ago disavowed slavery support a nation fighting to keep it?

Pope Pius IX, in a session with a Confederate envoy months later, suggested that an announcement of even "gradual emancipation" would greatly assist the Southern cause. The envoy gave the standard reply—his government had no control over slavery, which was a matter for its constituent sovereign states.

The Union was militarily strong and now, in the words of the "Battle Hymn of the Republic," was marching in the glory of the coming of the Lord. But the might of the Union's army, like the freeing of slaves, was a great potential. Stalled Federal troops still shivered along the Rappahannock, and hundreds of thousands of slaves were still in bondage. The Emancipation Proclamation, reflecting Lincoln's respect for the Constitution, left slavery untouched in Missouri, Kentucky, Maryland, and Delaware as well as in those areas of Virginia and Louisiana held by Federal occupation troops.

From the presidential mansion in Richmond, Jefferson Davis watched the crumbling of the Confederacy's common cause. One day women paraded through the streets demanding bread. Suddenly their march became a minor riot; they darted into shops and grabbed up food, clothing, and shoes. Davis climbed onto a wagon and addressed them. He promised a distribution of food—and volleys from a party of armed policemen if they didn't go home. Though the crowd scattered, the city remained restless, and Davis knew that calls to patriotism could not quell cries of discontent.

A chasm was growing between the rich planters and the yeomen soldier-farmers. Inflation and price-gouging hurt all but the wealthiest. Ten pounds of bacon, which had cost Richmond shoppers $1.25 in 1860, cost $10 in 1863. The price of five pounds of sugar climbed from 40 cents to $5.75, three pounds of butter rose in price from 75 cents to

Twin victories hearten the Union in mid-1863. Autumn brings serenity to Little Round Top (left) at Gettysburg, where Lee met defeat.
At Vicksburg, Rebel cannon, such as this British-made "Widow Blakely," blasted Federals until the town yielded to Grant's siege.

$5.25. Lacking coffee, families made do with roasted okra seeds or rye, parched corn, chicory, and other unsatisfactory substitutes. A War Department clerk wrote in his diary: "My wife, today, presented me with an excellent undershirt, made of one of her dilapidated petticoats. A new shirt would cost $30."

Hard-core believers in states' rights detested Davis. As one Alabama politician bluntly told him, he had "scarcely a friend and not a defender in Congress or in the army." Citizens turned to state officials. A volunteer wrote to Governor Zebulon Vance of North Carolina: "Now Govr. do tell me how we poor soldiers who are fighting for the 'rich mans negro' can support our families at $11 per month? . . . our soldiers are poor men with families who say they are tired of the rich mans war & poor mans fight. . . . A mans first duty is to provide for his own household the soldiers wont be imposed upon much longer."

Confederate impressment agents, who paid as low as 20 percent of market prices, took farmers' crops, livestock, and wagons. Even Secretary of War James A. Seddon admitted that impressment was "a harsh, unequal, and odious mode of supply." Farmers also gave a tenth of their crops or livestock as a tax-in-kind—and this on top of an income tax. Former Secretary of State Robert Toombs told the Georgia legislature that farmers "have been the great sufferers in this war, both in blood and in treasure." Many farmers were the victims of both Confederate and Union troops. All soldiers destroyed crops, killed livestock, and tore up fences and buildings for firewood.

Confederate officers and civilians complained about the guerrillas who waged a terrorist war against Unionists. Their murderous raids, in bitterly divided Missouri and bordering Kansas, won some cautious support from Confederate leaders. But the ultimate verdict came from Maj. Gen. Thomas C. Hindman, C.S.A.: The guerrillas were "doing no good, but much harm, in every way."

In the first glow of patriotism, men had gone to war without questioning the South's cause. Now desertions steadily increased. In April 1863, when the Confederate armies reached their peak strength of 498,000, about 138,000 men were declared missing. Reports of widespread civilian disloyalty came flowing into the War Department. Secret anti-war societies sprang up in several states. An Alabama regiment

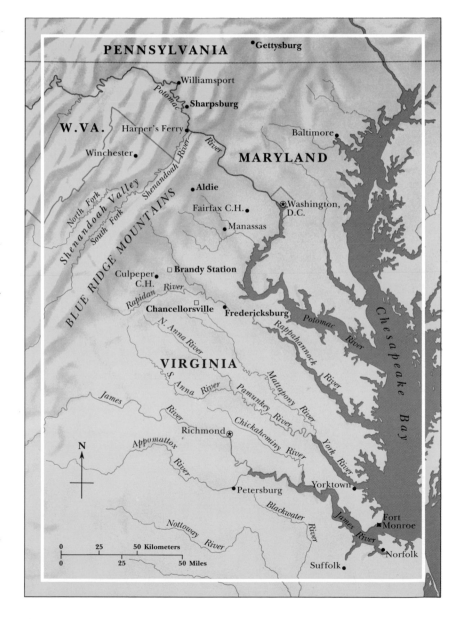

CHANCELLORSVILLE | *Rare and crucial in the tangled Wilderness, open vantage points provided key artillery positions in the battle fought here in early May. Below, the Chancellor family cemetery caps Fairview Heights.*

Here, Union gunners waged an artillery duel with Rebels on the grassy plateau called Hazel Grove (opposite). Maj. Gen. Joseph Hooker, in a fatal mistake, withdrew a division and yielded the plateau to Jeb Stuart, who brought

up his guns. "There has rarely been," wrote a Southern general after the war, "a more gratuitous gift of a battle-field."

The stone wall at Marye's Heights above Fredericksburg gave no protection to Rebels outflanked by John Sedgwick's men on May 3—but Sedgwick's corps missed the major battle going on at nearby Chancellorsville: a Union defeat.

Melzi Chancellor's house (below), also called Dowdall's Tavern, served as headquarters for Maj. Gen. O.O. Howard, whose corps broke under a surprise attack from the rear by Stonewall Jackson. Chancellorsville—

not a town but a fine house—burned under Rebel shellfire on May 3. A few days earlier a Union soldier had seen "quite a bevy of ladies" in spring finery on the "upper porch" of the big house.

"ran away almost in a body." In that state the Union recruited two companies of cavalry. So many deserters hid in the swamps of Florida that the governor appealed to Davis for help to root them out.

Many soldiers deserted because they put loyalty to their families over any other duty. On the poorest farms, wives or aged mothers struggled to do both their work and the work of their missing husbands or sons. Women petitioned Davis and Seddon. "If you dount send him home," an 81-year-old mother wrote, "I am bound to louse my crop and cum to suffer." Another woman pleaded: "I ask in the name of humanity to discharge my husband . . . thare is no use in keeping a man thare to kill him and leave widows and poore little orphen children to suffer while the rich has aplenty to work for them."

Davis tried to win the sympathies of poor and non-landed families by appealing to their sense of patriotism, fanning hatred of Yankees, and enlisting religion on the side of the Confederacy. By contrasting Federal barbarism with Southern chivalry, Davis sought to stake out a high moral ground for Southerners and their cause. He portrayed the North as a cesspool of "depraved" evildoers, denouncing Yankees as "the offscourings of the earth" and "demons" whose crimes ranged from "the burning of defenseless towns to the stealing of silver forks and spoons." He proclaimed special days for national prayer and solemnly urged fasting—fasting "in the midst of famine," a Confederate official sneered.

In January 1863 Davis ended a month-long tour of the embattled western region, hoping to "arouse all classes to united and desperate resistance." Crowds cheered at his stops, and the news was generally good. Grant's campaign against Vicksburg had failed. On the Yazoo River, an electrically detonated mine (then called a torpedo) had sunk the Union gunboat *Cairo*, the first vessel in naval history to be destroyed by a land-controlled mine. Confederate steamboats, "armored" with cotton bales, had driven the Yankees from Galveston and broken the blockade. John Hunt Morgan, the daring raider, had led 2,500 men into his adopted home state of Kentucky, burned railroad trestles and bridges, torn up tracks, and taken nearly 2,000 prisoners.

Morgan's exploits in Tennessee and Kentucky, like "Prince John" Magruder's success at Galveston, soon were eclipsed by confusing

Icon for Southern homes, the engraving below portrays Lee as majestic commander, Stonewall Jackson as deferential, in their last meeting on May 2. In fact, although Jackson was riding Little Sorrel, Lee was on foot, watching the column pass by to outflank Hooker. Shot that night by his own men, Jackson died on May 10. His grave at Lexington, Virginia, became a shrine. The unknown visitors may have been photographed after October 22, 1870, when Lee—then president of the town's Washington College—died after a brief illness. While Jackson awaited the end, Lee had written him an eloquent letter: "I should have chosen for the good of the country, to be disabled in your stead."

reports arriving in Richmond from Tennessee. "God has granted us a happy New Year," Gen. Braxton Bragg telegraphed, saying that a large Union force, led by Maj. Gen. William S. Rosecrans, had been stopped at Stone's River, near Murfreesborough. Bragg had indeed won a tactical victory on New Year's Eve, and a day's lull in the fighting had allowed his men time to relish it, but things went badly when he ordered another attack. The Federals held firm, their artillery punished the Rebels severely, and Bragg decided to retreat. He pulled back southward, allowing Rosecrans to occupy the town, a key position for control of middle Tennessee. He had also lost a reported 11,739 casualties from a force of 37,000, and the confidence of officers and men. One of his brigadiers wrote that they would now "enter action without hope of honor or renown and retreat with sullen indifference and discontent." Rosecrans had lost 12,906 of 41,400—but could claim a success.

Stone's River excepted, the New Year did not bring good news to Lincoln. Burnside's men along the Rappahannock were deserting by the thousand in the wake of the December disaster at Fredericksburg. Nevertheless, Burnside wanted to try again—and strike "a mortal blow to the rebellion." Against the counsel of his generals, Burnside planned to cross the river, outflank Lee, and take Richmond.

The Army of the Potomac, burdened by pontoon-laden wagons, marched out of its winter camps under a sunny sky that soon turned gray. A three-day storm came on. "It rains great guns," noted a staff aide, "and blows a harricane." Rain beat down on men and beasts, churning the dubious roads into what a soldier called "rivers of deep mire." Of all the war's bad road conditions, this episode probably saw the worst, a blend of misery and farce. A chaplain recorded details: "Here a wagon mired and abandoned; there a team of six mules stalled, with the driver hallooing and cursing; dead mules and horses on either hand—ten, twelve and even twenty-six horses vainly trying to drag a twelve-pounder through the mire." Even officialdom adopted the name "Mud March," although the word march glorified the infantry's mile-an-hour pace. Mules drowned, cannon sank, and some disgusted soldiers wandered off.

Lincoln removed Burnside and named as his successor Maj. Gen. Joseph Hooker, an officer Burnside had wanted to dismiss. Hooker

At ease on a fine June day, Union staff officers and foreign observers loll under a tree near Fairfax Court House; a white mustache identifies Count von Zeppelin of Prussia; Lt. Frederick Rosencrans of Sweden grips the hilt of his sword.

A hiatus followed Chancellorsville. Then, on June 3, Lee began moving men northward. Cavalry screens protected both armies. In a fight at Aldie, sharpshooters of the 5th Virginia Cavalry (bottom right) fell into Federal hands.

had told a war correspondent that what the nation needed was a dictator. Lincoln wrote a fatherly letter to his new commander: "Only those generals who gain successes, can set up dictators. What I now ask of you is military success, and I will risk the dictatorship."

No longer could Lincoln fight the war with volunteers. Congress passed a conscription act—weaker than the Confederate law—in March. Enforcement produced disturbances in many communities and a notorious draft riot in New York City in July. Many of the rioters there were Irish immigrants who hated black workers as competitors and strikebreakers; they lynched as many as a dozen blacks before police, militia, West Point cadets, and Federal units quelled the violence.

Of the 162,535 men ultimately called up for the draft, 116,188 would hire substitutes. A total of 86,724 other men would pay $300 apiece for an exemption. As intended, however, the law did prompt

volunteering and the Union managed to get the manpower it needed.

Hooker, known as "Fighting Joe," spent the rest of the winter taking care of the men he had. He got them their back pay, and improved morale by improving the food. He replaced the intelligence chief, private detective Allan Pinkerton, whose diligent work had produced overblown reports of Rebel numbers, with a colonel who organized a Bureau of Military Information. This improved the quality of operational intelligence. But it was no match for the information that Confederate war planners got from Virginians loyal to the South.

Late in April Hooker began his grand maneuver to capture Lee's army, declaring, "may God have mercy on General Lee; for I shall have none." From Falmouth, on the Rappahannock, he marched about a third of his 134,000-man army 30 miles or more up the narrowing river to Kelly's Ford. Two other corps crossed at a ford closer by.

Photographed sometime in the year at a Union wagon park near Brandy Station, 240 canvas-capped wagons—including ambulances, ordnance, baggage, and commissary vehicles—stand ready to support the Sixth Corps of the Army of the Potomac. To supply 8,000 men, these wagons would string out nearly two miles on a narrow dirt road. In the campaign that led to Gettysburg, each army utilized about 4,000 such vehicles; on one road these would extend more than 30 miles, exclusive of marching space for infantry. Lee moved at a disadvantage in June, entering enemy territory with a highly vulnerable line of communications, far from supporting railheads, and with a growing shortage of horses and mules.

The Union forces converged near Chancellorsville, a brick house in a hundred-acre clearing at a crossroads about ten miles west of the Rebel lines at Fredericksburg. Maj. Gen. Darius N. Couch, commander of the Second Corps, later sketched the scene: "the general hilarity pervading the camps was particularly noticeable; the soldiers, while chopping wood and lighting fires, were singing merry songs and indulging in peppery camp jokes." Another corps commander, Maj. Gen. George G. Meade, gave Hooker one of his rare compliments: "Hurrah for old Joe; we are on Lee's flank, and he does not know it."

Two other Federal corps crossed the Rappahannock below Fredericksburg. Lee seemed trapped between two steely claws. War correspondents got a briefing from Hooker: "The rebel army is now the legitimate property of the Army of the Potomac."

Hooker's plan, however, looked better on his inadequate maps than on the terrain where his army struggled—dense second-growth woods called the Wilderness of Spotsylvania. The troops stumbled through marshes and snarls of stunted, vine-covered pine and scrub oaks, the remnant of a forest that once supplied fuel to nearby ironworks. The brush was so thick that men, unable to shoulder their guns, carried them at trail or used them to fend off branches and briars. Union observers in balloons could see little but the green canopy.

To escape from Hooker's trap, and still guard the road to Richmond, Lee chose to send troops under Stonewall Jackson toward the advancing Federals and left only about 10,000 men to hold Fredericksburg. Jackson moved swiftly and entrenched along a cleared ridge facing an edge of the Wilderness. A Confederate artillery officer clinically described what the site gave him: "Any charging line is brought to a halt by the entanglement, and held under close fire of musketry and canister, while the surrounding forest prevents the enemy from finding positions to use his own artillery."

Three Union columns marched against the Confederates, who stopped only one. But Hooker ordered all three to pull back and dig in around Chancellorsville, giving up a good artillery position on high ground. Meade, commander of one of the columns, could not contain his anger. "If he thinks he can't hold the top of the hill," Meade muttered, "how does he expect to hold the bottom of it?"

That night, May 1, Jeb Stuart brought news from a scouting mission—to the west of Chancellorsville, the right flank of Hooker's line was open to attack. Lee and Jackson planned the next move, sitting on cracker boxes. Maj. Jedediah Hotchkiss gave them a map, prepared with the help of a local clergyman who was serving as a chaplain. Jackson traced a route to the west; he would go around this way, to strike Hooker's army from the rear.

"What do you propose to make this movement with?" Lee asked.

"With my whole corps," Jackson replied. That meant taking 30,000 men away from Lee, leaving him with 14,000 troops against the main Federal force of 73,000.

Never divide your forces in the presence of a superior enemy, say the manuals of war. But Lee had confidence in Jackson. He agreed.

Jackson moved off the next morning, putting his men, wagons, and artillery onto a narrow road through the forest for a 12-mile march around toward Hooker's right flank. The column stretched 10 miles behind him. When he reached the point of attack, it would take about five hours for the rest of his corps to arrive.

Hooker, standing by his headquarters tent, saw the enemy column passing by. Retreating without a fight? He must have hoped so. He did send a warning to one-armed Maj. Gen. O.O. Howard, the corps commander on the right, to expect a flank attack, but by afternoon the threat seemed to have vanished.

About 5:15 Jackson's men—in three lines two miles across—moved quietly up behind Howard's position. Rabbits and deer stampeded before them. Federal soldiers eating supper saw the animals and had a moment of curiosity before they heard the bugles and the heart-stopping Rebel yell and saw the bayonets rushing toward them.

Howard saw a division break and vanish in minutes. "It was a terrible gale," he remembered. "The rush, the rattle, the quick lightning from a hundred points at once; the roar redoubled by the echoes through the forest. . . ." He tried to make a stand. But Confederate troops routed his panic-stricken men.

The fading sun gave way to a rising full moon. "Push right ahead," Jackson ordered, riding over a battlefield where men in flight collided with both friend and foe. With his staff, he went scouting beyond his

BRANDY STATION | *Velvety pasture stretches beyond "Farley," in turn headquarters for W.H.F. "Rooney" Lee, Jeb Stuart, and the Union's John Sedgwick. Abundant hay (opposite, in modern rolls) would have helped fill Lee's need for fodder. In this vicinity a day of charges and countercharges ended pretty much in a draw. Brandy Station proved, however, a morale booster for Union cavalry and an embarrassment for Stuart. One general thought it right that Stuart should get the blame because he got "all the credit" for "anything handsome." Perhaps to make up for this, Stuart went adventuring apart from Lee's northbound infantry and left Lee in the dark about enemy moves.*

"This is the place I want it to be," said Lt. Gen. A.P. Hill, C.S.A., upon learning that the Army of the Potomac was gathering near Gettysburg. Generals of both armies recognized the strategic advantages here—defensible hills and ridges, open ground, good roads converging on the little Pennsylvania market town—and John B. Bachelder recorded them carefully in a bird's-eye view made soon after the battle.

pickets—close to the Federal position. He turned back toward his own lines, where the 18th North Carolina opened fire. "Cease firing! Cease firing!" his officers shouted. "You're firing on your own men!"

"It's a lie!" a Tar Heel officer shouted. "Pour it into them, boys!" Two bullets smashed into Stonewall Jackson's left arm, a third pierced the palm of his right hand. Aides lowered him from his horse and placed him under a tree. He spoke calmly of wounds "from my own men." Stretcher-bearers, under Federal artillery fire, carried Jackson to a field hospital, where a surgeon amputated his arm near the shoulder.

Like so many of the wounded of both sides, he would die within days. "He has lost his left arm, but I have lost my right," Lee would mourn. "Any victory would be dear at such a cost."

All night, patches of the Wilderness burned, and men who lay wounded there died in the flames. By dawn Hooker had recovered enough to forge a defensive line anchored on the Rappahannock and Rapidan. On the porch at Chancellorsville, he was knocked down when a cannonball struck a pillar he was leaning against. Dazed, he staggered to his feet, managed to mount his horse, and rode off in personal

retreat. "Everything could yet have been saved; yet all was lost," a colonel wrote in his diary. "Hooker was no longer Hooker."

Union troops who had crossed the river below Fredericksburg, men of "Uncle John" Sedgwick's Sixth Corps, were also thrown back, many falling exactly where other men in blue had fallen five months earlier. Of the 104,891 troops Hooker had put into action in the widespread battle, 17,278 were killed, wounded, or missing. The Confederates, about 60,800 strong at the beginning of the battle, suffered some 13,000 casualties—22 percent of Lee's army. In the grim arithmetic of

war, Lee had been hurt more than Hooker. But the battlefield victory clearly went to Lee and Jackson.

The Army of the Potomac began withdrawing to their camps at Falmouth. "The batteries lumbered on slowly through the mud, and the infantry with them; men and horses were all more than half asleep," an officer wrote. Here they were again, waiting for the next move from Lee. "If possible," Lincoln urged Hooker on May 7, "I would be very glad of another movement. . . ." There would be movement, but it would come from another Union general half a continent away.

Control of the Mississippi, strategists in two capitals agreed, would determine the future of two nations—or one. And control would be settled by Maj. Gen. U.S. Grant's campaign against one city—Vicksburg, the upriver stronghold of a 250-mile stretch of the valley still held by the Confederacy. The downstream bastion was the well-fortified outpost at Port Hudson, Louisiana. It would probably fall quickly if only Grant could take Vicksburg.

"We may take all the northern ports of the Confederacy," Lincoln had said, "and they can still defy us from Vicksburg. It means hog and hominy without limit, fresh troops from all the states of the far South, and a cotton country where they can raise the staple without interference." Grant had made his assessment in a soldier's grimmer image: The conquest of Vicksburg, he said, equaled "the amputation of a limb."

Vicksburg lay atop 200-foot bluffs on a sharp bend of the river. No ships, no army assaulting those bluffs could escape fire from the batteries there. North of the town spread the impenetrable swamps of a 200-mile-long delta formed by the Mississippi and Yazoo Rivers.

Somewhere in Arkansas was a Rebel army that in theory could aid Vicksburg. But no one even knew how many men this army had: Richmond officials thought it had 55,000; actually there were at most 27,000. The Confederate high command treated the Mississippi as the dividing line between zones of action: one bounded by the Appalachians and the river; the second the sprawling immensity to the west, called the Trans-Mississippi. The Federals treated the Mississippi as a single theater.

Grant had tried to take Vicksburg by amphibious operations along the river and by slogging through the bayous north of the city. He had even had his men dig a canal to try to route ships out of range of

Vicksburg's guns. Finally, late in March 1863, he launched a campaign to attack the city from its landward side.

He marched most of his army southward along the west side of the river, from Milliken's Bend, 20 miles northwest of Vicksburg, to Hard Times, Louisiana. David Dixon Porter, acting rear admiral, ran a fleet of gunboats and transports past Vicksburg, defying the cannon on the bluffs. Sherman, meanwhile, made menacing moves north of Vicksburg, and a Union cavalry force galloped into Mississippi from Tennessee. Both moves diverted attention from Grant.

Porter's 11 ships—the transports "armored" with wet bales of hay, cotton bales, and sacks of grain—took several hits. One ship sank without loss of life. The rest got through as did several more, to ferry more than 22,000 men across the river to Bruinsburg, Mississippi. "I felt a degree of relief scarcely ever equalled since," Grant recalled years later. ". . . I was now in the enemy's country, with a vast river and the stronghold of Vicksburg between me and my base of supplies. But I was on dry ground on the same side of the river with the enemy."

In 18 days Grant took his men 180 miles. He disposed of Rebels at Port Gibson and Raymond, then took Jackson, the Mississippi capital. He next turned toward Vicksburg, winning a stiff fight at Champion Hill and an easy one at a railroad bridge on the Big Black River, a natural barrier a few miles east of the city. He saw his string of victories as a prelude to an inevitable breach of Vicksburg's defenses. But Confederate engineers, making good use of ravines and gullies, had strung a line of entrenchments at the rear of the city. Rifle pits, and parapets 20 feet thick, laced the land and shielded its defenders.

Grant attacked, and lost 1,000 men. He tried another attack three days later, and again the Rebels fought ferociously. Federal troops pierced the line at one strongpoint but got no farther. Once more Grant's men were repulsed, this time with a loss of 3,200 men. Grant decided that Vicksburg would have to be taken by siege, not storm. He would "outcamp the enemy," he said, and "incur no more losses."

The Federals built their siege works, digging more than 11 miles of trenches and 89 artillery emplacements for 220 guns. As the land forces were short of proper siege guns, Admiral Porter lent a battery of heavy naval ordnance. Grant fired as many as 2,800 shells into the city every 24 hours. Other shells arced in from U.S. Navy gunboats and mortar scows on the river.

Families dug caves into the soft earth of the bluffs and, abandoning shell-pocked homes, moved into their holes. In some caves, carpets covered the dirt floors, parlor furniture gleamed by candlelight, and flowers and books filled niches carved in the walls. "All day and all night the shells from the mortars are falling around us," a woman wrote in her diary, "and all day from the guns around the fortifications. . . . It is a most discouraging sort of warfare."

Sharpshooters on both sides aimed at any upraised head or hand. Where the trenches were close, men lobbed hand grenades at each other. Sunstroke, sickness, bad water, and spoiled food felled besieged civilians and soldiers. "It got to be Sunday all the time," a survivor of the siege told Mark Twain. "Seven Sundays in the week. . . . We hadn't anything to do, and time hung heavy." Rationing was imposed: two biscuits, two slices of bacon, a few peas, and a spoonful of rice per day. Flour sold at $200 a barrel, rum at $100 a gallon. The Vicksburg *Daily Citizen*, which eulogized "the luxury of mule-meat and fricasseed kittens," ran out of newsprint and began publishing on wallpaper. And, night after night, day after day, the shells kept falling.

At the eastern end of the Confederacy's thousand-mile front, Robert E. Lee, still mourning Jackson, was weighing possibilities for his army. He could stay on the defensive, and risk being forced toward Richmond, or strike northward, which he had been thinking of since February. In Pennsylvania he could gather horses, food, and possibly matériel; and a great victory there would shake Union morale. Davis and his Cabinet endorsed Lee's invasion plan and gave him a free hand in reorganizing his army. In Jackson's stead, A. P. Hill and Richard Ewell would become corps commanders, with many other changes as well. Volunteers and draftees replaced the missing, and Lee now had 75,000 men ready to march. "There never were such men in an army before," he said. "They will go anywhere and do anything if properly led." Under Lee, they thought victory as certain as sunrise.

Jeb Stuart's cavalry screened the troops as they marched northwestward from Fredericksburg. On June 9, at Brandy Station, Federal cavalry, dispatched to probe the Rebel *(Continued on page 202)*

GETTYSBURG | *Autumn sun warms rolling fields and pastures where, on the afternoon of July 3, Confederates formed for a legendary attack. In an assault that became a byword for valor and futility, Pickett's Charge, 12,500 men undertook to break the Union center. Reluctant to give the order, Lt. Gen. James Longstreet wrote years later: "That day at Gettysburg was one of the saddest of my life." Lee said, "it is I that have lost this fight...."*

"Peace Eternal in a Nation United" reads the inscription on the Eternal Light memorial, dedicated on July 3, 1938. For the battle's 75th anniversary, 1,800 veterans met on the field for the final Joint Reunion of the Blue and the Gray.

GETTYSBURG | *Benign as a baseball diamond in the afternoon sun, the Peach Orchard betrays nothing of the fight that raged here on July 2. Without Meade's approval, Maj. Gen. Daniel Sickles advanced to this orchard, creating a salient and leaving the Round Tops open to capture. Alertness and quick action by Brig. Gen. G.K. Warren and Col. Strong Vincent kept Southerners from taking Little Round Top and turning the Federal line.*

July 3 brought stiff fighting for Massachusetts volunteers of the 1st Andrew Sharp-Shooters. The bas-relief that honors this company offers stern Yankee wisdom: "In God We Put Our Trust But Kept Our Powder Dry."

"Ulysses don't scare worth a d--n," said a man of the 5th Wisconsin on May 10, 1864. The general was sitting on a fallen tree writing a dispatch when a shell burst in front of him; he glanced up, then went on writing.

Grant had led his first foray against the enemy, he recalled in his *Personal Memoirs,* for lack of "the moral courage to halt and consider what to do." He found the Rebel camp deserted and saw that its colonel "had been as much afraid of me as I had been of him." After that he "never experienced trepidation upon confronting an enemy, though I always felt more or less anxiety."

Born in Ohio in 1822, to a family of old New England stock and modest means, he surprised himself by passing West Point's entrance exam at 17. Army paperwork turned his name from Hiram Ulysses to Ulysses Simpson; unable to win a correction, he just put up with the change. His whole career showed this lack of fuss. Grant became an all-time rarity among generals, said an English admirer of that rank, by accepting things as they were and trying to make the best of them.

Grant never intended to stay in the army, but served as a quartermaster in the Mexican War. This war he always detested as "one of the most unjust ever waged by a stronger against a weaker nation."

His happy marriage to Julia Dent, sister of a classmate and daughter of a slave-owning Missouri planter, began in August 1848. Duty on the Pacific coast kept them apart; rumors of drunkenness clouded his name; he resigned in 1854. Supremely businesslike in war, he failed in one business venture after another. He was clerking in his father's leather store at Galena, Illinois, in April 1861.

West Point connections did nothing for Grant, but he took on some volunteers known as "Governor Yates's Hellions" and soon had them in order. Most of them, he said, favored discipline. At 5 feet 8 inches and 135 pounds, in the simplest of uniforms, he had no dash, no

ULYSSES S. GRANT

gift of oratory at all, but men obeyed him.

Starting in obscurity, he developed his command skills battle by battle, with larger and larger forces. He didn't repeat mistakes. He relied heavily on a staff of small-town civilians for routine help, on himself for essentials. He wrote orders in his own hand (and spellings), and a junior noted that "no one ever has the slightest doubt as to their meaning." He showed flexibility as well as stubbornness in his long Vicksburg Campaign.

Given command of all the Union armies in March 1864, he shaped a coherent plan for victory. As Lincoln had noted, other generals promised success if the President would give them something unavailable (usually cavalry); Grant had no such "pet impossibility." He found roles for the political generals that Lincoln needed for a unified war effort and for reelection: Butler, Banks, Sigel. For the crucial fighting he relied on his ablest subordinates. He sent Philip Sheridan, age 33, to secure the Shenandoah Valley; supported his old friend "Cump" Sherman during the invasion of Georgia and the Carolinas; kept Meade in command of the Army of the Potomac. He stayed with that long-tried force until he brought Lee to the point of surrender.

"Let us have peace" was Grant's message when the Republicans nominated him for President. Elected in 1868, he served for eight years that tarnished his fame. He lacked the political skills to ensure Federal protection for the former slaves, whose cause he had at heart. He was baffled by the Gilded Age sharpies who tainted his administrations with scandal, and lost his modest new fortune to a swindler.

Smitten by throat cancer after years of cigars, he provided for his family by writing his memoirs—a book, said a great critic, that has the reader on edge to know how the Civil War is coming out. Grant's account of Appomattox reveals the man who had known humiliation and had no desire to impose it on the vanquished.

Union dugouts pockmark the yellow loess slopes in siege lines northeast of Vicksburg. Federal troops held this ground for 47 days under fire, twice assaulting Rebel defenses. Grant took the city's surrender on July 4, 1863, giving the Union a decisive victory.

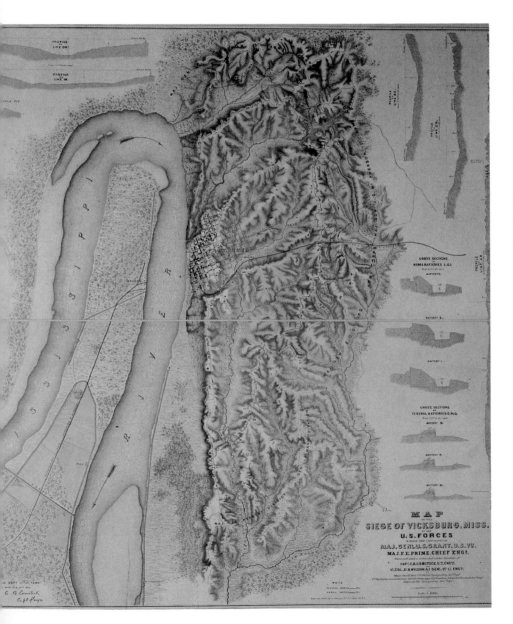

MAP
OF THE
SIEGE OF VICKSBURG, MISS.
U. S. FORCES

movements, pounced on Stuart. "Hundreds of glittering sabers instantly leaped from their scabbards, gleamed and flashed in the morning sun," a Confederate officer recalled. About 10,000 men from each side galloped into this storybook battle. Stuart held the field, but the Federal troopers proved at last that they could hold their own against the legendary Rebel horsemen.

The Confederates moved rapidly out of Virginia, pouring men into the rich farmland of Pennsylvania via the Shenandoah Valley and western Maryland. Hooker belatedly took up the pursuit, not quite certain just where Lee was heading. In response to Hooker's vague telegrams about the Rebel movements, Lincoln wired this message: "If the head of Lee's army is at Martinsburg and the tail of it on the Plank road between Fredericksburg and Chancellorsville, the animal must be very slim somewhere. Could you not break him?" Hooker could only look for the animal's tracks, and by June 26 he had still not found them. Secretary of the Navy Gideon Welles noted in his diary that Lincoln "observed in Hooker the same failings that were witnessed in McClellan after the Battle of Antietam—a want of alacrity to obey and a greedy call for more troops...."

On June 28, at a Union camp near Frederick, Maryland, an aide awakened Maj. Gen. George G. Meade, commander of the Fifth Corps, and handed him a letter: On Lincoln's orders, Meade was to relieve Hooker and take command of the Army of the Potomac's 94,974 men. Meade protested—he knew nothing of Hooker's plans—but in vain. Reportedly he said to the aide, "Well, I've been tried and condemned without a hearing, and I suppose I shall have to go to execution."

Leading elements of Lee's army were closing in on Harrisburg, capital of Pennsylvania. Then, on June 28, Lee learned from a spy that Union forces were near Frederick. He had thought them still in Virginia; he had heard nothing from Stuart's cavalry in days. Shocked, he began concentrating his forces at Cashtown, near a gap in South Mountain. From there he could go southeast to Gettysburg, a hub of good roads. He had heard that his old friend Meade was now the enemy commander, and although he respected his skill he thought the abrupt change would work in favor of the army that had beaten all of Meade's predecessors.

Gettysburg, July 1. Two armies meet at a place neither army has chosen. An American epic begins.

On a hot morning, two Confederate brigades approached the town and met a thin line of dismounted Union cavalry. The outnumbered Federals had breech-loading carbines; they could get off eight or ten rounds per minute against the Rebels' three, and they stopped the Confederate advance. Both sides brought up reinforcements as quickly as possible and the battle flared up into fury.

It was combat between veterans, fairly matched in skill and discipline, and therefore fought at searing cost. One North Carolina company of 91 would end the battle with everyone killed or wounded. The first day alone cost the First Corps (U.S.) 65 percent of its 8,200 men, and the 147th New York lost half its strength within minutes. Madness and slaughter, legends and valor—all was swirling here in a kind of ultimate battle. The 16th Maine had started the day with 298 men. By sundown it had 66, many with bits of flag in their pockets. Fearing the loss of their colors, they had torn up the flag and distributed the bits, like communion, among the living.

Thousands of Federals had managed to reach Cemetery Hill, high point on a ridge south of the clogged center of town. They expected to make a last stand in the fading light, but no attack came.

As night fell, the Federals had a defensive line three and a half miles long. It resembled a huge fishhook, and the landmarks that formed it would become part of the epic of Gettysburg: Cemetery Ridge was the shank, bending at Cemetery Hill; a rocky hill, Little Round Top, was the eye of the hook; Culp's Hill was the barb.

A mile across an open plain, the Confederates drew up their army along Seminary Ridge. Their campfires, thick as the heaven's stars, flickered a message of power and threat. Lee had assembled at least 50,000 men. He faced, by dawn, about 60,000 Federals, with about 20,000 more on the way. "The enemy is here," Lee told his corps commanders, "and if we do not whip him, he will whip us." That summed up the mood of both sides. The action on the second day amounted to finding out if part of the fishhook would break.

The Confederate attacks added bloody new names to the war's mournful litany—the Peach Orchard, the Wheat Field, Devil's Den.

Blood puddled the rocks and tinted the brooks. The "edge of the fight," said an officer, "swayed back and forward like a wave." When the wave finally ebbed at dusk, the fishhook was dented but intact.

At 1 p.m. on July 3, Lee's 150 guns along Seminary Ridge hurled "a tornado of projectiles" at the Federal line. One hundred Union guns responded, then broke off to conserve ammunition. Some 12,500 Rebel troops, arrayed in perfect lines, stepped out of the woods and in the sudden silence marched forward across the upward sloping field, rifles shouldered as if on parade. A breeze from the west cleared the gray pall of battle smoke and set the flags to rippling. When the Confederates had covered about 300 yards, Union cannon began to cut them down.

Men, torn by the iron hail of canister, fell in bloody clumps. The gaps quickly closed and, in the words of an awed Federal lieutenant, "Right on they move, as with one soul, in perfect order. . . . magnificent, grim, irresistible." Now at last came the rifle fire—veterans had learned the importance of waiting to fire in unison at close range. "Volley after volley of crashing musket balls sweep through the line and mow us down like wheat before the scythe," wrote a Virginia soldier wounded in the charge. Some of the Federals were cheering, shouting "Fredericksburg! Fredericksburg!"

The mile-wide line shriveled and out of it surged a mass of men rushing toward a clump of trees, the center of the Union line. The only Confederate general still with them, Brig. Gen. Lewis Armistead, raised his black hat on the tip of his sword. He sprang over a stone wall that jutted out from the trees. Behind him scrambled about 200 men. "Come on, boys! Give them the cold steel!" Armistead shouted. An instant later he fell, mortally wounded by several bullets. Federal troops fired into the clot of attackers at the wall, then mobbed them and hit them with whatever they had—cannon rammers, sabers, pistols, clubbed rifles. "Every man fought on his own hook," a bluecoat remembered. The men who fought here would call this the Bloody Angle; later it would be called the high-water mark of the Confederacy.

The survivors started back, some still able to run, some walking backward and still firing. About 6,000 men did not go back. Maj. Gen. George Pickett's division suffered the most. Of the 5,000 men who marched off with him, only 800 mustered (Continued on page 210)

VICKSBURG | *Bronze cavalryman on the Wisconsin State Memorial takes a bead on a long-vanished Confederate. Grasses soften once-raw earthen siege works, part of an 11-mile system thrown up by Union forces.*

Infantry turned engineers, one recalled; "they bored like gophers and beavers, with a spade in one hand and a gun in the other." Still, the Rebels held out for six weeks, repulsing every assault, before surrendering—near starvation and

without hope of relief—on July 4. "The Confederacy totters to its destruction," said its Pennsylvania-born ordnance chief, Josiah Gorgas, when the news reached Richmond.

Only one man entered the Civil War a private and emerged a lieutenant general: Nathan Bedford Forrest of Tennessee. No general in the war killed more enemies hand to hand: at least 30. "War means fightin' and fightin' means killin'," he said with his usual curt realism.

His career brings the racism of the era into clear focus: "If we ain't fightin' to keep slavery, then what the hell are we fightin' for?" To the Southern elite he kept the stigma of a slave dealer. The odium of a "massacre" of black troops at Fort Pillow still marks him, although scholars agree that his role in it cannot be determined now. They also agree that for a year or so in the late 1860s the "Wizard of the Saddle" was Grand Wizard of the Invisible Empire, the white resistance movement of the Ku Klux Klan.

"My life has been a battle from the start," he said as he faced its end in 1877. Fatherless at 15, he pitched in on the farm to support his mother and ten siblings. He scraped up some learning. He could read; he mastered numbers well enough to build a fortune. From deals in land and his "nigger-yard at Memphis," he had accumulated about $1,500,000. In 1860 one of his plantations made 1,000 bales of cotton.

Authorized by the governor to raise a battalion of mounted rangers, Forrest had some 650 men and a commission by November 1861. He relied on Colt revolvers ("navy sixes") and double-barreled shotguns until he could import Enfield rifles (with his own funds) or capture U.S. equipment, always a favorite source of supply. His first actions revealed ferocious courage and lightning-quick decisions. A rare letter in his own hand, dated May 23, 1862, reports "a small brush with the Enamy on yesterday I Suceded in gaining thir rear . . . they wair not looking for me I taken them by Suprise they run like Suns of Biches." Clerks and adjutants turned this idiom into formal prose.

NATHAN BEDFORD FORREST

Once a hulking recruit rejected an order: "Ah ain't agoin' to do hit." Forrest, 6 feet 2 and broad of shoulder, picked him up and tossed him into an icy river (after which the boy did pretty well). If Forrest disagreed with a superior, he might show deference or might not. He scorned some, defied others, told off one to his face: "You have played the part of a damned scoundrel, and are a coward." Consistently his insight outranked theirs. Once he questioned Lt. Gen. Richard Taylor about an assignment until—as Taylor saw—he had "isolated the chances of success from causes of failure with the care of a chemist experimenting in a laboratory."

In spur-and-saddle days, professional soldiers studied Forrest's mounted-infantry tactics: using horses for mobility, fighting on foot for massed firepower. Then they studied his deep-penetration strategy: leading a fighting force far behind enemy lines to hold an area, seize its resources, and deny the use of it to the enemy. Forrest excelled at this. As one scholar explains, he "had an intuitive and almost unique ability to handle his commands with enemy forces all around him." He was a master of deception and bluff. By 1864 his name alone could rattle a Federal outfit—put them "under cover," as Sherman expressed it. He was more than a match for his Union counterparts.

Looking back, Sherman called Forrest "the most remarkable man our Civil War produced on either side," an unpredictable genius of strategy. An American original, Forrest suggests ol' Bubba as Ares, god of war, or Genghis Khan with a cracker accent. Without his ignorance and "social disadvantages," said a South Carolina aristocrat, "he would in all probability have been the most conspicuous and useful general in the Army of the Confederate States." His farewell to his men, as published, defines an ideal valid on both sides: "I have never, on the field of battle, sent you where I was unwilling to go myself."

Known by Sherman as "that devil Forrest," Nathan Bedford Forrest helped win the Battle of Chickamauga for the South during two of the war's bloodiest days, September 19-20, 1863. The battle began north of Lee & Gordon's Mills (opposite) on Chickamauga Creek in Georgia.

next day. The attack would be called Pickett's Charge, but of the 46 regiments taking part, he commanded only 15. "This has been my fight," Lee told Pickett, "and upon my shoulders rests the blame." He had lost about 28,000 men in three days; Meade had lost about 23,000.

With characteristic prudence, Meade judged his forces too battered to launch a counterattack. The battlefield fell silent, except for the moans of the wounded and dying. Men went out to bury the dead and gather the wounded.

Among them was John Ketcham. He and his brother Edward, both Quakers, had gone to Gettysburg as lieutenants, Edward in the infantry, John in the cavalry. "Edward was the first man killed in the regiment," John wrote their mother. A bullet "struck him in the temple, and went through his head. He put up his hand, and said, 'Oh!' and fell on his elbow, quite dead." John had seen this, and fought on.

After the battle, a captain came by, saw John with his brother's body, and said, "If he were a brother of mine, I would bury him on the field of glory." And so John did, "under an oak tree, in his soldier's uniform, wrapped in a shelter-tent." His headstone, marked with his name and regiment, was "a piece of a young oak cut off by a rebel shell." Three months later, John died in a Confederate prison camp.

On the Fourth of July, as Lee sent his wounded back to Virginia in a wagon train 17 miles long, starving Vicksburg surrendered to Grant.

FOLLOWING PAGES: *Powerful currents of the Tennessee River rush through a narrow gorge known as "The Suck" and require use of a windlass and lines to haul a steamboat upstream toward Chattanooga. In late September and October, Rebel control of this stretch of river forced the Federals into a 60-mile overland route to supply their comrades trapped in the city; the effort used up 10,000 mules. On October 23, Grant arrived to break the siege. He managed to get 1,800 men downriver, floating past Rebel pickets in pontoon boats at night, to gain a bridgehead on the bank at Brown's Ferry. Then a shortcut over Raccoon Mountain sped supplies to the city. "Full rations, boys!" cried the men when the first steamer arrived.*

Port Hudson, 250 river miles down the Mississippi, fell five days later. "The river of our freedom," said Sherman, "is free as God made it."

"We are now in the darkest hour of our political existence," Jefferson Davis told one of his generals. His messages to his dispirited people dwelt now on the horrors of conquest: Yankee brutality, and frenzied slaves turning on their masters—"nothing less than the extermination of yourselves, your wives, and children."

In this darkest hour the Confederacy lost some 70,000 arms at Gettysburg and Vicksburg. Chief of Ordnance Josiah Gorgas became almost entirely dependent upon matériel from Europe via Bermuda and the Bahamas. From there, swift blockade-runners sped to Southern ports. The ships managed to get some 185,000 arms through the blockade between January 1862 and July 1863.

The Confederacy paid for the imported goods through loans, which in turn were paid off with government-owned cotton. The government built a huge press at the runners' principal port, Wilmington, North Carolina, where slaves packed thousands of bales a month. Gorgas's two-way blockade-running would bring the Confederacy about 330,000 weapons (most of them Enfield rifle-muskets), nearly 2 million pounds of saltpeter, and 1.5 million pounds of lead.

Gorgas had less trouble with foreign suppliers than he had with some officials at home. The governor of Georgia balked at relinquishing control over the distillation of alcohol needed for munitions making. Plain citizens showed more cooperation. Answering an urgent call for lead, Charlestonians contributed their window-sash weights and citizens of Mobile chipped in some unused water mains. Tons of spent lead were also gleaned from battlefields.

Late in the year the fall of Ducktown, in southeastern Tennessee, a seemingly inconsequential place, meant the loss of mines that produced virtually all the copper in the Confederacy. Without copper, guns were useless; it was essential in percussion caps for rifles and primer tubes for cannon. Gorgas commandeered the copper in stills that distilled turpentine, applejack, and corn squeezings.

The loss of Ducktown was one of the last mishaps the South could blame on Braxton Bragg, whose quarrelsome ways had made him a host of enemies on his own side. In June, Bragg was facing Rosecrans in middle Tennessee. Union commanders feared that some of Bragg's men would be sent to help Vicksburg; Confederates feared an attack on Chattanooga. To keep the Federals busy, Bragg authorized a quick raid by John Hunt Morgan into Kentucky. Morgan led 2,480 horsemen on into Indiana and Ohio, losing men and horses in skirmishes along the way. He and 364 exhausted survivors surrendered in late July at Salineville, Ohio, near the Pennsylvania line.

Meanwhile, Rosecrans's 60,000-man Army of the Cumberland had skillfully outflanked Bragg, who fell back to Chattanooga—from a fertile area to a meager one. At best, Bragg's men were victims of the commissary system. They lived on short rations when the harvests around them went to depots in Atlanta and then to Richmond. When Bragg learned that Rosecrans had crossed the Tennessee River and could cut his supply lines, he abandoned the city, the Confederacy's last defensible stronghold in the state of Tennessee.

Rosecrans put a garrison in Chattanooga and sent the rest of his army in pursuit of the Rebels, who withdrew into Georgia to await reinforcements coming from Mississippi and Virginia by rail. The Virginia troops had a long and maddening journey full of delays caused by differences in track gauge, wrecked bridges, and decrepit rolling stock.

Rosecrans split his army into three columns to utilize three roads in a 40-mile front, while Bragg gathered new strength behind the screen of north-south mountain ranges. He compared the terrain to "the wall of a house full of rat-holes. The rat lies hidden at his hole, ready to pop out when no one is watching." In the end, however, as one of his officers said, Bragg was befuddled by numerous rats from different holes—he wasted his chance to beat them one by one. By September 18 neither commander knew where the other was. The armies finally bumped into each other along Chickamauga Creek, north of Lee & Gordon's Mills. That night the generals made hasty tactical plans. Next morning, in the murky, tangled woods, Rebel and Federal fought a "soldiers' battle," unseen and often uncontrolled by the generals. In some places, a Confederate surgeon reported, "an enemy could not be seen until the opposing lines were within a few yards of each other."

On the second day of fighting, thanks to a Union blunder, the Confederates broke through a gap in the Federal line, driving off every

Lookout Mountain, a 2,126-foot peak on the south bank of the Tennessee (bottom), had little tactical value—but the Federal capture of it on a misty November 24 inspired dramatic art, such as the engraving below, and the post-war name

"Battle Above the Clouds." A shrewd photographer shot souvenirs at the summit: Company B, 9th Pennsylvania Cavalry, poses in the picture opposite. Securing Chattanooga gave Sherman a good base for his drive into Georgia.

Maj. Gen. George H. Thomas (right), called the "Rock of Chickamauga" for saving the Union army there, commanded with stolid valor in Georgia as he did throughout the war.

ranking officer except Gordon Granger and George H. Thomas. The "Rock of Chickamauga," as Thomas would be hailed, reformed a line, held off the Rebels until night, and—in good order—followed his fleeing comrades to Chattanooga. The last retreating Federals heard exultant yells from the field as the hard-used Army of Tennessee celebrated its one great combat success.

Bragg's victory had cost him 16,000 wounded or dead plus 2,000 taken prisoner—nearly a third of the army he had hurled into battle. Union losses totaled more than 11,000 dead and wounded and 5,000 prisoners. Bragg, ignoring the pleas of his subordinates, did not chase the Yankees. Instead, he laid siege to Chattanooga.

Confederates threatened road and railway routes into the city and blocked the Tennessee River. The only way into the city was via a steep, treacherous mountain road. The bodies of 10,000 mules, killed by Rebels or by starvation, littered the road. Up that road on October 23 came U.S. Grant, now in overall command of the Union forces of the West. He had replaced Rosecrans with Thomas, who had vowed to "hold the town till we starve."

On the cold rainy night of Grant's arrival, men and beasts already were starving. When a wagon managed to reach the city, soldiers followed it, picking up grains of corn that dropped out. Trusted troops guarded horse and mule troughs to keep hungry men from stealing the animals' food. "One of the regiments of our brigade caught, killed, and ate a dog that wandered into camp," a Kansas soldier wrote.

Grant moved swiftly to crack the siege. He launched an amphibious operation that drove Rebels away from the river, opening up a supply system that the jubilant troops named the Cracker Line. Reinforcements had arrived by a rail journey that wound through Washington, Baltimore, Columbus, Indianapolis, Louisville, and Nashville: 15,000 men of the Army of the Potomac, under Fighting Joe Hooker. From Mississippi, via boat, rail, and hard march, came 17,000 men under Maj. Gen. William T. Sherman, Grant's replacement as commander of the Army of the Tennessee; they arrived in November.

The Confederate siege line ran from Lookout Mountain to Missionary Ridge. The Federals first took Orchard Knob, an outpost in front of the ridge on November 23. Then others clambered up Lookout

Though Fort Sumter protected Charleston—where "rebellion first lighted the flame of civil war"—Confederate control galled the Federals more than its military value warranted. Rear Adm. Samuel F. du Pont, U.S.N., spoke of a "morbid appetite in the land to have Charleston." With heavy cannon—including the 200-pounder Parrott gun famed as the "Swamp Angel"—poised a few miles away, Union forces battered at the fort and the city. Southerners held on doggedly. Hasty repairs with gabions—sand-filled wickerwork—patch breaches (right) in Sumter's north outer wall. All told, the fort took some 46,000 projectiles. Bricks and mortar crumbled at the impact of shells, but turned into rubblework on which explosions had little effect. Sumter slumped but did not collapse; with other forts it continued to defend the harbor, which one Federal compared to a "porcupine's quills turned outside in." Union failure to take Sumter provided a rationale for the heroic, but ill-fated, attempt by the black soldiers of the 54th Massachusetts Regiment to capture Fort Wagner, a strongpoint a couple of miles down the coast.

Mountain and, in a clash romanticized as the Battle Above the Clouds, swept the Confederates from the crest.

Stubborn defenders extended the battle into a third day, which ended with the ridge defenses shattered and Confederates in headlong flight. A Kansas soldier recreated the scene: "Gray clad men rushed wildly down the hill and into the woods, tossing away knapsacks, muskets, and blankets as they ran. Batteries galloped back along the narrow, winding roads with reckless speed, and officers, frantic with rage, rushed from one panic-stricken group to another."

A little later, Grant and his staff came upon a long line of Confederate prisoners. Guards halted the line to allow the Union officers to pass. One of the prisoners recorded what happened next: Grant "lifted his hat and held it over his head until he passed the last man of that living funeral cortege. He was the only officer in that whole train who recognized us as being on the face of the earth."

As the year wore down, the eloquence of Abraham Lincoln twice illumined a war that now seemed no longer a series of defeats.

A week before victory at Chattanooga, Lincoln went to Gettysburg, where he dedicated a cemetery and, in words that would endure in hearts and in stone, called for another dedication: "that we here highly resolve that these dead shall not have died in vain—that this nation, under God, shall have a new birth of freedom—and that government of the people, by the people, for the people, shall not perish from the earth."

The day after the victory at Chattanooga, Thursday, November 26, was the first national Thanksgiving Day. On that day, Lincoln had proclaimed, Americans should be thankful for "the blessings of fruitful fields and healthful skies" and should "implore the interposition of the Almighty Hand to heal the wounds of the nation."

If there were reasons for dedication, for thanks, and for prayers, there were fewer reasons for despair. But once more a year of the war ended with two armies hibernating in their familiar winter camps—Lee along the Rapidan, Meade between the Rapidan and the Rappahannock. "We have fought for two years and a half," an officer on Meade's staff wrote as the year ended, "but it takes no wiseacre to see that we yet have much to learn."

At Greatest Risk: Black Servicemen

Washington, April 23, 1861. To the Secretary of War: "Sir: . . . I know of some 300 reliable colored free citizens of this city who desire to enter the service for the defense of the city. . . . Yours, respectfully, Jacob Dodson (Colored)."

Virginians were arming just beyond the Potomac; the capital had only a handful of defenders; and Dodson, a Senate employee, was offering loyal volunteers. Like others who sent similar letters, he received a chilly reply: "this Department has no intention at present to call . . . any colored soldiers. With respect, &c."

In law, it had no power to. The Militia Act of 1792 barred nonwhites from the land forces of the United States. The Navy had no such ban. It accepted "boys" at $10 per month, and eventually more than 9,000 blacks served on the saltwater and mud-water flotillas of the Union.

Ironically, the first Civil War soldiers of African descent appeared in the Confederacy. Louisiana's *gens libres de couleur*, free persons of color, had enjoyed privileges since colonial days. Many lived in comfort and some were rich, masters of plantations and of slaves.

At New Orleans they recalled with pride how their forebears had

fought under Andrew Jackson to defeat the British in 1815. They formed a regiment of "Native Guards," which was mustered into state service in March 1862 and stayed in the city when the Federals took it in April.

With relief, the Guards offered to help put down "this unholy rebellion." Benjamin F. Butler, a Massachusetts lawyer and *pro tem* general, cited the law and rejected them.

In Kansas, legality didn't keep

Senator James H. Lane, a veteran of border strife, from recruiting blacks; he promised equal treatment and pay. His informal ways caused trouble for his 1st Kansas Colored Volunteers later on, when red tape replaced chains, but his men were fighting Rebel bushwhackers by the fall of 1862.

On July 17, 1862, Congress revised the law: Now the President could accept men "of African descent" for army service. The next month Ben Butler called for volunteers from the free black militia of Louisiana, and on September 27 the 1st Regiment of Louisiana Native Guards became the first black troops mustered into Federal service.

In the Sea Islands of South Carolina, Col. Thomas Wentworth Higginson, a Harvard man, took charge of a regiment of newly freed slaves. As a test case, this venture attracted visitors who could wrangle a pass. One mutinous incident, said the colonel, and "the party of distrust" might have squelched any plan for arming blacks. And if slaves had broken out in insurrection, many "of our army would have joined with the Southern army to hunt them down." Such horrors aside, even people of goodwill doubted the ability of men reared in slavery.

Known only as Jackson, this young Confederate servant became a Union drummer. Soldiers of the 2nd U.S. Colored Light Artillery (opposite) wait for a train at Johnsonville, Tennessee, on November 23, 1864. At Nashville, they helped to end the Army of Tennessee's last drive northward.

Abolitionists, Colonel Higginson concluded later, "had underrated the suffering produced by slavery" but "overrated the demoralization." His men proved apt at drill, eager to learn, proud of their identity as the 1st South Carolina Volunteers (U.S.), realists about risk.

Bullets, canister, and shellfire in the field were any man's hazards. Black soldiers faced dangers all their own. Confederate War Department General Orders, No. 60, of August 21, 1862, warned that Union officers recruiting and arming slaves were "outlaws" and would be subject to execution as felons when President Davis gave the order. And all "slaves captured in arms" would be handed over to state officials. Law in the slave states made death the penalty for rebellious bondsmen. Colonel Higginson spoke for his brother officers: "we all felt that we fought with ropes round our necks." His men said: "Dere's no flags ob truce for us. . . . When de Secesh fight de *Fus' Souf*, he fight in earnest."

New Year's Day, 1863, brought Lincoln's Emancipation Proclamation into effect. The "First South" formed on the parade ground to hear it read and to receive their flags. As the banners changed hands, the newly freed spectators broke into song: *My country, 'tis of thee, Sweet land of liberty*. "Just think of it!" mused the colonel; "the first day they had ever had a country."

Soon the governor of the Bay State formed the first black regiment from the North, the 54th Massachusetts (Colored) Infantry. Yankee aristocrats like Col. Robert Gould Shaw led the officers, all white; noncoms and privates included educated men like two sons of Frederick Douglass. By June the regiment had reached the combat zone.

Minor actions had already given evidence that blacks could fight. Lane's Kansans had shown their mettle. Higginson's men had made a foray into Florida and occupied Jacksonville. But the first major test came at Port Hudson, Louisiana, a Rebel stronghold on the Mississippi south of Vicksburg.

Nathaniel P. Banks, another two-star politico from Massachusetts, had replaced Butler and reversed his policy with the Native Guards. Only whites, Banks assumed, had intelligence enough to be officers, and he forced many blacks to resign. But Capt. André Cailloux, a man of wealth, Lt. John H. Crowder, a poor but brilliant teenager, and others remained with the 1st to lead the assault of May 27, 1863.

If a commander with good sense had examined the Confederate position, says a modern scholar, the assault by the 1st and 3rd Native Guards would never have been ordered. The Rebels had infantry and artillery in strong works on high ground; the only approach road was a deathtrap. The attack failed, and Cailloux, Crowder, and nearly 200 others were lost in combat.

Raw recruits met Rebel veterans at Milliken's Bend, north of Vicksburg, on June 7. A Union captain called this fight worse than Shiloh and his black freedmen as brave as any soldiers he had ever seen. They faced a charge "with considerable obstinacy," reported the Rebel general; the "white or true Yankee portion ran like whipped curs."

MEN OF COLOR

To Arms! To Arms!

NOW OR NEVER

THREE YEARS' SERVICE!

AND JOIN IN FIGHTING THE

BATTLES OF LIBERTY AND THE UNION

FAIL NOW, & OUR RACE IS DOOMED

SILENCE THE TONGUE OF CALUMNY

VALOR AND HEROISM

PORT HUDSON AND MILLIKEN'S BEND.

ARE FREEMEN LESS BRAVE THAN SLAVES

OUR LAST OPPORTUNITY HAS COME

MEN OF COLOR, BROTHERS AND FATHERS!

WE APPEAL TO YOU!

In the sand dunes near Charleston, at dusk on July 18, the 54th Massachusetts advanced on Fort Wagner, a well-armed fieldwork of sand, turf, and palmetto logs. At 200 yards, recalled a survivor, it "became a mound of fire." Sgt. Lewis Douglass called this a "trying time." A bursting shell would clear a 20-foot area; the men would close up and go on. At the double-quick they rushed an outer trench, an inner ditch, and the parapet. Tens of attackers met hundreds of defenders on the rampart. There Sgt. William H. Carney planted the Stars and Stripes; and Colonel Shaw, sword held high, was shot through the heart. When the Federals fell back in the dark, Carney—wounded in the arm, breast, and both legs—brought the flag away safely.

Fort Wagner became a byword for valor, probably the most famous of the black troops' battles. In the South, it set a precedent. Two captured noncoms were taken to a state court, which threw out the case. Unhappy authorities finally chose to treat free blacks as prisoners of war.

Perhaps, said Colonel Higginson icily, the Rebels would grant a black soldier the rights of war when the Union granted him "the ordinary rights of peace"—pay equal to a white soldier's.

Congress had balked at that. A white private earned $13 a month plus $3 for clothing. A black private earned $10 minus $3 for clothing. A black noncom had no more, while his white counterpart had $17 to $21. Even $36 a year would buy fuel for a family in Massachusetts, as a corporal of the 54th wrote to the President: "We have done a Soldiers Duty. Why cant we have a Soldiers pay?" His outfit and others proudly refused to take anything less than equal payment. Congress passed various measures to equalize and increase pay, but not until March 1865 did it make these retroactive to the day of enlistment. The true obstacle may have been suspicion that equal pay could imply social equality.

Fears of that kind ran deeper in the Confederacy. In theory a slave labor force could be a military asset, available on demand for such work as building defenses. In practice the rich planters grudged the time of their bondsmen. Nathan Bedford Forrest broke the pattern by taking 45 of his hands to drive wagons, promising them freedom in victory. Many owners might let the army hire a cook or farrier or teamster, and a gentleman of any rank might take his body servant to the field.

Legally or not, a few slaves appeared on the muster rolls—Jacob Jones, musician with the 9th Virginia, for example. A few free men of color served in the Rebel Navy, three aboard C.S.S. *Chicora* at Charleston.

As casualty and desertion figures mounted in the winter of 1863-64, Maj. Gen. Patrick R. Cleburne, C.S.A., took action. An Irishman who had immigrated in 1849, he had a detached view of slavery and a clear view of military needs. He drafted a plan to begin training "the most courageous of our slaves" and to guarantee freedom to all "who shall remain true to the Confederacy." He spelled out his scheme with eloquence and sent it up through channels. It appalled the brass, Davis ordered it suppressed, and it remained unknown for 32 years.

By the summer of 1864, Southern opinion makers were urging the use of black troops. Diehards like Howell Cobb objected: "If slaves will make good soldiers our whole theory of slavery is wrong." Early in 1865 General Lee let his views be known: Blacks could be "efficient" soldiers and should fight as free men. An appropriate law was not passed and signed until a month before Appomattox. By then some 179,000 had served as United States Colored Troops (the final official designation), and more than 100 had held commissions,

Recovering from wounds, William Carney supports himself with a cane as he holds the 54th's battle-worn flag. He had fought to serve "my country and my oppressed brothers." He and his regiment had indeed served both.

13 as chaplains and 8 as surgeons.

After the war, some officers tried to help black veterans; others showed no concern. Some of the men remained in the occupation forces; some became the famous "buffalo soldiers" of the Regular Army in the West. In the South, black veterans met insults, violence, even murder. Elsewhere they often met complacent prejudice. On the Fourth of July they would march in the local parade, bringing up the rear. Some prospered; many struggled. As they grew older, in the 1880s and '90s, things grew worse and the government more indifferent.

The Navy had acted quickly to bestow the seven Medals of Honor awarded black sailors. The Army moved slowly for 16 blacks (and for many whites as well). Sergeant Carney didn't receive his bronze and ribbon until May 23, 1900. He had returned home to take charge of New Bedford's gas street lamps, had tried his luck in California for a bit, then got a Federal job. With a twinge in the old wounds when the weather changed, he carried the mail through the old whaling town for 31 years. He married and brought up a proud family; he addressed brother veterans and other patriots on memorial occasions. He was working at the State House in Boston in his last days, and his flag is still there. The silk grows more fragile from year to year—but the service it represents shines brighter.

1864

CRISIS OF DECISION

In the East Room on a March night, the ladies and gentlemen became what one of them called "the only real mob I ever saw in the White House." They cheered and they shoved each other to get a glimpse of one of the guests. "Ladies suffered dire disaster in the crush and confusion; their laces were torn and crinolines mashed. . . ." The guest retreated to a red plush sofa and, reluctantly, stood on it. Ulysses S. Grant, blushing and sweating, briefly endured being "the idol of the hour."

Abraham Lincoln watched, beaming. At last, he believed, he had found the general he wanted, the general he needed in this presidential election year. The next day, Lincoln gave Grant his commission as lieutenant general—a rank previously held only by George Washington and Winfield Scott—and the man from Galena became the general-in-chief of all Union armies.

Escaping the distractions and intrigues of the capital, Grant set up his headquarters at Culpeper, Virginia. There he began working on his plan "to bring pressure to bear on the Confederacy" by getting all his armies "to move together toward one common center" and destroy the enemy's "will to fight."

He selected two good professionals to meet the enemy's best: Meade against Lee and the Army of Northern Virginia; Sherman against Joe Johnston and the Army of Tennessee.

He had useful assignments for the political generals whom the administration needed. Franz Sigel was to destroy a key railroad in the Shenandoah Valley and deny Rebel troops the region's ripening wheat. Benjamin Butler, with more than 30,000 men, was to threaten Richmond from the south by moving up the peninsula between the James and Appomattox Rivers. And Nathaniel Banks, who had begun a joint army-navy operation up the Red River in Louisiana toward Texas, got a new mission: to take Mobile, Alabama, the last Rebel port on the Gulf. Banks remained bogged down on the river, but by May 1 the rest of Grant's grand design was smoothly taking shape.

Grant had given himself the delicate job. He would be directing Meade's operations, and the Army of the Potomac looked upon Grant as their new leader. Grant thought the army "in splendid condition." The men, he said, "feel like whipping somebody." The troops, however, did not feel like praising him. Their one particular hero had been

Flanking a stately red cedar, a flag and a stone soldier stand guard at Virginia's Cold Harbor National Cemetery. Here Confederates checked a major Union assault. Spring 1864 renewed intense conflict in the Wilderness (above), where Rebels had routed Federals a year earlier.

"It is a beautiful spring day on which all this bloody work is being done," wrote a Rebel soldier, caught up in the fighting in the Wilderness, where light now filters through a tangle of dogwoods. Grant pursued Lee's dwindling, but skillfully entrenched, army through this region of dense second-growth forest. Here the rivers and fords, thick woodlands, and steep ravines had served Lee well in earlier offensives. Now he made them defensive assets.

McClellan—who had let it be known that he would accept the Democratic nomination in 1864—and since then they had served under a number of losers.

Newspapers hailed Grant as a savior, the winning general from the West. This publicity embittered the soldiers of the East, combat-hardened men who had also been winners, on the bloody fields of Antietam and Gettysburg. Officers told Grant what enlisted men probably thought: "You have not faced Bobby Lee yet."

Grant's arrival in Virginia underscored the differences between the armies of East and West. In the East, soldiers preened and paraded. In the West, they slouched and looked sloppy when their generals let them get away with it—Thomas didn't but Sherman did. Grant was the ultimate western officer: battered hat, wrinkled uniform, hands in pockets, looking, said an eastern colonel, "for all the world like a country storekeeper or a western farmer."

The same distinctions marked the Confederates. Lee's soldiers showed more discipline than the western forces. But no matter where a Rebel marched, it was usually to his own drum. And now Southern soldiers had a realistic notion of the forces against them. They took refuge as always in humor and increasingly in religion. Revivals were popular. When a soldier at one service led his brethren in prayer for more courage, a peg-legged veteran shouted: "Hold on with that-thar prayer! Why don't you pray for *more provisions?* We've got more courage now than we's got any use for!"

They still fought for their states, for their homes, for honor, and in the Army of Northern Virginia they fought for General Lee. But doubts were growing. A captured Georgian, packed with other prisoners in a boxcar, told of hearing a young South Carolina officer "from the 'fire-eating' class" go on and on about the justice of secession. "He impressed me," the Georgian said, "as one who had an undue rice-eating mentality, and needed a cornbread diet. However, when the great doors of the penitentiary opened to receive us, he said, 'Boys, I don't know but that South Carolina *was* a little hasty.'"

The Confederacy's conscription system was breaking down. At one point in 1864, officials in Mississippi enrolled 537 conscripts; 302 of them deserted. One general said half the troops from the Tennessee

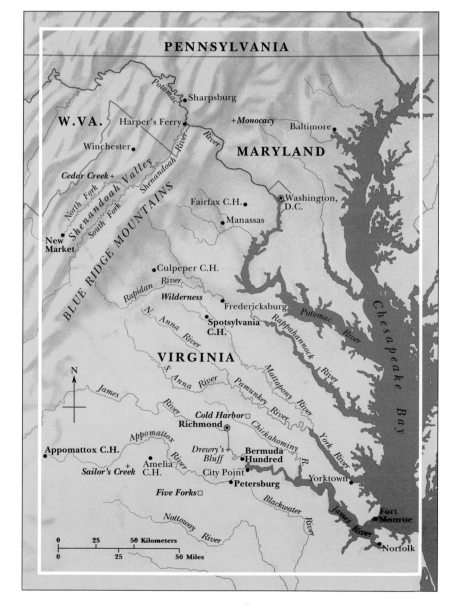

SECTOR OF ATTRITION |
The Union army, wrote Massachusetts cavalryman Charles Francis Adams, Jr., "has literally marched in blood and agony from the Rapidan to the James." The Rapidan and Rappahannock Rivers *(below) meander to their confluence north of the Wilderness region. Tame waters and changing hues of autumn give no sense of the savage battles that Grant fought here in May. Weeks of combat, from the Wilderness to* *Spotsylvania, culminated on June 3 at Cold Harbor (opposite). Here, charging an entrenched enemy, several thousand Federals fell within an hour.*

Drawn-out battles marked these weeks in Virginia. A map drawn in 1867 (detail, below) delineates terrain at Cold Harbor. Charging westward from their lines near Old Cold Harbor (dark blue), Federals plunged into a zigzag maze of Rebel

entrenchments (red) near New Cold Harbor. They faced rifle and artillery fire that "piled . . . men like cordwood." In mid-May the two armies found themselves in a series of clashes at Spotsylvania Court House, climaxing,

on May 12, in hand-to-hand combat as Federals assailed the "Mule Shoe" salient. A monument honors the 15th New Jersey Volunteers, who had shown "highest steadiness" in the Wilderness.

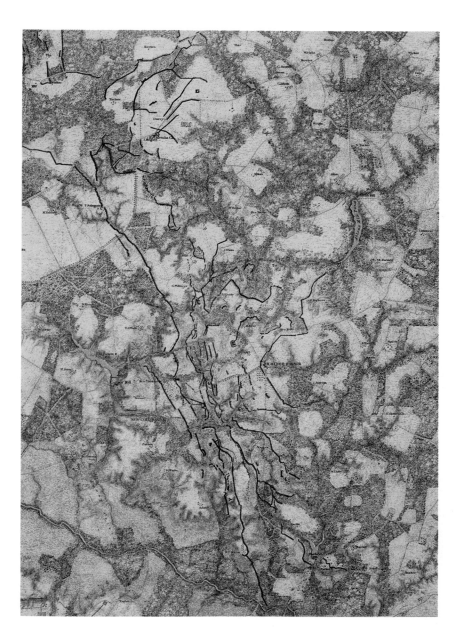

and North Carolina mountains were not reliable. Diarist Robert G. H. Kean, head of the Bureau of War, wondered about a "curious secret society"—the Order of the Heroes of America, commonly called the Red Strings. Members used a scarlet thread as a badge, as in the Old Testament story of Rahab and the spies of Joshua, and tried to organize opposition to the war.

The South was losing its ability to staff and supply its forces. Death and injury had claimed many able officers; some replacements were promoted more for courage than for skill. And they had less and less to fight with. For lack of horses, cavalrymen marched to battle and artillery batteries stood immobile. If a Rebel scavenger collected a Federal trooper's repeating rifle, he couldn't get ammunition for it. Thoughtful and influential citizens on both sides suspected that the Confederacy was doomed.

So, thought others, was the Union. On April 8 an Ohio Congressman, Alexander H. Long, called for recognition of Confederate independence. "I am reluctantly and despondingly forced to the conclusion that the Union is lost never to be restored." Long was a Copperhead, a Democrat who opposed the war, but he made a point worth pondering: "I see, neither North nor South, any sentiment on which it is possible to build a Union."

Lincoln had the political skills to make sure he would be renominated. But he would be asking voters for the first re-election since Andrew Jackson's. He would be asking them to fight on, and to accept nothing less than the Union as a goal. How many more casualties would the public accept as the price?

On May 4, Grant, with more than 115,000 men, crossed the Rapidan. Lee did not oppose the crossing; he was content to see Grant march into the Wilderness, that immense dark tangle where the Federal artillery would be of little use. Next day he pounced on the moving columns and blind, chaotic fighting began. At a small swamp, men relied on splashing noises to locate a target. In smoke-shrouded brush, men were firing steadily—but firing, as somebody said, "by earsight." Brushfires spread in the dry leaves; soldiers tried to save the wounded from being burned alive, but not all were rescued.

The second day was like the first: hours of swirling bedlam. One

survivor likened the noise of unseen battle to "the noise of a boy running with a stick pressed against a paling fence, faster and faster until it swelled into a continuous rattling roar." Men fired at assumed enemies. Rebel bullets brought down their own James Longstreet, gravely but not fatally wounded. The two days cost the two armies an estimated 25,800 total casualties.

"More desperate fighting has not been witnessed on this continent," wrote Grant, who could use Shiloh as a standard.

On the night of May 7, Federal troops began pulling out of their lines. Once again they had crossed the Rapidan, once again they had been savaged by Lee, once again a vaunted new leader seemed about to retreat. But then Grant's party came up, riding south—south to fight again. The men recognized him and broke into cheers. They set pine knots on fire, an aide noted, as if to light a triumphal procession. As Grant told a correspondent that night, "There will be no turning back."

If he took the shortest route to Richmond, Grant would head for a hamlet called Spotsylvania Court House. Lee had men there on the 8th, with the Po River to protect his left flank, when Federal units arrived. The Rebels had started digging trenches and throwing up parapets, and they fought off Union assaults.

At one area where high ground would give artillery an advantage, the Confederate line curved northward in a mile-deep salient, called the Mule Shoe for its shape. On May 10, 24-year-old Col. Emory Upton led a storming column of 12 regiments that smashed into the salient in hand-to-hand combat, but Gershom Mott's supporting division flubbed its attack and the Federal effort failed.

Grant planned to hit the salient again, this time with one whole corps plus two additional divisions. On the eve of the assault, he wrote a dispatch for Washington. He told of "very heavy fighting" in which he estimated he had lost 20,000 men, and declared: "I . . . propose to fight it out on this line if it takes all summer."

Rain pelted down on the 12th, which a Confederate officer recalled as "one continuous roll of musketry from dawn until midnight." At what forever would be known as the Bloody Angle—far worse than the one at Gettysburg—men fought in knee-deep mud. Wounded men were trampled and drowned in the muck. As once before in this

campaign, Lee undertook to lead a counterattack in person and his officers and men simply balked: *General Lee to the rear! Go back, General!* They would not charge until he withdrew; then they went yelling into the melee. In that salient, bullets cut down an oak 22 inches thick. After almost 24 hours of continuous butchery, a survivor looking for an officer found his body in the reddened mire; "not four inches of space" on his person lacked a wound.

By the time the dispatches reached the War Department, the horrors had been filtered out. At the White House, Lincoln told a cheering crowd about Grant's "if it takes all summer" vow. But Grant had yet to defeat Lee. With enlistments expiring, enough men to fill 36 infantry regiments were going home. Replacements were green at best, useless at worst. And it was still a long time until election day.

Grant was never able to get between Lee and Richmond. The two armies—110,000 Federals and 60,000 Confederates—sparred and

sidestepped. Finally, at Cold Harbor, within ten miles of Richmond, Grant hurled half his army at the center and southern part of Lee's six-mile line. Grant's men knew the odds. Many performed the soldier's pre-battle rituals: sewing or pinning a label onto his uniform to identify his body; throwing away cards and dice. One man wrote a last-minute note in his diary: "June 3. Cold Harbor. I was killed."

At 4:30 a.m. they charged. Several thousand were killed or wounded. One was the prophetic diary writer.

Next Grant struck toward Petersburg, only to be thwarted there. Both armies settled in for a siege.

Grant's grand design looked far less grand than it had a month before. The Confederates had Ben Butler's army penned up at Bermuda

Hundred—as useful, said Grant, "as if it had been in a bottle strongly corked." Sigel's campaign in the Valley had failed. In Georgia, crafty Joe Johnston had frustrated Sherman by refusing to give battle, although giving up ground. Sherman tried frontal-assault tactics at Kennesaw Mountain, near Marietta, and lost about 3,000 men.

One bit of good news for the Union came from the sea. On June 19 the Confederate raider *Alabama,* which had captured or burned 67 Federal merchant ships in two fiery years, steamed out of the French port of Cherbourg to challenge the U.S. Navy's *Kearsarge.* Firing starboard to starboard on a circular course, with the range finally closing to 500 yards, they fought for more than an hour. A Union sailor said the battle reminded him of "two flies crawling around on the rim of a saucer." At last the *Alabama* struck her colors, sinking; spectators aboard a British yacht rescued her captain, Raphael Semmes, and some of the crew he called his "precious set of rascals."

July brought Lincoln bad news close to home. Jubal Early swept north through the Shenandoah, crossed the Potomac into Maryland, and took Hagerstown, imposing a $20,000 fine for Federal depredations in the Valley. He created a flurry, with calls for men from New York and Pennsylvania to give emergency service for 100 days. Early couldn't hope to hold Baltimore or Washington if he struck either one, but a quick foray through the capital—burning official buildings, raising the Rebel flag, forcing the President to flee—would humiliate the Lincolnites. It would certainly do them no good in the fall election.

Grant had rushed one division and some dismounted cavalry up to meet the threat—just enough and just in time to delay Early in a fight on the Monocacy River on July 9. He had added the rest of the Sixth Corps and offered the Nineteenth as anxiety grew.

As Early approached Washington, office workers took up arms. Invalid soldiers limped out of hospitals to the forts that ringed the city. A steamer stood ready to take Lincoln to safety. He preferred to inspect the defenses. For two days in a row he came under fire at Fort Stevens. Early's pickets shot at anyone who moved on the parapets, but Lincoln seemed concerned with one thing—defeating the enemy—and his Sixth Corps reinforcements came in time to do that. He saw his troops fall when they made a sortie and drove off the Rebels. Early slipped

Gentle contours of the Blue Ridge drop down into the broad Shenandoah Valley, a rich granary for Lee's army. In early summer Jubal A. Early bedeviled Federals sent to destroy crops and disrupt Rebel communications in the Valley.

In July, Early marched his troops north into Maryland. At Frederick he extracted $200,000—in lieu of burning— retribution for David Hunter's devastation in the Shenandoah. Then he swooped toward Washington,

defended only by skeleton forces. Now Grant sent out to the Shenandoah his trusted Philip Sheridan, who vowed that "the Valley, from Winchester up to Staunton, ninety-two miles, will have little in it for man or beast."

away to Virginia. On July 9, he had collected a $200,000 ransom from Frederick instead of burning the town. Congress later promised to give that sum to the town, but the money never came.

The threat of a Confederate raid—or invasion—had passed. But Lincoln's subsequent call for 500,000 new volunteers emphasized to voters the endless casualty lists, the endless war. And the news was getting worse, especially from Petersburg, where bungling spawned what Grant called "the saddest affair I have witnessed in the war."

Lt. Col. Henry Pleasants, commander of the 48th Pennsylvania at the siege of Petersburg, had been a mining engineer before he went to war. He was staring at a strongpoint in the Rebel lines one day when he heard an enlisted man mutter, "We could blow that damned fort out of existence if we could run a mine shaft under it." He was sure the coal miners in his outfit could do just that. Army engineers scoffed at the idea and offered neither help nor equipment.

But Pleasants won approval, got his men extra rations of whiskey, and put them to work for nearly a month with short-handled picks and cracker boxes as wheelbarrows. The men dug a tunnel 511 feet long with a wooden duct to bring in fresh air. They hauled out 18,000 cubic feet of dirt, dumped it along a nearby railroad grade, and covered the dirt with brush. At the end of the tunnel they carved two galleries where they put four tons of gunpowder, surrounding the powder kegs with sandbags to channel the blast upward.

Plans called for three divisions to exploit the breach, and two black brigades were chosen to lead the attack. They trained ardently, singing a new song: "We looks like men a-marching on, We looks like men er war." Then Meade objected: If the attack failed, it would be said that the generals didn't mind wasting colored troops. A white division with a shaky record was chosen, by lot, to take the lead; it got no special training, or even special orders.

At 4:44 a.m. on July 30, a startled witness heard a "slight tremor of the earth for a second, then the rocking as of an earthquake, and, with a tremendous blast . . . a vast column of earth and smoke" shot upward, "its dark sides flashing out sparks of fire." Down poured "showers of stones, broken timbers and blackened human limbs." The Confederate fort and two guns vanished; 278 men in the fort were killed or wounded. For nearly a quarter of a mile on either side, dazed Confederates were stumbling out of their lines.

Almost simultaneously, 164 Union cannon and mortars roared in support of the infantry assault. The brigadier commanding the lead division, James Ledlie, was in the rear, drinking. Instead of dashing around or through the pit, many of the attackers crammed themselves into it. Rebels rushed mortars into nearby trenches and lobbed shells onto the mob below. Of more than 3,000 new men of war, 1,327 were lost in the Crater or just beyond; about 2,500 white Federals were killed, wounded, or captured.

Confederates, shaken by the blast and enraged by any use of black troops, clubbed and bayoneted both blacks and whites before the fighting died out. Federal officers later accused the Confederates of using the bayonet on black troops who tried to surrender—much as other Rebels had been accused after they captured Fort Pillow, in Tennessee, in April. Southerners denied the charges, and precise details remained obscure; but surrender, usually surprisingly easy between Yank and Secesh, turned perilous between white and black.

"Remember Fort Pillow!" became a war cry for blacks east of the Mississippi. West of the river the cry was "Remember Poison Spring!" At this spot in Arkansas, reported the colonel of the 1st Kansas Colored, many of his wounded were killed out of hand. The 2nd Kansas Colored sent no prisoners to the rear in a victory at Jenkins' Ferry on April 30.

As a matter of policy, the Confederates had refused to recognize captured blacks as prisoners of war, promising to treat them as rebellious slaves. (They had made an exception for men of the 54th Massachusetts, who were obviously free volunteers.) Davis's worst threats proved idle, but black prisoners certainly suffered at Rebel hands— some were sold, some reported shot while trying to escape. Arrangements for exchange of prisoners had already bogged down; now the special problems of the black soldiers brought exchanges to a stop.

Prison camps had been places for temporary detention. Now they were needed for the duration. Both sides set up new camps; each denounced the other for inhumane treatment of prisoners. In fact, death and disease did not take sides: 25,976 Confederates died in Northern prison camps, 30,218 Federals in Southern camps.

IN EARLY'S PATH | *By the Monocacy River, 3,300 veteran troops and 2,500 largely green home guards held their ground against Early's 17,000, giving the capital city an extra day to gather seasoned defenders. The heaviest fighting centered around "Araby," the Keefer Thomas family home (below). The Thomases and some neighbors huddled in the cellar through it all. Opposite, plowed fields hug contours of rolling hills near Chambersburg, Pennsylvania.*

A Federal officer told the builder of one Union camp that barracks should be "mere shanties, with no fine work about them." Rebel prisoners were given scant rations, left in rags, and allowed to freeze to death in unheated hovels. Union officials justified their treatment of prisoners as retaliation for Confederate abuses.

The most notorious Confederate prison was Andersonville in southern Georgia, where 45,000 men were confined from the time it opened in February 1864 to the end of the war. "Since the day I was born," wrote a survivor, "I never saw such misery." About 13,000 died from disease, malnutrition, or other maltreatment. There were no proper barracks. Prisoners dug holes to live in or made huts out of logs. After the war, a U.S. military commission tried Swiss-born Capt. Henry Wirz, the commandant of Andersonville. Judged guilty of "murder, in violation of the laws and customs of war," he was hanged—the only uniformed Confederate, it is said, executed for his role in the war.

Even without the horrible details of the prison camps, Union voters looked at a dark picture. By August, Federal casualties for the year had exceeded 70,000. On the 23rd, Lincoln had his Cabinet members sign a document he did not let them read. What he had written was this: "This morning, as for some days past, it seems exceedingly probable that this Administration will not be re-elected. . . ." His team would have to save the Union before their term expired, because the new President's campaign positions would keep him from saving it later.

The Democrats met in Chicago and adopted a peace platform. They nominated McClellan as a war candidate. Just two days later, on September 2, Sherman entered Atlanta. McClellan disowned the platform, endorsed the war effort, and hoped for victory.

Sherman, however, was finally scoring conspicuous successes in a campaign that had gone steadily forward since early May.

After his defeat at Kennesaw Mountain, Sherman had relentlessly pressed Johnston, methodically destroying Confederate railroads along the way. Union wrecking crews built bonfires of railroad ties, stuck ripped-up tracks into the flames, then bent the red-hot rails around trees. The troops called their handiwork "Sherman's neckties."

Sherman followed Johnston to the outer fortifications of Atlanta. Now, for the Union, came the luckiest happening of the campaign:

Superior seapower afforded the Union a distinct advantage over the Confederacy. Trained sailors like those of U.S.S. Kearsarge (right), more powerful guns, and numerous ships let Federal forces blockade Southern ports and destroy

Rebel commerce raiders. Traditional cruisers like the Kearsarge—*wooden-hulled screw steamers rigged for sail—did the blue-water fighting. In 1864 the* Kearsarge *sank the raider C.S.S.* Alabama *off France. Joint operations*

President Davis replaced wily Joe Johnston with Gen. John Bell Hood. The move, a Georgia officer said, "unwittingly hit the Southern Confederacy a heavy blow." Lee had told Davis, tactfully, that Hood was "a bold fighter" who seemed to lack "other qualities necessary."

Hood, a classic example of a man promoted above his level of competence, was determined to drive Sherman from the gates of Atlanta. In a series of ill-conceived attacks he lost more than 20,000 men and then evacuated the city.

Soon after Sherman entered Atlanta he ordered all its civilians into exile, to get them out of the way. When city officials protested, Sherman said, "War is cruelty and you cannot refine it. . . . You might as well appeal against the thunder-storm as against these terrible hardships of war. They are inevitable. . . ."

Hood, striking at Sherman's lines of communication, hoped to draw him northward. Sherman did pursue him for a while, then returned to Atlanta. Hood headed for Tennessee, planning to roll up the Federals as far north as Kentucky and eventually rejoin Lee.

The first obstacle to Hood's scheme was a 22,000-man force under Maj. Gen. John M. Schofield. He eluded Hood long enough to set up a strong defense line, anchored on riverbanks, at Franklin, south of Nashville. In a hopeless frontal assault, Hood attacked Schofield, sending 18 brigades of infantry, drawn up in line of battle, across two miles of open fields. It was a tragic repetition of the fatal charge at Gettysburg on an even larger scale. "For the moment," a Federal officer wrote, "we were spellbound with admiration, although . . . we knew that in a few brief moments, as soon as they reached firing distance, all that orderly grandeur would be changed to bleeding, writhing confusion. . . ."

Irish-born Pat Cleburne of Arkansas, a gallant, storied general, "the Stonewall of the West," had two horses shot from under him during the charge. Running before his men, brandishing his sword with his by the Union navy and armies captured coastal forts and towns; by late 1864 Wilmington, North Carolina, was the South's last major port. At Hampton Roads, an armada prepares to attack Fort Fisher, which protected Wilmington.

In a naval attack followed by an army assault, a force of 59 warships and 8,000 men—the largest amphibious operation in American history until World War II—took Fort Fisher on January 15, 1865; Wilmington fell on February 22.

Clumsy and unseaworthy, ironclads served only in coastal or inland waters. The ram Albemarle disabled the side-wheeler U.S.S. Sassacus in May of 1864; her boiler repaired, Sassacus helped bring down Fort Fisher.

cap on the point, he was shot through the heart—one of five Confederate generals killed in that orderly grandeur. Six others were wounded, one mortally, and another was captured. About 7,000 of lesser rank were casualties as well. The fighting lasted into the night.

Schofield, who suffered about 2,300 casualties, withdrew during the night to Nashville. Then, in a week of mild weather, Hood put up breastworks fronting the Federal lines. The second week of December, one long storm of snow and freezing rain and sleet paralyzed everything. At his headquarters in Virginia, Grant fretted over the delay. Then, after a thaw, a Federal force under George H. Thomas emerged and, in two days of fighting, sent Hood reeling. Bedford Forrest's "powerful rear guard," Thomas reported, "did its work bravely to the last," but the rest of the Army of Tennessee "had become a disheartened and disorganized rabble of half-armed and barefooted men." Some units would fight again, but in fact that army was gone. Survivors made their way to Mississippi, and the heaviest fighting west of the Appalachians was essentially over.

Sherman's victory at Atlanta presaged Lincoln's at the polls. McClellan, who lost most of the soldier's vote, carried only New Jersey, Delaware, and Kentucky. Now the year that had begun with the promise of Grant would end with the merciless marches of Sherman in Georgia and Sheridan in the Shenandoah.

Grant had sent Sheridan into the Valley with orders to drive Early out of the Shenandoah and make it useless as a Confederate larder. "Carry off stock of all descriptions and negroes so as to prevent further planting," Grant ordered. "If the War is to last another year we want the Shenandoah valley to remain a barren waste."

Sheridan, in his first major attack, drove Early out of Winchester and reported 2,500 prisoners. But he failed to move against the railroads supplying Lee and Richmond. Nor did he impede the passage of reinforcements to Early. The showdown finally came when Early's troops, shrouded in morning fog, swooped down on a Federal camp at Cedar Creek. Sheridan, on the road from Winchester, heard gunfire and instantly set off toward the battle. His men were in headlong retreat when he rode up, waving his hat and urging them to turn back. The troops began cheering him. "Face the (Continued on page 259)

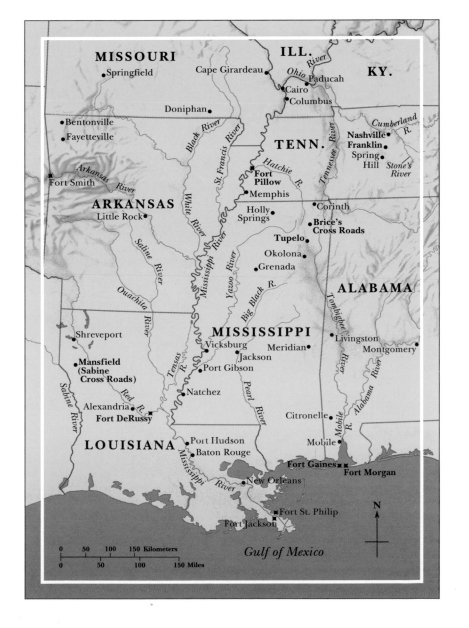

AT MOBILE BAY | *Lone cannon awaits a phantom attack at Fort Gaines, across from Morgan at the entrance to the bay. Gaines fell first, with little resistance. Morgan held out longer under Brig. Gen. Richard Page.*

Designed to shelter cannon but blocked by sand as protection against the new rifled artillery, Morgan's casemates (opposite) housed offices, hospital space, and food and ammunition. "It was necessary for my garrison of 400 men to labor hard day and night," Page reported, to prepare for the attack. He recalled "furious fire." When flames threatened the magazines, Page ordered 30 tons of powder flooded—and surrendered to Farragut and Maj. Gen. Gordon Granger.

He was a sensible man, said Sherman, and only did sensible things. He won the confidence of veterans in the hard-used Army of Tennessee, involuntary experts on flawed generalship. He figured in many noteworthy Civil War conflicts, including quarrels that simmered on into post-war years.

Precisely because he became a general of few successes and many controversies, Joseph E. Johnston explains a good deal about the fate of the Confederacy.

Born in 1807 in piedmont Virginia, a grandnephew of Patrick Henry, he entered West Point at 18. Robert E. Lee became his friend. Graduating 13th in a class of 46, he campaigned against Chief Black Hawk and was wounded by the Seminoles in Florida.

In 1845 he married Lydia McLane, of a prominent Delaware family. They had a happy, but childless, marriage. Her social ties helped his career until she came to be at odds with Mrs. Jefferson Davis.

JOSEPH E. JOHNSTON

him severe wounds, and Lee replaced him.

Not fully healthy by December, Johnston took up theater command in the West. "Great ends to be secured, high expectations formed, and most inadequate means furnished"—so Braxton Bragg summed up conditions no Confederate general could do much about.

Like President Davis then, soldiers today think Johnston might have risked more in his efforts to save Vicksburg, but everyone gives the Richmond brass some blame for that defeat and for others incurred by Bragg.

"Boys, this is Old Joe," said Maj. Gen. Frank Cheatham, introducing their new commander to the glum, staunch veterans of the Army of Tennessee, in winter camp at Dalton, Georgia. Old Joe, stern in retraining but warm in handshaking and liberal with rations, quickly won their hearts. When Sherman started southward in May 1864, Johnston conducted a masterly fighting re-

Johnston distinguished himself in the Mexican War at the cost of five wounds. He was brigadier, and quartermaster general, when he resigned on April 22, 1861, to "go with Virginia."

He did himself proud at First Manassas, but soon was deep in a murkier struggle. As he understood Confederate law, his U.S. rank made him "first general" in his new nation. President Davis and the Congress made him a full general but fourth in seniority. He wrote at length complaining of this "studied indignity," this tarnish on his "fair fame." Davis penned a terse rebuff. Jealousy over rank plagued both sides all through the war, but was worse in the South with its cult of honor. Davis was as touchy as Johnston; both tried to set their cause above their quarrel and neither succeeded. Their cause suffered accordingly.

Defending Richmond against McClellan in May 1862, Johnston failed to smash a Union corps isolated at Seven Pines (Fair Oaks to the Federals). His juniors bungled. A bullet and a shell fragment gave

treat—nobody could have done it better, U.S. Grant observed. Johnston had his army, overmatched but intact and confident, in defensive works outside Atlanta in July. Then Davis, convinced that Johnston would evacuate Atlanta, gave his role to John Bell Hood, a bold fighter but untried in charge of an army. "I confess I was pleased at the change," Sherman wrote his wife; another Federal general spoke of "universal rejoicing." Hood went on the offensive and wrecked his army. Its dauntless survivors joined Old Joe in the Carolinas in March 1865, after public clamor forced Davis to send Johnston into the field again. Nothing availed. Sherman gave generous terms when Johnston surrendered on April 26 near Durham's Station in North Carolina.

In peace, Johnston refought his battles in print—especially those with other Southrons. He died in 1891. Fragile with 84 years and heart disease, he had insisted on standing bareheaded in winter cold at Sherman's funeral; Sherman, he said, would have done as much for him.

Atlanta's outskirts bristle with palisades, rifle pits, and rows of spiked logs called chevaux-de-frise, part of a 12-mile defensive ring that Confederate engineers began in 1863 and strengthened in 1864 to protect the city from Sherman's three advancing armies.

"As dangerous to assault as a permanent fort," in Sherman's words, dirt-and-timber entrenchments sheltered Johnston's troops at New Hope Church (below). The Rebels dug in on Kennesaw Mountain (opposite), and easily repelled

Sherman's attack. Johnston's strategic retreat and entrenchment during the Atlanta Campaign occupied Union troops for ten weeks. In July the pugnacious John Bell Hood replaced the prudent Johnston as Confederate commander.

FOLLOWING PAGES: Formidable Rebel defenses could not save Atlanta; Sherman's men entered the city on September 2, then marched through Georgia—and the Carolinas in 1865— wreaking destruction at will.

other way, boys," he shouted. "Turn back! Turn back!" Rallied, they counterattacked, smashed Early's army, and devised refinements of Grant's order to strip the Valley.

Winter came to a ravaged Shenandoah. Farm animals starved to death. Both Sheridan and Grant said that a crow flying across the Valley would have to carry its own rations. Lee's soldiers went on one-quarter rations, and on some days had no rations at all.

In Atlanta, Sherman burned down factories and whatever else would serve the war, and with 60,000 men began his march to the sea. His men set off with flags flying, gun barrels glittering in the sunlight, bands playing—"Battle Hymn of the Republic," "Lorena," "Yankee Doodle," and sometimes "Dixie." Like a scythe with a stroke 60 miles wide, his armies stripped the land, tearing up rails, burning bridges and factories, looting farms, rustling cattle. Georgians, though angry and frightened, marveled at the rank on rank of "strong, healthy, well-fed" men. A South Carolinian noticed, "There was not a broken shoe or a ragged elbow among them."

Sherman's men drove herds of cattle and sheep, stole goats and hogs, killed and left to rot the beasts they did not take. Men on horseback, the mistress of a plantation wrote, rode off "with bunches of turkeys, bunches of chickens, ducks and guineas swinging both sides of the horse like saddle-bags. Then the wagons—Oh! the wagons—in every direction—wagons! wagons!"

Another woman told of Yankees storming into her home. "One man came in, stuck his bayonet in a ham, and marched out with it; another did the same; and in a moment everything was swept off the table—plates, knives, forks, everything. A hundred men were in the house at a time, searching every part of it, breaking open doors, closets, drawers, trunks, in their 'search for arms.'" Most of the marauders were, as one woman noted, "curiously civil and abstaining from *personal insult*," though they shocked Southerners by stealing from slaves. The slaves—or ex-slaves, now—did not inflict the atrocities that the South had dreaded so long. Many just went off to the Yankees, to follow the liberators wherever they might go.

Sherman's men tore up fences and camped in front yards, raided smokehouses for bacon and hams, chopped through walls where slaves

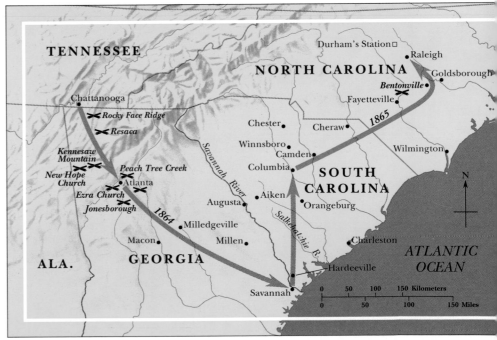

He "never clearly won a battle," remarked a biographer, "nor ever failed to win a campaign." Sherman was always a man of contradictions. Serving in the South as a young officer, he became enchanted with its culture and a good friend of many families; but as a Civil War general he made himself the most hated of Yankees.

Born of New England stock in Ohio in 1820, he lost his father in 1829. Influential friends secured his chance at West Point. He finished sixth of 43 in 1840, never getting beyond the rank of private.

Sherman saw limited action against the Seminoles in Florida. In the Mexican War he shuffled papers as a quartermaster in California. He resigned his commission to try banking, then law. In 1859 he became the first superintendent of Louisiana's new military academy, which he left "with much regret" when the state seceded. To Sherman the Constitution, not slavery, was the only great issue at stake.

From the start Sherman showed strategic vision at the level of genius. In 1860 he told Southern friends that they were "rushing into war with one of the most powerful, ingeniously mechanical and determined people on earth." They would make early headway, but "surely fail" in the end. After Sumter he predicted the course of the war with remarkable accuracy, declaring that the Mississippi Valley would be the key to victory. He once defined strategy as "common sense applied to the art of war," and he showed a highly professional grasp of the art.

Although he had never commanded more than a company by 1861, he rose steadily: brigade, division, corps. When Grant became general-in-chief in 1864, Sherman took over operations in the West. In the Atlanta Campaign he was, in present-day terms, an army group commander—the first in American history. He led three armies totaling 100,000 men, and soldiers today study this campaign as a master-

WILLIAM TECUMSEH SHERMAN

piece of planning, administration, and maneuver, as well as an instructive model for operations deep in a hostile area. He would not tie himself to a single route; with alternatives, he said, "I can take so eccentric a course that no general can guess at my objective."

Often seen as omens of modern "total war," Sherman's harsh ways with enemy civilians followed official instructions published by the government in 1863. He characterized his destructive sweep as "statesmanship"—it would demonstrate to the South (and the world) the will and power of the Union. It had "one sole object—successful war and consequent peace."

Sherman was least impressive as a tactician, but he averaged only 62 casualties per 1,000 engaged (as against 113 for Grant, 149 for Lee). He was the only Civil War general whose memoirs included a chapter on the war's military lessons.

Until his death in 1891 he was a Union hero, his name always linked with that of his good friend Grant. As fine a soldier as Grant in many respects, he could not have equaled him as wartime general-in-chief. Sherman's outspoken contempt for politicians and his constant troubles with the press would have undercut his effectiveness in that role.

For 14 turbulent years he did command the little peacetime army. He set its intellectual agenda for study and reforms. But twice, exasperated by wrangling in Washington, he left the capital, once by moving army headquarters to St. Louis and once by taking a long tour of Europe. There he met Count von Moltke, the great German chief of staff, who had reportedly compared Civil War armies to "armed mobs." Asked later about the truth of this, Sherman snapped: "I did not ask him that question because I did not presume that he was such an ass as to say that." Nothing could convince Sherman that his army was not "as good an army as the Prussians ever had"—equal to any in the world.

Smoldering rubble of Atlanta's passenger depot reflects the ruin of the vital rail center that had sent food, supplies, and troops throughout the Confederacy. Sherman's capture of Atlanta boosted Union morale—and President Lincoln won reelection.

Crammed with refugees and their goods, the last evacuation train waits to leave the Atlanta passenger depot, soon to be a wreck like the roundhouse at right. Sherman's troops destroyed tracks and equipment, then torched the city.

FOLLOWING PAGES: Nashville stayed in Federal hands despite Hood's best efforts in mid-December. His two-day battle proved a decisive defeat. He lost 6,000 men: no less than 25 percent of the valiant Army of Tennessee.

had hidden wheat and grain. They looted while claiming they were foraging and looking for weapons. An infuriated Southern woman read the truth in a letter dropped by a Yankee lieutenant. He had written his wife: "We have had a glorious time in this state. Unrestricted license to burn and plunder was the order of the day.... Gold watches, silver pitchers, cups, spoons, forks, etc., are as common in camp as blackberries.... Officers are not allowed to join in these expeditions without disguising themselves as privates.... I have at least a quart of jewelry." "The coming, the going of this Army was a horrible nightmare," said another woman. "We awoke from it to realize we were destitute. The Confederacy seemed suddenly to have changed, a glory had passed from it, and, without acknowledging it, we felt the end was near."

So did Grant and Sherman and Lincoln, whose year of hope and despair ended with a telegram from Sherman: "I beg to present you as a Christmas gift the city of Savannah...." Sherman had reached the sea, but his march had not ended. Neither had Grant's.

Wartime Mapmaking: Art, Craft, and Victory

Strategy, said the Swiss military theorist Baron de Jomini in the 1830s, is "the art of making war upon the map." Like the hand-in-blouse pose for generals, this concept came from Napoleon.

Before the French Revolution, armies were small enough to march along a single road and to fight under the eye of the commander. The mass armies of the Napoleonic wars changed that. The emperor organized specialized services to provide maps. His engineers depicted relief with hachures—short lines drawn in the direction of slope—or contour lines, which were more accurate but less emphatic.

West Point followed the French in training topographical engineers, who mapped rivers and coastlines and surveyed routes for canals and railroads. When war broke out in 1861, the U.S. Coast Survey provided "valuable service" to naval squadrons blockading Southern ports and to Union armies in the field. No one, however, had prepared for war on home soil.

In June 1861 the Survey began a detailed map of northern Virginia, but it wasn't ready by the first battle of Bull Run. Although General McClellan ordered maps for his Penin-

sula Campaign the next spring, his subordinates encountered serious difficulties. "Correct local maps were not to be found," he reported; often their streams and roads ran in the wrong direction.

Surprisingly, the Confederates, fighting in their own backyard, also lacked decent maps—as well as topographical engineers. In the Seven Days, General Lee issued to his division commanders maps that "proved unworthy of the name." Poorly acquainted with the ground north of the Chickahominy River, he hoped to overwhelm an isolated corps

thought to be deployed near Powhite Creek. His plan miscarried when the Union forces fell back behind a sluggish, heavily wooded stream called Boatswain's Swamp—a feature not shown on Lee's map. Stonewall Jackson attempted a flanking march that proved nearly twice as long as the map indicated.

The commander of a Louisiana brigade, Richard Taylor, wrote later that his colleagues knew no more about the area than "about Central Africa." Within a day's march of Richmond they were "profoundly ignorant of the country, were with-

out maps, sketches, or proper guides, and [were] nearly as helpless as if we had been suddenly transferred to the banks of the Lualaba."

The situation in the West was no less confusing. In January 1862 two Union commanders in southern Kentucky, closing in on the enemy yet separated by a day's march, tried to coordinate their plans by courier. Confusion developed because their maps showed different road patterns and place-names. Fortunately for them, they met at the last minute, recognized the problem, and made their maps agree; otherwise the engagement at Logan's Cross Roads (also known as the battle at Mill Springs or Fishing Creek) might have been a Rebel victory.

In March, General Jackson summoned his topographical engineer, Jedediah Hotchkiss, and told him to prepare a map of the Shenandoah Valley from Harper's Ferry to Lexington, "showing all the points of offence and defence." Self-taught as a mapmaker but also a geologist and experienced surveyor, Hotchkiss was the best the South had. He had an instinct for terrain and a flair for expressive sketches, drawn with colored pencils. He was at Jackson's side in the field, making sketches on

In the war, maps proved essential—and often unreliable. In 1863 the South's best topographer, Jedediah Hotchkiss, mapped Chancellorsville, Salem Church, and Fredericksburg battlefields (above) in just 29 days. Beside a level on a tripod, a model poses with dividers and other tools.

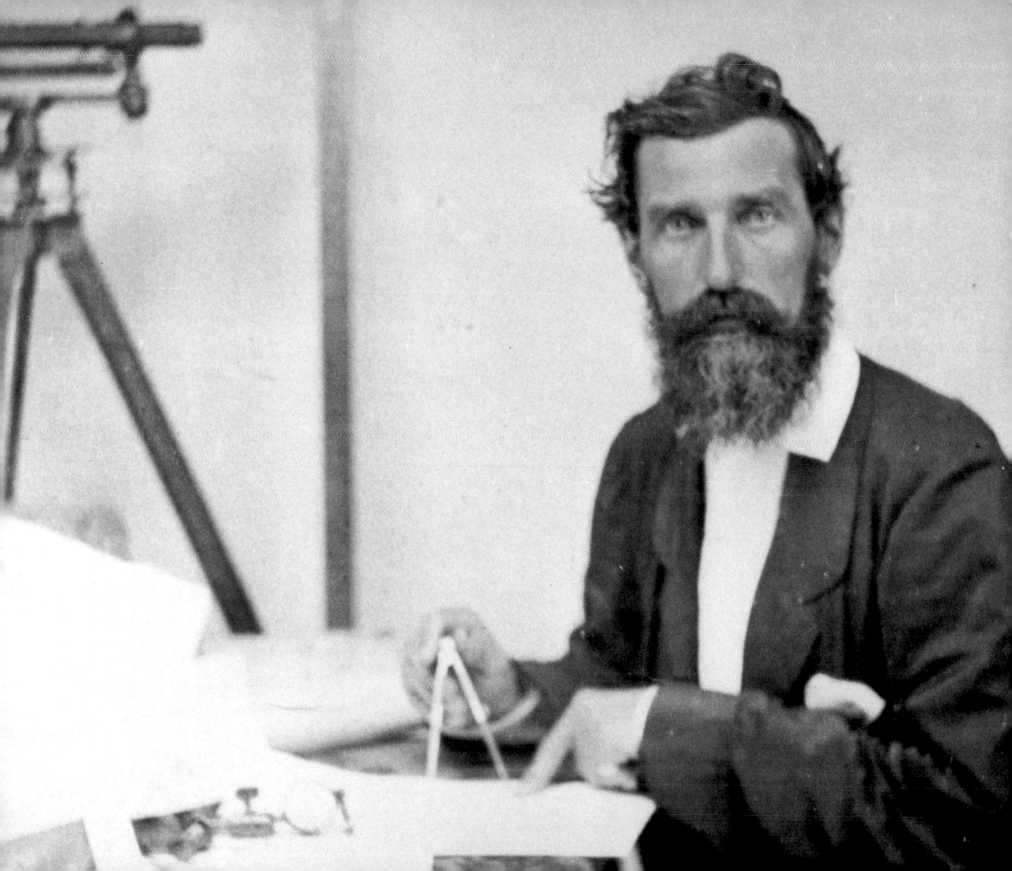

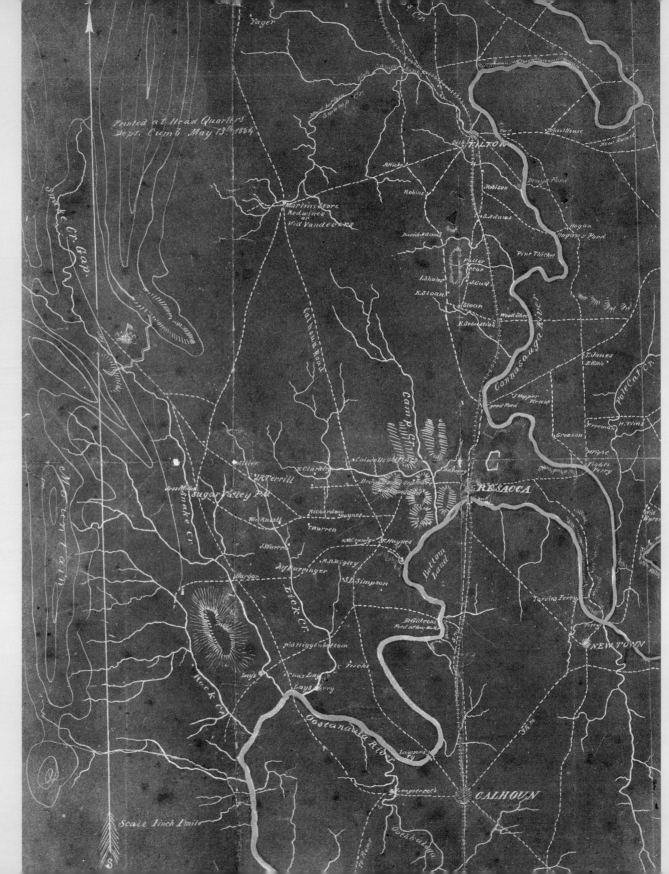

Photocopy, 1864: Sunlight striking through a tracing-paper overlay darkened a sheet coated with silver nitrate; ink lines on the overlay appear white on the copy. This tinted map shows Snake Creek Gap and Resaca, Georgia.

the march or during engagements, and his work proved its value in the Valley Campaign of May and June.

In February 1863, when Lee was beginning to think of invading Pennsylvania, he wanted a map of the Valley "extended to Harrisburg, Pa., and then on to Philadelphia." Hotchkiss adapted county maps borrowed from headquarters, integrating "other collected data" (perhaps from spies). In about three months he had a map duly showing Harrisburg and extended east as far as Baltimore. Drawn to the scale of 1:160,000, it included mills, forges, taverns, schools, the names of farmers—the details that let people find their way around in those days. Roads appeared in red, with fords marked at rivers.

A large-scale map like this let corps and division commanders move from one designated point to another on adjacent roads, with units close enough for mutual support but separated for speed, ease of march, and foraging. This was an absolute necessity in such a campaign. On a single road Lee's wagons alone would have made a 40-mile column. The Army of the Potomac, with men four abreast and wagons and guns well closed up, would have been 70 miles long: an ideal target for the enemy.

As both armies advanced into Pennsylvania, officers rounded up county maps for added details,

including terrain. Hotchkiss had rendered major mountains in brown hachures but left out tactical features. At Gettysburg even such an imposing height as Big Round Top was missing.

What is obvious on Lee's map is that Gettysburg was the hub for at least eight roads, the factor that would draw both armies to the town. (A glance at a map the previous summer had led McClellan to suspect that Lee's objective then might be Gettysburg; the "Young Napoleon" understood war—on the map!)

If properly trained, cavalry scouted the countryside for up-to-date particulars. By 1863, Maj. Gen. George H. Thomas, U.S.A., had his horsemen reporting the condition of roads and bridges; the location of forage and drinkable water; natural defensive positions; "and the other minutiae necessary to rapid maneuver over a strange terrain." Time permitting, topographical engineers transferred the most vital information onto maps that were printed in the field and issued throughout the Army of the Cumberland.

The smaller forces operating west of the Mississippi had less need of maps, and along the river not only county maps but also U.S. surveys were available. Late in 1862, when Sherman started an ill-fated effort to attack Vicksburg, he gave each division commander a copy of a map "compiled from the best sources."

This, sensibly enough, was the same map used by the Navy, and Sherman urged his juniors to make as many copies as possible, "being very careful in copying the names."

No Civil War general made more creative use of maps than Sherman, who once ordered a subordinate to post a regiment "not far from the letter M or O in the word 'mountain.'" In the Atlanta Campaign he made tactical use of maps to guide division commanders and occasionally even to coordinate artillery fire—standard now but a rarity then.

Planning his drive into Georgia, Sherman studied maps rich in 1860 census data on crops and industry and commerce, maps prepared and kept secret by the War Department. He chose his objectives accordingly.

Meanwhile his cartographers developed a campaign map. For a base they used a five-year-old state map that showed county names and boundaries, roads, railroads, and towns; it highlighted topographical features with hachures. The portion depicting northwestern Georgia was enlarged to a scale of one inch to the mile so that important details could be added easily.

As soon as Sherman announced the date of advance, the master copy was cut into 16 pieces and divided among draftsmen who worked night and day tracing the original on thin paper in a special transfer ink. Four adjacent sections would be placed on

a large lithographic stone and 200 copies would be printed. Mounting and binding the sheets was slow work, but all was done in two days. When the commanding generals set out, each had a bound copy; before they struck the enemy, every corps, division, and brigade commander had his own. Copies for the cavalry were printed on muslin, which was slow to tear and easy to wash if soiled. (Staff and infantry officers often carried maps printed on handkerchiefs.)

New details came in as officers questioned spies, prisoners, and local residents. "The best illustration of the value of this," noted a historian of the Army of the Cumberland, was the discovery of Snake Creek Gap, "through which our whole army turned the strong positions at Dalton and Buzzard Roost Gap. . . ." None of the maps available had shown this feature.

A corrected field map of the vicinity could be made at once, by a portable photoprinting device. Capt. William C. Margedant, a topographical engineer, had invented

MAP OF
NORTHERN GEORGIA

A map of northern Georgia—compiled in 1864 from engineering surveys, Cherokee land maps, and details from informants—served as the principal reference in the opening stages of the Atlanta Campaign. The Federals' discovery of Snake Creek Gap, not shown on other printed maps, allowed a surprise outflanking movement on Rebel forces at Resaca—a technique that was used repeatedly and ultimately led to the fall of Atlanta. In 1863 the U.S. Army assigned its topographical specialists to the Corps of Engineers. As war continued, their mapping expertise improved and demand increased. In 1865 the Corps delivered 24,591 maps to armies in the field.

their perennial shortages of paper and equipment, the Confederates were making "sunprint" maps as good as the Federals' by 1864.

Grant's specialists in northern Virginia spent the winter of 1863–64 preparing 29 new maps for the spring fighting, all on the scale of one mile to the inch. They were lithographed, said former staff officer Theodore Lyman, "printed in true congressional style on wretched spongy paper" that soon wore out, and full of errors. For the Wilderness area, "only eight miles by nine," one landmark was 30 degrees out of position and another, 45. Todd's Tavern was a mile too far north; a bend of the Po River two and three-quarter miles too far west; Spotsylvania Court House two and a half miles west. Roads ran "quite wild," with three major exceptions: stretches of the Orange Plank, Brock, and Catharpin Roads. (On May 7, 1864, Grant issued an order putting two corps near a road junction that existed only on paper.)

"The effect of such a map," recalled Lyman in bitter summary, was "utterly to bewilder and discourage the officers who used it, and who spent precious time in trying to understand the incomprehensible."

But as the army advanced south of the Rapidan, the engineers ran compass surveys, estimating distances "by paces, by the gait of their horses, or by angles," and corrected

photoprint maps were rushed into use—1,600 copies before the fall of Petersburg on April 2, 1865.

Not every road on the operational maps led to a battle, and battle maps—portraying "war on the ground"—belong in a category of their own. By their very nature they could only be drawn after the event, and once an army retreated, its mapmaker had to work in part from memory. If you want to find the entrenchments deep in the woods of the Wilderness, you can easily follow the Federal battle map on plate 55 of the *Official Military Atlas of the Civil War*. If you rely on Hotchkiss's map, plate 83, you can easily get lost.

Jed Hotchkiss may have been the finest topographical engineer of the war; but as often happened, the South had a gifted individual and the North had a rich organization. In producing good military maps, the Union enjoyed a decisive edge.

Ironically, 30 years after the war, the Antietam Battlefield Board hired Hotchkiss to draw the base map for the newly created national military site. He failed to submit his sketches within the specified 60 days, and was fired. His employer said he could still depict strawstacks (which had figured in the action), but in other respects the state of the art had passed him by. If the old man needed comfort, he could remember that never once, during the war itself, had he failed Jackson or Lee.

this. The map was traced onto thin paper and laid over a sheet coated with nitrate of silver. Sunlight would darken the paper while the ink lines left their image in white. Copies by this quick method cost so much that only chief commanders got them, but several revisions could be printed in a single day.

Maj. Albert H. Campbell, C.S.A., thought up the same procedure, noting that expert photographers considered it "impracticable, in fact impossible." Though hampered by

1865

THE CROWDED FLAGS

About two o'clock on a rainy morning early in March, Gen. Robert E. Lee summoned Maj. Gen. John B. Gordon to headquarters, on the outskirts of Petersburg. Gordon found him alone, standing at the fireplace, his head resting on his arm, his look pained and faraway. Never before had Gordon seen his commander openly despondent. But the hour had come when Lee "could no longer . . . entirely conceal his forebodings of impending disaster."

Lee handed Gordon reports showing that around Richmond and Petersburg there were about 35,000 men fit for duty. Against them, Lee estimated, Grant had 150,000 troops, with 50,000 more on the way. In the East, the Confederacy could muster 65,000 against 280,000.

At Lee's request, Gordon gave his view of possible actions: surrender with the best terms possible; abandon Richmond and join Johnston in North Carolina; or fight on here. After a conference in Richmond, Lee summoned Gordon again. Lee saw only one choice: to fight. "To stand still was death. It could only be death if we fought and failed."

He made a desperate plan. He would strike Grant, forcing him to shorten his 37-mile siege line at Petersburg. With a shorter front to

defend, Lee could send men to Johnston in North Carolina. There, he hoped, the Confederates could defeat Sherman; then they could wheel and fight Grant.

The plan would not work unless Gordon could capture Fort Stedman, which he thought "the most inviting" point for a night attack, and in the end it failed; but the attempt left a poignant incident in Gordon's memory.

As a first step, Gordon ordered his own strong defenses dismantled during the night of March 24. The noise alerted a Union picket, who yelled across the lines, "What are you doing over there, Johnny? What is that noise? Answer quick or I'll shoot." The pickets had long since been on easy terms. A private at Gordon's side called, "Never mind, Yank. Lie down and go to sleep. We are just gathering a little corn. You know rations are mighty short over here." A narrow strip of corn stood between the lines. The Federal replied, "All right, Johnny; go ahead and get your corn. I'll not shoot at you while you are drawing your rations." Gordon told the private to fire a single shot, the signal for the attack. He hesitated. "Fire your gun, sir," Gordon repeated. The private shouted, "Hello, Yank! Wake up; we are going to shell the woods. Look out; we are coming."

Morning shadows evoke the horror of the Battle of the Crater at Petersburg, where on July 30, 1864, the Union lost some 4,000 men. Walking through the ruins of Richmond, two women mourn their fate and that of the Confederacy.

PRECEDING PAGES: *Members of the well-fed, well-shod Company B, 170th New York Volunteers, play cards, read, and smoke while relaxing in the field. This regiment suffered high casualties in 1864 fighting on the North Anna.*

On February 17, 1865, Sherman took Columbia, South Carolina; fires spread by brisk winds ravaged nearly two-thirds of the city (below). Charleston fell that day. An accidental fire on December 11, 1861, had destroyed the Circular

Congregational Church, where free black children sat together on the portico in 1865 (opposite). The city endured Union blockade and attacks for four years.

Gordon later absolved his young private: "He was going into the fearful charge, and he evidently did not feel disposed to go into eternity with the lie on his lips."

Death, honor, valor, desperation, hunger—these were the realities of the final days for the Confederacy. As a nation, the Confederate States of America had shriveled to parts of Virginia, North Carolina, and South Carolina, along with small areas farther south and isolated holdings in the Trans-Mississippi. Richmond was jammed with the human wreckage of war—wounded and dying soldiers, deserters, refugees with no other place to go, speculators with little to speculate on.

Lee's men around besieged Petersburg, dependent for supplies upon ramshackle railroads, at best ate quarter rations: a handful of meal and a quarter of a pound of meat a day. The meat was usually "Nassau bacon," rancid pork brought through the blockade. Thousands deserted, slipping across to the Union lines or making their way home to farms awaiting the spring plow.

In battered Petersburg, the new year promised worse suffering. The Federals had taken Fort Fisher, which guarded Wilmington, the last port of the blockade-runners. Wilmington fell in February; the sealing of its harbor sealed the fate of the South.

With the loss of Nassau bacon and the other supplies that had flowed through Wilmington, Richmond and Petersburg began to starve. In Richmond, a barrel of flour cost $1,250. People traded recipes for cooking rats. (In Washington, Secretary of the Navy Gideon Welles,

"I had a good many bloody struggles with the musquetoes," he recalled. "I can truly say I was often very hungry." Thus, in 1848, Congressman Lincoln made fun of himself as a military hero.

When the noted chief Black Hawk invaded Illinois in 1832, neighbors elected Abe Lincoln, age 23, captain of volunteers. He served just 36 days as an officer—inventing phrases of command, losing a wrestling match with another captain for the use of a good campsite—and he never met the enemy warriors. He told a friend in 1859 that his election to the captaincy "gave me more pleasure than any . . . since."

Lincoln summed up his schooling in one word: "defective."

He was briefly postmaster at New Salem, partner in a store that "winked out," and self-taught surveyor. Mainly self-taught as a lawyer, he shared a loose-jointed practice in a dusty 20-by-22-foot office in Springfield; he argued cases about land deals and divorces, slander and stray hogs. His files included his stovepipe hat and a big bundle of papers labeled "If you can't find it anywhere else look in here."

Such, on the face of it, was the military and administrative track record of Abraham Lincoln, candidate for President in 1860. As his trifling cousin Dennis Hanks put it, there was "suthin' peculiarsome" about him.

His frontier childhood belongs to the American epic. An Indian killed his grandfather. His father grew up barely literate, but good at farming. Abe, born in 1809, was seven when the family moved from Kentucky to Indiana—from slave state to free. He was already reading and writing. He heard the howl of wolves, the panther's scream, the squeal of a shoat in the claws of a bear. He killed a wild turkey with his father's rifle, and never fired at anything larger again. Big for his years, he was given an ax; he built up strength using it "almost constantly" for 15 years. He learned, and disliked, farm skills such as plowing.

Growing toward 6 feet 4—exceedingly tall for his times—he excelled in local sports, hurling a crowbar or a heavy maul, lifting weights, racing and jumping. He didn't cuss, smoke or chew, or drink "fool

ABRAHAM LINCOLN

water," but he could claim to be the big buck of his salt lick.

His baby brother died about 1812, his mother in 1818, but the trouble that seemed to haunt him was the madness that struck a schoolmate. In a burst of mania this boy attacked his parents and himself; years later Lincoln brought the tragedy into a somber poem. (Lincoln's verse, if not up to his prose, was better than most poems about him.)

Always thoughtful, often brooding, Lincoln suffered at times from "hypo" (hypochondria), a deep gloom. Once he wrote: "I am now the most miserable man living. If what I feel were equally distributed to the whole human family, there would not be one cheerful face on the earth."

That torment stemmed from romance, it seems. Lincoln had overcome his shyness and proposed to the bewitching Mary Todd, a belle from Kentucky. She could chatter in French, waltz with grace, flirt with a fan or a comment on politics. She was daring enough to accept this unsuitable admirer, generous enough to release him when his confidence faltered, adult enough to say yes when he took heart and proposed again. Mrs. Lincoln liked to say that she had chosen him because he would be a great man, even President—"for you can see he is not pretty."

Short of cash as a bridegroom in 1842, Lincoln often charged $5 or $10 for a case; $100 was a large fee. But he prospered, modestly; in 1844 he bought his frame house in Springfield. He had learned law by making it, with four terms in the state legislature, and working hard at it. He spent years sharpening his sense of fine distinctions, mastering the arts of analysis and questioning. He cheerfully conceded minor points and fought for essentials. His personality appealed to voters and clients, judges and juries. His arguments were persuasive: clear, terse, often pungent and funny, sometimes majestic. He spoke of the wolf and the lamb like the prophets of Scripture, which he knew well.

His partner W. H. Herndon described Lincoln as a speaker. At first he stood awkwardly, "inclined forward," hands behind him, his voice unpleasant. But he "never acted for stage effect." He was cool, careful, fair to opponents. When he warmed to the occasion "his shrill,

"Plainly the sheep and the wolf are not agreed upon a definition of the word liberty...."

Abraham Lincoln

squeaking, piping voice became harmonious, melodious, musical." His face would glow. Then "he rose up a splendid form, erect, straight, and dignified." He raised both hands high at a 50-degree angle in moments of "greatest inspiration." He gripped his left lapel with his left hand and gestured with his right "to drive home and clinch an idea."

Lincoln called his ideas "short and sweet, like the old woman's dance" in his first campaign—he favored a national bank, a high tariff, and internal improvements. In his only congressional term he challenged, unsuccessfully, President Polk's case for war against Mexico. In the 1850s he was defending the bedrock of his political faith: equality as defined by the Declaration of Independence. He detested a trend toward exceptions for "*negroes . . . and foreigners, and Catholics.*"

Slavery, the flagrant exception, called forth his greatest eloquence, his sharpest analysis, his most careful distinctions. "If all earthly power were given me," he said in 1854, "I should not know what to do as to the existing institution." He had always hated slavery, he opposed any expansion of it beyond the slave states, but he did not propose to attack it there, where the Constitution protected it.

Once, talking with a client, Lincoln denounced the Fugitive Slave Law: "It is ungodly! No doubt it is ungodly! But it is the law of the land. . . ." The client pointed out that Republicans wanted to make Lincoln President: "How would you look taking an oath to support what you declare is an ungodly Constitution, and asking God to help you?" Lincoln answered, after a melancholy pause, that it was "no use to be always looking up these hard spots."

Before long he was taking the presidential oath and leading a war to preserve the Union, ungodly laws and all. Hard spots abounded. Even the soft spots of political routine would have strained a Chief Magistrate now. Lincoln managed. For his Cabinet he chose his greatest rivals and other able men, unifying his party; he controlled them with easy confidence. He did the grubby essential work of patronage, doling out postmasterships and other jobs—and officers' commissions. Shrewdly, he chose foreign-born men ("Schim-mel-fen-*nig* must be appointed") and "War Democrats" like N. P. Banks; such leaders might lose battles, but the war could not be won without their followers.

During the conflict, says one specialist, "the nearest thing to a research and development agency was the President himself." Lincoln intervened to help T.S.C. Lowe get his balloons into action. A fine shot, he tested the Spencer repeating rifle in person and worked to get such breechloaders into use. He watched tests of naval ordnance, new explosives, rockets, flamethrowers. He liked inventors, however quirky; he got a good chuckle from a scheme to bombard C.S.S. *Virginia* with red pepper (presumably to blind and choke her crew).

Once he found able commanders, Lincoln let them manage the fighting, but he set policy. Twice, early on, abolitionist generals invoked martial law to free the slaves of local Rebels. The President revoked these orders—no general would make law by say-so, or force the hand of his Commander in Chief. His own Emancipation Proclamation did not touch slaves in Union-held areas. Only a constitutional amendment could ensure an end to slavery, and he did some arm-twisting before Congress approved one on January 31, 1865. Those maneuvers remained hidden, like much of his work and thought. As Billy Herndon said, his "nature was secretive, it was reticent, it was 'hush.'" Even his jokes and anecdotes—the "little stories" he was so often reminded of—could conceal his mind as well as reveal it, and his humor led some to dismiss him as a lightweight.

Lincoln's character, however, slowly became as unmistakable as his figure. He was not—Herndon again—"a man who could be successfully threatened." His administration jailed hundreds of citizens for disloyalty, real or suspected; those who called him a tyrant had something to go on, but he had prisoners released as soon as possible. In victory he rejected any hint of vindictiveness. On the morning of Good Friday, April 14, he told the Cabinet he wouldn't take part in punishing Rebel leaders, "even the worst of them. Frighten them out of the country, open the gates, let down the bars, scare them off." And he threw up his bony hands like a farm boy scaring sheep.

That night he was shot. His murder surely changed public life for the worse, but nobody could say just what he would have done in peacetime. As usual he had kept his own counsel; and, as he said in his youth, "Towering genius disdains a beaten path." He keeps his unique place in American hearts as the man who freed the slaves and saved the Union, the funniest, least fussy, and most eloquent of Presidents.

weary from yet another levee, noted in his diary, "The season has thus far been one of gaiety. Parties have been numerous.")

Some Southern politicians still hoped to preserve the Confederacy. One was Vice President Alexander H. Stephens. He and Lincoln met as old friends in a five-man conference aboard the *River Queen* off Fort Monroe on February 3, but Lincoln insisted on nothing less than the Union as a condition of peace for "one common country."

After long resistance, the Confederate Congress in March authorized the use of slaves as soldiers, but none ever fought.

Lincoln, sensing imminent victory, pondered a just peace. On March 4, in his Second Inaugural, he promised to fight if God so willed "until every drop of blood drawn with the lash shall be paid by another drawn with the sword. . . ." Yet he offered hope for one common country: "With malice toward none; with charity for all; with firmness in the right, as God gives us to see the right. . . ."

In South Carolina, vengeful troops under Sherman were wielding the torch, not the sword. Sherman himself said his army "is burning with an insatiable desire to wreak vengeance upon South Carolina. I almost tremble for her fate. . . ." Although he issued the same orders he

had in Georgia—destroy only property of military value—his men rampaged far more savagely in South Carolina than they had in Georgia. "The army burned everything it came near," an Illinois major wrote his wife, ". . . not under orders, but in spite of orders. . . ."

Joe Johnston could scarcely believe the speed of the Union advance through rain and mud. Sherman's army was "making its own corduroy roads at the rate of a dozen miles a day and more, and bringing its artillery and wagons with it." Johnston decided that "there had been no such army in existence since the days of Julius Caesar."

When Sherman left Savannah, he feinted toward Charleston and Augusta. But instead of striking either city, he bypassed both and wrecked the railroad between them. Charleston, long under blockade and now cut off from rail supply, surrendered on February 18. By then Sherman was in Columbia, a capital city in flames.

To save his city from battle, the mayor surrendered it. But fleeing Confederates had already set fire to bales of cotton. After dark the wind came up, while mobs of escapees—criminals from jail and freed Union prisoners of war—roamed the streets, as did liberated slaves. Drunk, wild, and bent on vengeance, the mobs set more fires. Dawn brought vistas of chimneys and smoldering rubble.

One of Sherman's most vindictive officers was Maj. Gen. Judson "Kill Cavalry" Kilpatrick. As the broad-winged Union cavalcade swept into North Carolina, Kilpatrick's troopers rode on the left wing. They were bivouacked near Fayetteville when Rebel cavalry pounced on them. While Southern horsemen slashed their way though the camp, Kilpatrick ran out of his farmhouse headquarters in his drawers and shirttail and fled into a swamp. Left behind on the porch, shivering in her shift, was a spectacular blonde later identified as a very unofficial member of Kilpatrick's staff. While minié balls whizzed around her, a Confederate dismounted and gallantly carried her to the safety of a ditch. She and Kilpatrick survived—he as a Union hero, she as a heroine of many (wealthy) conquests. Confederates remembered the skirmish as the Battle of Kilpatrick's Pants.

The Federals pressed on toward Goldsborough, where Sherman planned to link up with Maj. Gen. John M. Schofield and his 30,000 men, on the march from Wilmington. The combined armies could head north to join Grant, wiping out any resistance along the way.

The Confederates in North Carolina had a cluster of renowned generals: Beauregard of Sumter and Shiloh. Bragg of Chickamauga. Hardee of Shiloh, "Old Reliable." Lt. Gen. Wade Hampton, five times wounded chief of cavalry. And cagey Old Joe Johnston of Seven Pines and the West, now commander of a patched-together army of about 20,000. Some of his regiments mustered only 50 or 60 soldiers, and one of his divisions had just 500 men.

Johnston gathered his men—and his boys of the North Carolina Junior Reserves—at a village called Bentonville. Sherman's left wing had wheeled away from the right, and Johnston hoped to defeat the isolated left. Battle flags were painfully close together when his shrunken regiments charged; Federal reinforcements came up; and Johnston decided to withdraw on the third day of the battle, March 21. That afternoon Hardee had ordered a cavalry charge. Among the men who fell was 16-year-old Willie Hardee, the general's only son, mortally wounded. He had become a soldier that very day.

While Sherman's army, joined with Schofield's, took time to rest and refit, the general rode to New Bern. There he boarded a steamer for a voyage to City Point and a meeting with Grant as well as a surprise visitor, Abraham Lincoln.

When Grant, Sherman, and Lincoln met aboard the *River Queen* with Rear Adm. David D. Porter, Lincoln had already inspected Fort Stedman. And Sheridan, fresh from victories in the Shenandoah, had crossed the James to join Grant. "Must more blood be shed?" Lincoln asked his generals, who told him that one last battle seemed inevitable. "My God, my God," Lincoln said. "Can't you spare more effusions of blood? We have had so much of it."

Lincoln and Sherman departed, and Grant turned once more to ending his war with Lee. On March 29, Grant ordered Sheridan to seize Five Forks, a road junction beyond the western end of Lee's Petersburg line. Sheridan's success cut Lee off from his meager supplies. In Richmond, President Davis discreetly asked Brig. Gen. Josiah Gorgas, head of the Ordnance Bureau, to mold cartridges for a small Colt pistol. Davis later gave it to his wife before sending her and their children to Charlotte, North Carolina. *(Continued on page 292)*

PETERSBURG | *The floor of the Crater, seen in a view to the northwest, has softened over the years. At nearby Fort Stedman (opposite) in the Union siege lines, Maj. Gen. John Gordon of Georgia tried a breakout on March 25.*

His men took the fort, only to be driven back by Federals within four hours; he lost about 3,500 from an army already hopelessly outnumbered.

FOLLOWING PAGES: *To prevent Federal gunboats from reaching Richmond, the Confederates sank some of their own. The remains of three appear in the muddy James River below Drewry's Bluff, north of Petersburg.*

289

As Union forces advanced on Richmond on April 2, the Confederates withdrew, setting fire to factories, warehouses, and arsenals. An inferno overwhelmed the city, destroying the riverfront Gallego Flour Mills (below) and much else.

Hopeful that the future would mean freedom, this group—perhaps a family— posed for a photograph beside the James River and Kanawha Canal near the city's "Burnt District."

Early on the morning of Sunday, April 2, Union forces smashed Lee's outer entrenchments. Gen. A. P. Hill fell, killed by a skirmisher. Shells struck Lee's headquarters as he rode toward the thin gray line of Petersburg's inner defenses. "I see no prospect of doing more than holding our position here till night," Lee reported to Richmond. There a messenger found Davis in St. Paul's Church. When he opened and read the dispatch, a worshiper saw "a sort of gray pallor creep over his face." He picked up his hat and left the church. That night Lee began to pull his troops out of Petersburg and Richmond. He expected to get supplies at Amelia Court House, 40 miles southwest on the Richmond & Danville Railroad; they did not arrive. Explosions rocked the capital as the Confederate Navy scuttled its ironclads on the James. Tobacco warehouses, torched by departing troops, went up in flames. Mobs stormed army depots to get rations. Convicts broke out of jail and roamed the streets on a looting spree. Rioting flared up and fires engulfed the city as the first Federals entered.

A young lady, writing amid "the din of the enemy's wagon trains, bands, trampling horses, fifes, hurrahs and cannon," described an inferno: "Along the middle of the streets smouldered a long pile, like street-sweepings, of papers torn from the different departments' archives of our beloved Government, from which soldiers in blue were picking out letters and documents that *(Continued on page 303)*

Occupation of Richmond gave the Union Army an assortment of abandoned Confederate artillery. At left, caissons and limbers holding projectiles and gunpowder, brass howitzers, a tool wagon, and a portable field forge cover a wharf; all await transport to the North.

FOLLOWING PAGES: Union officials in Richmond inspect the rubble of the Virginia State Arsenal, where pyramids of cannon balls remained ready for use. In the background stands the shell of the Franklin Paper Mill, one of more than 700 buildings left blackened and desolate. Rebels fired the three bridges that spanned the James River. Only stonework—like this single arch of the Richmond & Petersburg Railroad bridge—survived the fall of the Confederate capital.

The Women of a House Divided

I question," mused an Englishman who visited America in 1863, "whether either ancient or modern history can furnish an example of a conflict which was so much of a 'woman's war' as this. The bitterest, most vengeful of politicians in this ensanguined controversy are the ladies."

"Secesh" ladies, in particular, impressed wartime observers with their fierce loyalty from the outset. North or South, women were effective recruiting agents before conscription began, showering charms on volunteers and sending petticoats to laggards. But as Mary Ward of Rome, Georgia, later recalled, "if the Southern men had not been willing to go I reckon they would have been made to go by the women."

Though wiser heads recognized the North's superior resources, Rome was only one among hundreds of Southern towns where many women greeted secession with glee and illusion. Working feverishly, the women of Rome equipped its three companies with dress suits, fine linen, and embroidered slippers to ensure "a splurge in Washington when they should arrive there, which they expected would be very soon indeed."

Both sides were ill-prepared for conflict, rendering women's roles as outfitters and provisioners essential to the war effort. Lint-making and cloth-tearing for bandages turned New York parlors "fluffy since Sumter," wrote Jane Stuart Woolsey.

Only two weeks after war erupted, more than 20,000 aid societies had sprung up, their members furiously cutting, stitching, and knitting. Most were extraordinarily productive, even if occasionally mistaken about the troops' needs. Trainloads of exotica such as havelocks—tropical headgear—piled up, unused, in Union depots, near heaps of spoiling sweetmeats sent from home.

In the North, the new Women's Central Association of Relief looked after comforts for the boys and supervised nurses' training. The women of the U.S. Sanitary Commission organized local aid societies and fund-raising sanitary fairs into an efficient, highly profitable whole. Women of the Confederacy—loyal foremost to their states—formed no counterpart. But the success of numerous "Ladies Gun-boat Funds" paid for shipbuilding and enhanced Southern women's fame as patriots.

A remarkable number of women, not content to aid their cause from a distance, broke the domestic tether. At least 3,200 women served as paid nurses, mostly for the North. Several hundred more posed as men and enlisted. Some must have escaped detection altogether, for a few were unmasked only when they required medical treatment—as did a Confederate officer imprisoned on Johnson's Island who gave birth to a "bouncing baby boy."

On the other hand, Sarah Emma Edmonds (alias Frank Thompson, nurse) deserted the 2nd Michigan Infantry rather than be hospitalized when malaria struck. All the while undetected, Edmonds had served the Army of the Potomac as perhaps the most unusual of the war's colorful female spies: a woman disguised as a man disguised as female contraband; dry goods clerk; Confederate boy; and "Bridget," an Irish peddler with a brogue and a basket of pies. For her efforts, Edmonds eventually got a monthly pension of $12.

At encampments and cities alike, observers noted astounding numbers of prostitutes. "Boston absolutely swarms with strumpets," reported one journalist, while Washington counted more than 5,000 of them, a

---

Massachusetts cartridge-makers bend to their tasks in the risky setting of an arsenal. Need drove thousands of women to ill-paid munitions work.
A devoted Southerner, Rose O'Neal Greenhow (shown with her daughter) supplied facts of the Union advance before First Manassas.

"They had seen the magic of a scrap of writing sent from a master to an overseer, and they were eager to share such power . . . ," observed a teacher of former slaves. Such work with freedmen helped make teaching a woman's job by 1880.

Union surgeon Mary Walker (left) and other medical women endured the contempt of male doctors. Felicia Grundy Porter (center) led Tennessee's Soldiers' Relief Society; Sally Tompkins served the Confederacy as a hospital manager.

tenfold wartime increase. Richmond rivaled the Federal capital. More than anything else, the situation bespoke the desperation of women suddenly forced into wage earning—and the pitiful money paid for respectable work. In Richmond, one writer noted, female clerks were "lapsing into prostitution from their total inability to feed and clothe themselves with the[ir] pay."

Degradation was a relative thing, however, particularly for a well-born Southerner forced into the workplace. She might replace a male teacher or a Yankee schoolmarm, usually in one of the South's many private academies. But as young Sarah Morgan of Louisiana lamented: "I would rather die than be dependent; I would rather die than teach."

Southern state laws strictly forbade the education of blacks. This gave Northern teachers a vast and challenging new opportunity as early as the winter of 1861–62, when abolitionist and religious groups began sending idealistic young women to instruct the inhabitants of Federally held areas along the South Carolina coast. Many of the teachers, including a Philadelphia-born black abolitionist named Charlotte Forten, were troubled by the cultural gap they sensed between themselves and their charges—the "crude little specimens" of one school, the singers of "very wild and strange" spirituals, the wedding party in its "very unique and comical" finery.

The scarcity of men opened the way not only for female teachers but also for "government girls," or "department girls," first in the Treasury Departments and later in other agencies. But whereas the wartime demand for teachers outstripped the supply, competition for government jobs was keen, especially in the hardpressed Confederacy.

"Each vacancy brought a hundred applications," lamented Secretary of the Treasury Christopher Memminger. Petitioners often stressed their desperate plight as breadwinners to fatherless broods, as orphans, or as refugees whose homes and property were in Yankee hands.

A "Treasury girl" would be expected to sign or number 3,200 notes a day, earning $3,000 a year in 1864. By then flour cost $300 a barrel in Richmond, and butter, $25 a pound. Still, the War Department clerk earning half her pay or the Clothing Bureau seamstress making two dollars a shirt envied her.

Pay was even lower for munitions employees, working-class girls like Irish-born Mary Ryan, whose carelessness ignited an explosion that killed at least 43 women and 2 men at the Brown's Island Confederate States Laboratory in 1863. It and accidents in arsenals in Washington, D.C., Mississippi, Pennsylvania, and Connecticut accounted for the deaths of more women than died around battlefronts.

Wartime hardship and inflation occasionally led women to strike, sometimes successfully. Umbrellamakers in New York increased their piece rate from six or eight cents to eight or ten in 1863. Cartridge fillers at Brown's Island also won a raise. But female assertiveness was one thing in the industrial North, where factories and mills already employed

more than 270,000 women by 1860, and quite another in the agrarian, conservative South.

Beyond the workplace, demonstrations by women turned violent. Hundreds joined the murderous mobs of the New York draft riots in 1863. In Southern cities, scarcity and "the *Demon spirit* of speculation" ignited bread riots the same year. At Salisbury, North Carolina, dozens of ax-wielding women smashed up speculators' stores and carted away 20 barrels of flour—triggering a $20-a-barrel price drop. In Richmond, a thousand women looted warehouses and speculators' shops.

At first, Southern women of all classes had turned necessity to virtue by devising substitutes as shortages grew and domestic economies became more primitive. Aristocratic Virginia Clay of Alabama recalled that "old spinning wheels and handlooms were brought out from dusty corners, and the whirr of the wheel became a very song to us." Homespun, perhaps crowned by a palmetto leaf hat, signaled patriotism. Fashion took a particularly ingenious turn as coveted corset stays were replaced by ersatz versions of hickory or white oak. Squirrel skins or cotton-gin belts, fastened to a cracking scrap of old leather or a sole of wood, did for shoes; berry juice for ink; pan drippings for candles. Wives wrote letters to their soldier-husbands on wallpaper—the South

hadn't a single paper factory before the war. Food, though, was the main concern. Salt, butter, flour, corn, meat, and milk grew scarcer. Sugar, coffee, and tea disappeared. Substitutes were concocted.

The poor, of course, suffered first and longest, but eventually hunger and despair threatened most households. By the spring of 1862, many women were questioning the war's wisdom and its insatiable hunger for their menfolk. Beseeching Mississippi's Governor John J. Pettus to leave an able-bodied white man on each plantation, "A Planter's Wife" wrote that her slaves could be controlled only as long as food was plentiful; after that, "do you suppose they will hesitate to do that which the poor in many cities are on the eve of doing to secure the staff of life? Do you think that *then* woman's hand can keep them in check?"

Far more common was the kind of forthright plea for her husband's discharge that came from Alabamian Margaret Adams, the mother of eight: "i have nary friend in the world no won do nothing for me ant no other chance in the world only for me and my little ones to go without cloths and something to eat." But discharges on such humanitarian grounds seldom occurred. More and more soldiers, implored by destitute women, deserted.

An observer north of the combat zone would also have seen the

smooth-skinned girls wrinkled prematurely by unimaginable daily burdens, by constant anxiety, by the tragedies repeatedly visited upon a single family. In border areas of the Union states, Confederate soldiers invaded homes; in Minnesota, Dakota Territory, and elsewhere on the frontier, Indian attacks terrorized women without male protectors. Northern wives also urged their soldiers to come home—prompting one German-Jewish colonel to reply: "I would very much wish, if you would write me a little more incoraging as to my military career. . . ."

But the ravages of war and social upheaval in the South were immeasurably greater. Hundreds of thousands of Southern women lived in battle zones; at least 250,000 Southerners fled Northern armies, to become refugees. The dead were counted: one serviceman in four. Alabama alone had 80,000 widows. The chivalrous, patriarchal antebellum Southerner was another casualty. Men crippled for life went uncounted, but as one woman wrote, "the empty sleeve and the crutch made men who had unflinchingly faced death in battle impotent to face their future." Post-war observers began to remark that the Southern woman seemed "superior" to her brothers.

During the war, cherished ideals of womanhood teetered on a precarious pedestal as women's response to

home-front hardship mocked Victorian notions of female fragility. But the condition of black Southern womanhood had mocked those ideals all along. As the former slave Sojourner Truth told Women's Rights conventioneers in 1851: " Nobody eber helped me into carriages, or ober mud puddles, or gives me any best place and ar'n't I a woman? Look at me! Look at my arm! I have plowed, and planted, and gathered into barns, and no man could head me—and ar'n't I a woman? I could work as much and eat as much as a man (when I could get it), and bear de lash as well—and ar'n't I a woman? I have borne thirteen chilern and seen em mos' all sold off into slavery, and when I cried out with a mother's grief, none but Jesus heard—and ar'n't I a woman?"

Some women had likened the master-slave relationship to the husband-wife bond. And the war, though fought largely by white men over the rights of blacks, did lend relevance and passion to issues of women's rights. But black women remained caught in a web of prejudices. In the antebellum South, they had been the most vulnerable Americans: slaves among the free, black in a white-ruled world, female in a male-ruled world.

The Civil War erased only the first of these, even as it brought millions of women together in communities of shared experience.

Broken clouds sweep the sky above a 6-pounder reproduction cannon at Sailor's Creek, Lee's final battle site. Here, on April 6, the Federals captured 7,700 Confederates—eight generals among them. Lee exclaimed, "My God! Has the

army been dissolved?" Shaken but staunch, Mahone responded, "No, General, here are troops ready to do their duty." The day before, Lee's tattered soldiers had begun a forced march to obtain rations, which did not arrive.

They struggled on until Maj. Gen. Philip Sheridan outpaced them and blocked their retreat at Appomattox.

caught their fancy. . . . One gang of drunken rioters dragged coffins sacked from undertakers, filled with spoils from the speculators' shops. . . ." On April 4, Lincoln arrived in Richmond, sat at Davis's desk in the presidential mansion, and went out to tour the city. Jubilant former slaves surrounded him, called him "Messiah," and fell to their knees. An embarrassed Lincoln told them to rise, saying, "You must kneel to God only. . . ." Later, at a farewell concert aboard the *River Queen*, Lincoln asked a military band to play "Dixie." To surprised guests he explained, "That tune is now Federal property."

The Confederacy was fading away to the west—Lee's army staggering toward the Appomattox River, Davis's train carrying him and the remnants of government on a rickety 135-mile trip to Danville.

Lee's army lost about 7,700 as prisoners in a battle at Sailor's Creek. His men were starving. One haggard soldier described his ration as an ear of corn for himself and three for his horse. Joshua Chamberlain—a brevet major general of volunteers, repeatedly wounded, winner of the Medal of Honor for fighting at Little Round Top—gave a hero's tribute to his faltering foe: "We could not help admiring the courage and pluck of these poor fellows, now so broken and hopeless, both for their cause and for themselves."

Union troops followed a path marked by discarded rifles and blanket rolls and knapsacks. Abandoned wagons and cannon were stuck in axle-deep mire, dying mules still harnessed to them. Gaunt horses roamed for forage.

Lee soldiered on, day after day. On April 8 he stopped near Appomattox Court House, met with his staff, and ordered a breakout at daybreak the next morning, Palm Sunday. At 8 a.m. he dispatched an aide to Gordon, who was leading the thrust. Gordon, though still game, sent back an answer: "Tell General Lee I have fought my corps to a frazzle. . . ." "Then," said Lee, "there is nothing left me to do but to go and see General Grant, and I would rather die a thousand deaths."

Sheridan had arrayed his cavalry across Lee's front. Union infantry arrived—one column led by Brig. Gen. John Gibbon. Around 10 a.m., a Confederate officer bearing a flag of truce appeared with a message: "General Lee desires a cessation of hostilities until he can hear from General Grant as to the proposed surrender." Lee arranged to

meet Grant at the nearby brick home of Wilmer McLean. After the fighting on his land at Bull Run in 1861, McLean had moved as far away from war as he could imagine. Now the war would end in his parlor.

Lee, resplendent in a new uniform and gleaming sword, wore freshly polished boots and golden spurs. Grant, whose baggage had gone astray, rode up wearing muddy boots, his slouch hat without cord, his enlisted man's blouse wrinkled and unbuttoned. He did not carry a sword, and he did not ask for Lee's.

The soldier Grant, not vengeful politicians, set the terms: Lee's men would lay down their arms, sign paroles, and head for home. Anyone who had claim to a horse or mule could take one. Grant promised that officers and men would "not be disturbed by the United States authority so long as they observe their paroles and the laws in force where they reside." He sent 25,000 Federal rations to Lee's starving troops.

Lee rode Traveller back to his lines. Surrounded by the stunned and tearful survivors of the Army of Northern Virginia, he said, "Men, we have fought the war together, and I have done the best I could for you. . . ." His eyes brimming, he whispered, "Goodbye," and rode away.

Chamberlain was given the honor of receiving the formal surrender of Lee's infantry—about half the force he had led west: "men whom neither toils and sufferings, nor the fact of death, nor disaster, nor hopelessness could bend from their resolve," Chamberlain wrote. "The dusky swarms forge forward into gray columns of march. On they come, with the old swinging route step and swaying battle-flags . . . crowded so thick, by thinning out of men, that the whole column seemed crowned with red."

On his own authority, Chamberlain had given the order for a salute of honor. Down his line, regiment by regiment, the Union troops smartly shifted their rifles from order arms to carry—the marching salute. Gordon, riding at the head of the column, raised his downcast eyes at the sound of the shifting arms and ordered his men to return the salute. "On our part," Chamberlain wrote, "not a sound of trumpet more, nor roll of drum; not a cheer, nor word nor whisper of vainglorying . . . but an awed stillness rather, and breath-holding, as if it were the passing of the dead."

As the gaunt Rebels passed by, a man from Maine mumbled to a

ROAD TO APPOMATTOX | *Late afternoon sun casts long shadows near the Hillsman house (below), which overlooked the assault at Sailor's Creek. Still seeking food and rest, and pursued by Grant, Lee led the remnants of his army toward Appomattox Station. His Second Corps crossed on High Bridge (opposite). Firing the railroad span failed to deter Union soldiers, who extinguished the blaze and then used a wagon bridge for their crossing.*

At the village of Appomattox Court House on April 9, Lee found more than 60,000 Federal troops; most blocked his way to the west, while others began closing in from the rear. Although his advance units showed fight, Lee realized his forces had been trapped and further resistance was useless. Well aware that his army's surrender would mean the end of the Confederacy, Lee met with Grant that day to discuss terms of surrender. Sometime later, civilians and Union soldiers posed with stacked rifles in front of the Appomattox Court House. Everyone understood the significance of what had happened here.

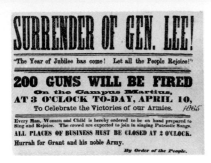
The day of Lee's surrender, someone sketched the pen-and-ink map below, noting the "house at which Gen'l. Lee received Gen'l. Sheridan afterwards Grant,—when agreement was signed." The news traveled quickly. Relieved that the killing was over, the Confederates mourned nonetheless; when Lee bade his soldiers farewell at Appomattox, they wept. By April 10 jubilation reigned throughout the North. Broadsides, like this one displayed in Detroit (left), appeared everywhere, announcing mandatory business closings and victory celebrations honoring General Grant and the Union armies.

comrade, "No wonder we didn't kill more of them; either one of them would split a minie-ball if it should strike him."

As the last brigade stacked its arms and handed over its bullet-torn banner, someone in the Union line called for three cheers, not for the victory but for the Rebel brigade. For this mark of "soldierly generosity," a Confederate colonel remembered, "Many of the grizzled veterans wept . . . and my own eyes were blind as my voice was dumb."

The next day, Thursday, April 13, Lincoln talked of rebuilding the Union before Congress reconvened. At the Cabinet meeting he casually mentioned that before nearly every important event of the war he had dreamed he was sailing in a strange vessel toward an unknown shore. "I had this strange dream again last night," he remarked, saying that he expected great news very soon. There was cheerful speculation about what it might be.

On Friday—Good Friday—retired Maj. Gen. Robert Anderson raised over Fort Sumter the same flag he had lowered exactly four years earlier. In Raleigh, North Carolina, Sherman received a message from Johnston proposing negotiations. In Washington, Lincoln invited General and Mrs. Grant to Ford's Theatre to see the comedy *Our American Cousin.* Grant sent a polite refusal.

During the second scene of Act III, John Wilkes Booth, a 26-year-old actor, opened the door to Lincoln's box and shot the President in the back of his head. Booth grasped the handrail of the box, dropped to the stage, and disappeared into the wings. Lincoln was carried to a boardinghouse across the street. There, next morning, he died.

Rumors of a Confederate conspiracy spread through Washington after the discovery that someone had entered the home of Secretary of State William H. Seward and tried to stab him to death in his bed. Chamberlain, marching his men from Appomattox, had two fears—a Rebel plan to seize Washington or "a frenzy of blind revenge" by his troops. In Raleigh, Sherman knew that "one single word by me would have laid the city in ashes." Grant ordered mass arrests in Richmond, then, regaining his coolness of mind, rescinded the order.

Neither vengeance nor a new spasm of fighting transpired. At the Bennett place, a modest farmhouse near Durham's Station on a railroad, Sherman showed Johnston the report of Lincoln's murder.

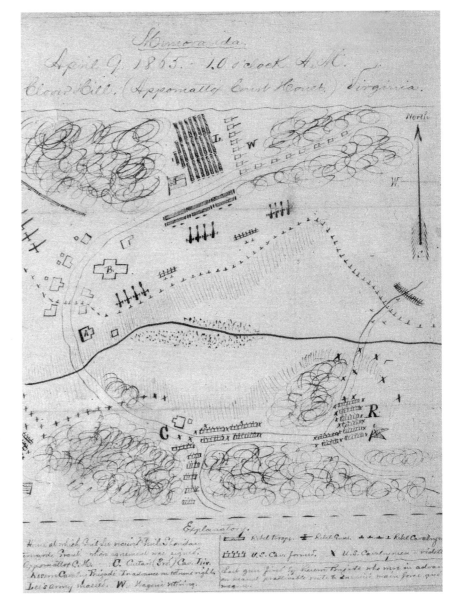

"The perspiration came out in large drops on his forehead," Sherman recalled, and he called the act "a disgrace to the age." Keeping in mind his conversation with Lincoln at City Point, Sherman wrote sweeping and generous terms for settling civil as well as military matters.

Andrew Johnson, now President, repudiated Sherman's agreement. Johnston, given the terms Lee had accepted from Grant, surrendered on April 26. That same day, near Port Royal, Virginia, Federal troops set fire to a barn to force out Booth and a companion. A soldier, thinking he saw Booth raise a gun, fatally shot him.

Federal cavalrymen captured Jefferson Davis on May 10 near Irwinville, Georgia, and he was taken to Fort Monroe. There he would be held, for a time in irons, expecting trial for treason. By the time he was caught, remnants of Confederate commands in Alabama and Mississippi had surrendered. On May 13, near Brownsville, Texas, a small Confederate force won the last skirmish of the war. On June 23, in the Indian Territory, Brig. Gen. Stand Watie of the Cherokee nation made the last surrender of Confederate land forces.

In Bering Strait, the Confederate cruiser *Shenandoah* was prowling for whaling ships flying the Stars and Stripes. On June 28, a neutral skipper told her captain, James I. Waddell, that the war was over. "You go to Hell," said the Rebel. He did not accept the news until August. Then, hunted by the U.S. Navy, he set sail for England, via Cape Horn. He had captured 36 ships, using several to send prisoners to safety, and became the last Confederate to lower the flag when he anchored in Liverpool on November 5. His was the only ship to circumnavigate the globe under the Southern flag.

For all but the *Shenandoah* and diehards in the West heading for Mexico or surrender, the war was over by May 23. That was the first day of the Grand Review, an extravaganza of trumpets and billowing flags in Washington. Thousands lined Pennsylvania Avenue to see the men of the Army of the Potomac stepping as smartly as they had when George McClellan had drilled them so long ago. On the next day came the rough-hewn armies from the West, marching "in good drill," as Sherman noted proudly, but keeping their long, free-swinging stride and singing "John Brown's Body." They brought along their mascots— an eagle, a raccoon, a tethered pig—and their notorious, camp-following

"bummers" with their laden mules. Black families who had attached themselves to the soldiers of the West still accompanied them.

East and West marched to different steps in peace, as North and South had marched apart in war. But a new nation was rising around these compass points, around these men who seemed so wildly unalike, around these ex-slaves, and around the men who were not on parade, the men of the South. Those men would limp or walk, sometimes in groups, sometimes in solitude, to a peace and a future that began at a place now restored to the Union. One of them, just turned 19, found himself walking with a Union colonel along a Virginia road. As they were parting, the colonel asked his former enemy where he was going.

The boy looked down the road. "Home, sir," he simply said. "Home." He did not name a state.

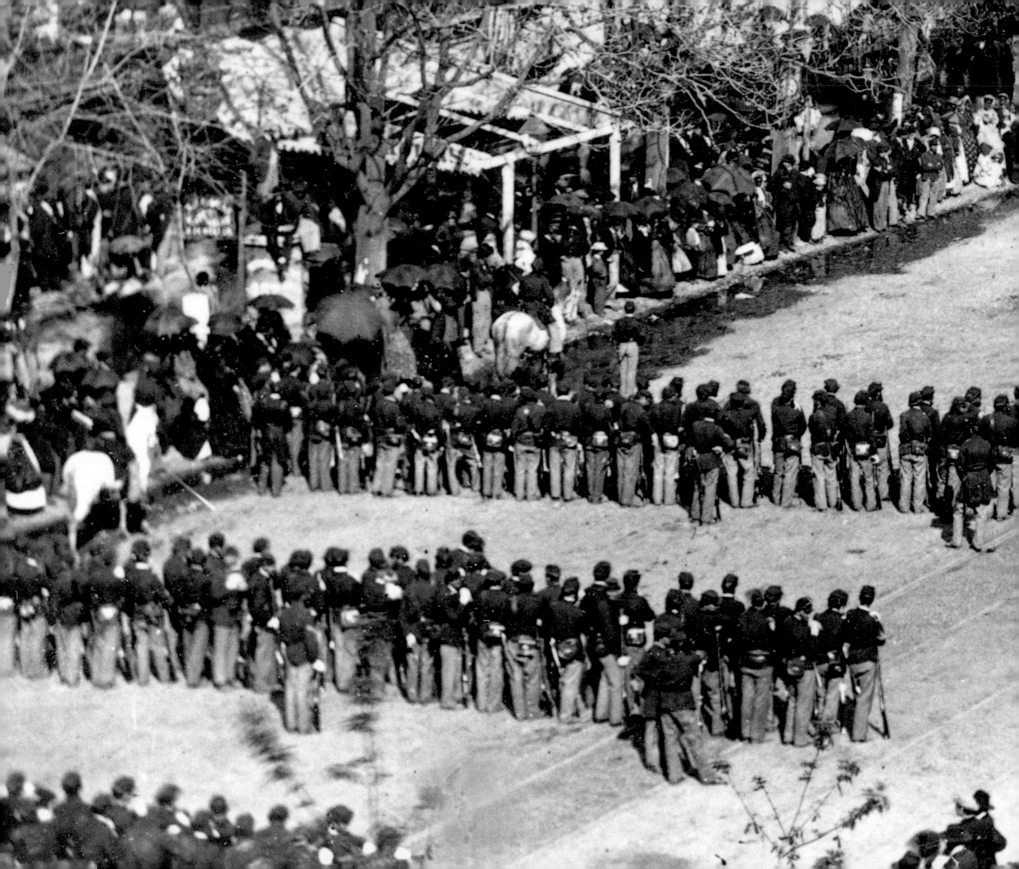

IN LATER YEARS

Not long after Gen. Joe Johnston surrendered, he overheard a man saying that the South had been "conquered but not subdued." Johnston asked the man what Confederate unit he had served in. The man sputtered something about circumstances preventing him from being in the army. "Well, sir, I was," Johnston said. "You may not be subdued, but I am."

In defeat, some Southerners did want to fight on—beyond conquest, beyond defeat, beyond reason. They echoed Jefferson Davis's last proclamation, a call for guerrilla warfare.

On the eve of surrender, the young brigadier E.P. Alexander pleaded with Lee to order "every man for himself, to take to the woods and make his way either to Johnston's army in Carolina, or to his home, taking his arms, and reporting to the governor of his State."

Lee politely refused, saying that the men "would supply their wants by violence and plunder.... A state of society would result, through the South, from which it would require years to recover...."

Southerners were not alone in expecting a guerrilla war. Sherman feared that "we will have to deal with numberless bands of desperadoes, headed by such men as Mosby, Forrest ... and others." Col. John S. Mosby's Partisan Rangers had staked out "Mosby's Confederacy" in northern Virginia early in the war. If any Rebels would take to the woods and fight on, these were likely candidates.

But Mosby put aside his red-lined cape and ostrich-plumed hat and declared, "We are soldiers, not highwaymen." He signed a parole, as did Forrest. In his farewell to his men, Forrest set them on the path that most Confederates took: "Neighborhood feuds, personal animosities, and private differences should be blotted out...." The Union government, he said, would be magnanimous.

As early as May 1865, President Andrew Johnson proclaimed a general amnesty for former Rebels who swore an oath of allegiance and endorsed the abolition of slavery. He exempted former leaders and the well-to-do from amnesty, but later issued many special pardons.

Even before Appomattox, about 6,000 Confederates had changed allegiance to get out of prison camps. These ex-Rebs, called "Galvanized Yankees," became U.S. Volunteers but did not have to fight their former comrades. They served on the western frontier, guarding telegraph stations and fighting Indians. The last of them were mustered out in 1866, and the role of Indian fighters passed in part to black recruits who signed up for service in the 9th and 10th Cavalry.

For the newly freed in the South, war's end was a time of jubilation. Parents could celebrate the birth of a child who belonged to no one but themselves; and relatives separated by sale found one another again. "Men are taking their wives and children," noted a Union officer in a letter to his own wife, "families which had been for a long time broken up are united and oh! such happiness."

Amid the joys of reunion, Confederate soldiers returned home to desolate farms, fire-gutted towns, a devastated land under bluecoat rule. The war had wiped out most railroads and shipping. Former slave-owners faced all sorts of readjustments—the family cook might tell a lady "if she want any dinner she kin cook it herself." Few people had any money. Most families in cities had no jobs, and many families in the country had lost most of their livestock, and families everywhere had lost someone—as a bitter epitaph at Shiloh recorded, "killed for defending home."

The war killed 260,000 Confederates, one out of every ten white males in the South. The Union lost 364,000 men, including 37,000 black troops. Some 400,000 men on both sides were wounded, and many of them would die young. Some veterans felt, like Oliver Wendell Holmes, Jr., that after the war the world never seemed quite right again.

Lincoln's Gettysburg Address had hallowed the first of many battlefield cemeteries for the Union dead. After the war, some Northerners, including Meade, suggested that the Confederate dead be buried alongside the men they fought. This did not happen officially, though mistakes were made. One Mississippi soldier still lies in the national

Untimely cold brings October snow to Union graves at Arlington, once the home of Robert E. Lee, now a national cemetery. Here, in the words of a war poet, "glory guards with solemn round / The bivouac of the dead."

cemetery at Gettysburg because somebody mistook *Miss.* for *Mass.*

Some of the most radical Republicans had contended that the seceded states themselves were dead. Thaddeus Stevens of Pennsylvania insisted that in defeat they were mere "conquered provinces." Charles Sumner and others preferred a notion of "state suicide" that reduced them to territorial status. Lincoln's moderation prevailed.

As Congress required by the Reconstruction Act of March 2, 1867, a Southern state faced this procedure: White and black voters chose delegates who drew up a new state constitution. Once the voters approved this document, the new state legislature convened to ratify the Fourteenth Amendment, which conferred citizenship on all persons born or naturalized in the United States. (The Thirteenth Amendment, which officially eliminated slavery, had been ratified in December 1865.) The last three states readmitted—Texas, Mississippi, and Virginia, all in 1870—were required to ratify the Fifteenth Amendment, which crisply guaranteed voting rights for male citizens "regardless of race, color, or previous condition of servitude."

Female citizens here and there suggested that a white gentlewoman might be as well qualified to vote as a former field hand, but that was a minor theme at best for white Southerners. They fumed as they saw blacks not only voting but being elected to office. Blacks used their new power with moderation, usually, in the style of the soldier who recognized a Rebel prisoner as his former owner and greeted him cheerfully: "bottom rail on top dis time!" But a white Democrat in the upper South had predicted: "When the bayonets shall depart . . . look out for the reaction. Then the bottom rail will descend from the top of the fence."

Even with Federal troops at hand, secret societies, such as the Ku Klux Klan, waged a kind of guerrilla campaign against blacks and their friends. After President Hayes took the troops out of the picture in 1877, the white rail did reappear at the top of the fence and the doctrine of white supremacy asserted itself anew. Some leaders talked of a New South, where industry would bring progress and wealth, but attitudes of the Old South persisted. The embattled North lived on as well, while evangelists of vengeance, "waving the bloody shirt," tried to shout down the advocates of reunion. But new prospects beckoned.

Over the horizon, for both Northerners and Southerners, there was a nation to expand, farms and ranches to carve out of the frontier. Thousands of families were drawn westward by the Homestead Act of 1862, which gave Federal land to people who would settle on it. Immigrants, mostly from Germany, Ireland, and England, had been pouring into the United States. Many of them fought for the Union, and came home to factory jobs in a flourishing economy.

Four years after the war, the first transcontinental railroad united the country. By 1900 the U.S. had a national system—all standard gauge—with 200,000 miles of track: more than all the rail mileage of Europe. By then the term Union was giving way to *nation* or *United States*, with *States* no longer considered plural.

Although the Fourteenth Amendment barred from state or Federal office almost all Confederate leaders, the pardoning of Southerners had begun even before the amendment was ratified. Many held high office, and in 1898 one enjoyed a glory all his own. In the Spanish-American War, "Fightin' Joe" Wheeler, a very youthful general under the Confederacy, took the field as a general of U.S. Volunteers. Near Santiago, in Cuba, he saw a Spanish force retreating and shouted happily, "We've got the damn Yankees on the run!"

Grant, who had done so much to achieve the Yankee victory, had done much to achieve reconciliation. Elected President in 1868, he did not hesitate to use troops to defend black interests, but he willingly signed the General Amnesty Act in his second term. He knew that the war's effect was profound—except for Grover Cleveland, every elected President until 1904 would be a veteran of Grant's armies—but he knew also that some day the grip of the past must loosen. In 1885, dying of cancer of the throat, he finished his memoirs with these words:

"I feel that we are on the eve of a new era, when there is to be great harmony between the Federal and Confederate. I cannot stay to be a living witness to the correctness of this prophecy; but I feel it within me that it is to be so. The universally kind feeling expressed for me at a time when it was supposed that each day would prove my last, seemed to me the beginning of the answer to 'Let us have peace.' "

Former Confederate and Federal officers were pallbearers at his funeral. On his tomb was carved his famous statement: *Let Us Have Peace*. The words face to the South.

Notes on Contributors

THOMAS B. ALLEN, a former National Geographic Society editor, writes frequently for the Society's books and magazines. Society books in which his work appears include *Guide to the National Parks of the United States, Field Guide to the Birds of North America,* and *Journey Into China.* His magazine story "Return to Pearl Harbor" appeared in the December 1991 issue. An authority on military subjects, Allen is the coauthor, with Norman Polmar, of *World War II: America at War 1941-1945,* a one-volume encyclopedia. He, Polmar, and F. Clifton Berry wrote *CNN: War in the Gulf,* a book on the 1991 conflict in the Persian Gulf. Allen's expertise is also brought to bear in *War Games,* which looks at gaming as a tool in determining national security policy. He and Polmar are the coauthors of *Merchants of Treason,* a report on modern espionage, and the biography *Rickover: Controversy and Genius.* Allen has lectured widely; he conducts writing workshops at the Writer's Center of Washington and serves on its board. A native of Bridgeport, Connecticut, he came to Washington, D.C., in 1965.

Staff photographer SAM ABELL, born and reared in Sylvania, Ohio, has been contributing images to National Geographic publications since 1970. His magazine stories include "The Wonderland of Lewis Carroll," "The World of Tolstoy," "The Shakers' Brief Eternity," and "Journey into Dreamtime," a vision of northwestern Australia. Among the Geographic books he has photographed are *Still Waters, White Waters: Exploring America's Rivers and Lakes* and *The Pacific Crest Trail.* In addition to his Society work, Abell has published five books, including *Contemplative Gardens, C. M. Russell's West,* and two volumes on the Civil War: *Distant Thunder: A Photographic Essay on the American Civil War* and *The Civil War: An Aerial Portrait.* In 1990, Abell's work was collected in a mid-career retrospective, *Stay This Moment,* which comprised a major book and exhibition at New York's International Center of Photography.

Writer SHELBY FOOTE, now living in Memphis, Tennessee, was born in Greenville, Mississippi, and studied at the University of North Carolina. He has written six novels: *Tournament, Follow Me Down, Love in a Dry Season, Shiloh, Jordan County,* and *September September.* While writing his three-volume history, *The Civil War: A Narrative,* he received three Guggenheim fellowships. His relationship with the Society dates from his use of its Civil War map (enclosed with this package). Foote wrote to the Society, "I had [it] within arm's reach all the time and referred to [it] so often that it became too tattered for further use, then was fortunate to have you issue a duplicate on plastic, which I used from then on out." For NATIONAL GEOGRAPHIC's July 1979 issue, Foote wrote "Echoes of Shiloh."

Acknowledgments

The Book Division gratefully acknowledges the patient and generous cooperation of all who have helped in the preparation of this volume: Federal, state, and local officials and agencies; historical societies and museums; the Fifth Avenue Presbyterian Church of Roanoke, Va.; and many individuals with specialized knowledge. We thank the helpful librarians of other institutions as well as Charles Brady, Anya Krugovoy, and Robert P. Radzyminski of our own.

We are particularly indebted to our general consultants, Edwin C. Bearss and Jay Luvaas, to the National Park Service, and to the following: Ted Alexander; Michael A. Allen; Michael Andrus; Cathy S. Beeler; David Berry; Russell K. Brown; James Burgess; Chris Calkins; Emory Campbell; Ann Childress; Ray L. Claycomb; Graham Claytor, Jr.; Carl Cruz; Larrie S. Curry; Warren Cutler; John R. Davis, Jr.; Herbert Doswell, Jr.; Dennis Frye; Franklin M. Garrett; Joseph T. Glatthaar; Susan L. Gordon; Vicki Greene; Ron Grim; Karl Hakala; F. Terry Hambrecht; Roy W. Harkness; Noel G. Harrison; D. Scott Hartwig; Alan Hawk; Tracy H. Hayes; David Hedrick; Robert Holcombe; Patricia N. Holland; Jean Hort; Carl E. Hyde, Jr.; G. Jeffery Jackson; Jim Jobe; David J. Johnson; Gordon L. Jones; Robert J. T. Joy; Suez B. Kehl; Dennis P. Kelly; Frances Kennedy; Bobby L. Lovett; Howard Madaus; B.B. Mitchell, III; Mark Nardini, George M. Neil; Jessica Norton; James Ogden, III; Susan Orsini; Donald C. Pfanz; Robert H. Prosperi; George Reaves; Lyle Rosbotham; Cynthia B. Scudder; David Shayt; Dale C. Smith; Whitney Smith; Wilson K. Smith, Jr.; Samuel Spangler; E. Gehrig Spencer; Marsha B. Starkey; Richard W. Stephenson; Emily Stewart; William N. Still; Damon Von Eiff; Daryl Watson; William D. Welge; Clare White; Jerry White; Ronald G. Wilson; Terrence J. Winschel; Thomas C. Wolfe; Michael Wurm; Paul D. Zastrow.

Illustrations Credits

ABBREVIATIONS: LC – Library of Congress; NA – National Archives; NYHS – New-York Historical Society, New York City; NYPL – New York Public Library; USAMHI – U.S. Army Military History Institute, Carlisle, Pa. (photographed by National Geographic Photographer Joseph H. Bailey); VM – Valentine Museum, Richmond, Va.; (t)-top; (b)-bottom; (l)-left; (r)-right; (c)-center.

FRONT MATTER: 1, LC. 11, NA. FOREWORD: 13, NA.

CHAPTER I: 15, LC. 16-17, Collection of the Pennsylvania Historical & Museum Commission's Drake Well Museum in Titusville, Pa. 19, (l) George S. Whiteley IV; (r) USAMHI. 22, North Carolina Division of Archives and History. 23, Baltimore & Ohio Railroad. 25, (t) Collection of the Public Library of Cincinnati and Hamilton County; (b) NYPL. 26, (both) LC. 27, NYHS. 28, Georgia Department of Archives and History. 29, LC. 30-31, NYHS. 36, Herb Peck, Jr., Nashville, Tenn. 36-37, Virginia State Library and Archives. 38, National Portrait Gallery, Smithsonian Institution. 39, LC. 40, Kansas State Historical Society. 41, (l) NYPL; (tr) LC; (br) Kansas State Historical Society. 46, Ohio Historical Society. 46-47, Baltimore & Ohio Railroad. 48, (l) American Antiquarian Society; (r) LC. 49, LC. 50, Lloyd Ostendorf Collection, Dayton, Ohio. 51-54, (all) LC. 55, NYPL. 56-57, LC. 57, NYPL. 58, (l) LC; (r) NA. 59, NA.

CHAPTER II: 61, George R. Rinhart Collection. 62-63, LC. 64-65, (both) NA. 66, (l) NA; (r) LC. 68, NYHS. 70-71, U.S. Military Library, West Point. 72, (tl) Collection of the Louisiana State Museum, copy photo by Jan White Brantley; (bl) VM; (tr) LC. 73, NA. 74-75, LC. 76-77, LC. 84-85, (both) LC. 86, Casemate Museum, Fort Monroe, Va. 86-87, LC. 88, Collection of the South Carolina Historical Society. 90-93, (all) LC. 94-95, (both) NA. 96, (t)(c) National Library of Medicine, Bethesda, Md.; (b) Congregation of the Sisters of the Holy Cross, Notre Dame, Ind. 97, Tennessee State Library and Archives, Nashville, Tenn. 98-99, NA. 99, Edward G. Miner Library, University of Rochester School of Medicine & Dentistry.

CHAPTER III: 101, NYHS. 102-103, LC. 105, (t) NYHS; (b) NA. 108-109, (both) NA. 113, N.C. Wyeth, 1910, M. Knoedler & Company. 114-115, (both) LC. 116-117, USAMHI. 118, LC. 120, from *Battles and Leaders of the Civil War, Vol. I.,* New York, Thomas Yoseloff, Inc., 1956. 121, (tl)(br) Official U.S. Navy Photograph; (tr) USAMHI. 122, LC. 124-125, Illinois State Historical Library. 130, VM. 131, LC. 132, USAMHI. 133, (b) USAMHI; (t) VM. 134-143, (both) LC. 144-145, (both) NA. 146-149, (all) LC. 154, NA. 155, LC. 156-157, LC. 157, (t) NA; (b) Minnesota Historical Society. 162-163, Western Reserve Historical Society. 164, Illinois State Historical Library. 165, State Historical Society of Wisconsin. 166-167, LC. 167-168, (both) collection of Dr. Thomas and Karen Sweeney. 169, LC.

CHAPTER IV: 171-178, (all) LC. 179, (t) USAMHI; (b) LC. 180, Dementi-Foster Studios, Richmond, Va. 181, Anne S.K. Brown Military Collection, Brown University Library. 182-191, (all) LC. 192-193, USAMHI. 200, NA. 201, Old Court House Museum, Vicksburg, Miss. 208, NA. 209, LC. 210-213, (all) NA. 216, (tl) NYHS; (bl) NA; (tr) LC. 217, Richard F. Carlile Collection. 218-219, (all) LC. 220-221, VM. 222, USAMHI. 223, LC. 224-225, LC. 225, The Library Company of Philadelphia. 226, (bl) LC; (tl)(tr) courtesy of Carl Cruz, great-great-grandnephew, photographed by National Geographic Photographer Joseph H. Bailey. 227, USAMHI.

CHAPTER V: 229, USAMHI. 230-242, (all) LC. 243, Chicago Historical Society. 248-249, NYHS. 250, USAMHI. 250-251, LC. 251, NA. 256, VM. 257-259, (both) LC. 260-261, Collection, The Museum of Modern Art, New York. 262-264, (all) LC. 264-265, NA. 266-267, LC. 269, George S. Whiteley IV. 271, (l) Hotchkiss Collection, Mary Baldwin College Library; (r) LC.

CHAPTER VI: 275-280, (all) LC. 282-283, NYPL. 283, NA. 284-291, (both) LC. 292, NYPL. 292-293, Metropolitan Museum of Art, Harris Brisbane Dick Fund, 1933. 293, NA. 294-295, Virginia Historical Society. 296, Courtesy of the Atlanta Historical Society. 297, LC. 298, (b) Penn School Collection, Penn Center Inc., St. Helena Island, S.C.; (tl) NA; (tc) LC; (tr) Eleanor S. Brockenbrough Library, the Museum of the Confederacy, Richmond, Va. 299, Lloyd Ostendorf Collection, Dayton, Ohio. 300, USAMHI. 300-301, International Museum of Photography at George Eastman House. 306, LC. 307, Courtesy of the Burton Historical Collection of the Detroit Public Library. 308, Illinois State Historical Library. 309, LC. 310-311, NA. 315, Dementi-Foster Studios, Richmond, Va.

MAP CREDITS: Maps from the Library of Congress, photographed by National Geographic Photographer Victor R. Boswell, Jr., appear on pages 82, 112, 119, 153, 202, 236, 268, 270, 272, 273, and 307.

Composition for this book by the Typographic section of National Geographic Production Services, Pre-Press Division. Color separations by Graphic Art Service, Inc., Nashville, Tenn.; Lanman Progressive Co., Washington, D.C.; and Phototype Color Graphics, Pennsauken, N.J. Printed and bound by R.R. Donnelley & Sons Co., Willard, Ohio. Paper by Mead Paper Co., New York, N.Y. Dust jacket printed by Peake Printers Inc., Cheverly, Md.

Library of Congress CIP Data
Allen, Thomas B.
   The Blue and the Gray / by Thomas B. Allen ; photography by Sam Abell ; prepared by the Book Division, National Geographic Society.
     p. cm.
    Includes index.
    ISBN 0-87044-876-5. -- ISBN 0-87044-877-3 (Deluxe)
   1. United States--History--Civil War, 1861-1865. 2. United States--History--Civil War, 1861-1865--Battlefields--Guidebooks. I. Abell, Sam. II. National Geographic Society (U.S.). Book Division. III. Title.
E468.A44 1992
973.7--dc20
92-13567
CIP

Index